Publication Team

GMS Series Co-ordinator: Rawwida Baksh
Project Managers: Elsie Onubogu and Linda Etchart
Production: Rupert Jones-Parry

Acknowledgements

The Commonwealth Secretariat would particularly like to thank Johann Galtung who coined the term 'conflict transformation' and who, together with Kai Fritjof Brand-Jacobsen, co-facilitated the Secretariat's Pan-Commonwealth workshop on 'Gender, Youth and Conflict Transformation'.

We would like to offer our deep gratitude to the many contributors to this publication, including Urvashi Butalia, Christine Chinkin, Neloufer de Mel, Herbert Gayle, Maria Hadjipavlou, Amena Mohsin, Kadi Sesay and Pamela Thomas, who presented papers at the regional symposia on 'Gender, Politics, Peace, Conflict Prevention and Resolution' and the Pan-Commonwealth workshop on 'Gender, Youth and Conflict Transformation', based on which the case studies in Part II of this book were compiled. The case studies by Helen Hakena and Christiana Solomon were contributed following these fora.

Special thanks are due to Rawwida Baksh who initiated and led the Secretariat's work on Gender, Democracy, Peace and Conflict from 1996 to 2003 and conceptualised this book, and to Linda Etchart who joined the Gender Section in 2001–2003 and worked with Rawwida to synthesise the analysis from the Commonwealth fora referred to above, as well as to integrate global developments on gender, development, democracy, peace, security and conflict into Part I of the book.

Part I has also benefited from other inputs. Chapter 1 was written by Victor Pungong and Elsie Onubogu. Chapter 2 includes sections on 'Conceptualising Peace-building' and 'Assessing Women's "Natural Role" as Peacemakers', which were adapted from Christiana Solomon's paper. Parts of Chapter 3 and Chapter 6 were drawn from a paper by Christine Chinkin on 'Post-conflict Reconstruction and Rehabilitation: Ensuring the Needs of Women'.[1]

We would like to express our sincere gratitude to Elsie Onubogu, who took over co-ordination of the project from

Linda Etchart as programme officer responsible for the Secretariat's work on Gender, Democracy, Peace and Conflict, and updated some of the material, and to Tina Johnson, who edited the book to its present format. In the event that we have inadvertently omitted any individual or organisation who contributed, we offer our sincere apologies and thanks.

Finally, this publication would not have been possible without the inputs of Commonwealth Secretariat colleagues, in particular, Victor Pungong and Lach Fergusson of the Good Offices Section of the Political Affairs Division; and Joel Kibazo, James Robertson and Rupert Jones-Parry of the Communications and Public Affairs Division.

Contents

Foreword   vii

Abbreviations   xi

PART I: GENDER, PEACE AND CONFLICT: 1
SETTING THE CONTEXT

1   Gender and Conflict Transformation in the   3
    Commonwealth
    Victor Pungong and Elsie Onubogu
    The Commonwealth's Core Values and Principles   3
    The Commonwealth Approach to Preventing and   4
    Resolving Conflicts
    Gender Mainstreaming in the Commonwealth   7
    Gender Mainstreaming in Conflict Transformation in   8
    the Commonwealth

2   Applying a Gender Lens to Armed Conflict, Violence   14
    and Conflict Transformation
    Linda Etchart and Rawwida Baksh
    The Impact of Armed Conflict on Gender Relations   15
    Masculine Identity and Violence   18
    Assessing Women's 'Natural Role' as Peacemakers   20
    War, Women and Women's Bodies   22
    Gender, Conflict Transformation and Peace-building   27

3   Achieving Gender Equality and Equity in Peace   34
    Processes
    Elsie Onubogu and Linda Etchart
    International Declarations and Resolutions   34
    Gender Balance and Gender Mainstreaming   36
    Obstacles to Women's Participation in Peace Talks   38
    Why Women Must Be Included in Peace Processes   39
    Women in Peace Movements and as Leaders   43
    A Framework for Gender Mainstreaming in   45
    Post-conflict Reconstruction
    Gender, Justice and Reconciliation   49
    The Role of Men and Boys in Achieving Gender   52
    Equality

Recommendations for Involving Men and Boys and   55
Addressing Their Concerns

4   **Progress in Gender Mainstreaming in Peace**   56
     Support Operations
     Linda Etchart
     International Calls for Women's Inclusion   56
     Implementation of Recommended Actions   63
     The Composition of Peacekeeping Missions   68
     The Role of Gender Training in Peace-building   71
     The Potential Negative Impacts of Peacekeepers   72
     Addressing the Negative Impacts of Peacekeepers   77
     Next Steps   80
     Recommendations to Facilitate Gender   81
     Mainstreaming in Peace Support Operations

5   **Gender Mainstreaming in Post-conflict**   82
     Reconstruction
     Rawwida Baksh
     The Gender Dimension of the Conduct of the War   83
     in Sierra Leone
     The May 2001 National Consultation   86
     Gender Equality in Political and Public   88
     Decision-Making
     Gender Equality in Human Rights and Legal Reform   89
     Gender and the Truth and Reconciliation Commission   90
     (TRC)
     Gender-Based Crimes in the Special Court   92
     Gender Issues in Poverty Eradication and Economic   93
     Empowerment
     Gender Equality in Education, Training and   95
     Employment
     The Role of Young Women and Men in Post-   96
     conflict Reconstruction
     Challenges Remaining   97
     Vision of the Women of Sierra Leone   98

6   **Creating an International Law of Peace**   99
     Christine Chinkin
     Sources of the New Law   99
     Benefits of an International Law of Peace   101
     Recommendations   103

PART II: NATIONAL AND REGIONAL EXPERIENCES   105

7   **Bangladesh: Women and Minorities in Conflict**   107
    Resolution
    Amena Mohsin
    Ethnic and Religious Differences   108
    Minority Women and the State   108
    Development, Displacement and Insecurity   110
    Militarisation and Insecurity   111
    Women as Agents of Change and Conflict Resolution   112
    Recommendations   115

8   **Cyprus: Peace Is Too Precious to Be Left to**   117
    Men Alone
    Maria Hadjipavlou
    'Choose Your Side!'   117
    Moving from a Conflict Mentality to a Peace   118
    Mentality
    Cypriot Women's Efforts in Peace-building   120
    Women and Men in Partnership in a Post-conflict   128
    Cyprus
    Some Lessons Learned   129
    Recommendations   131

9   **India: Legacies of Dispute**   132
    Urvashi Butalia
    The Complexities of Women's Experiences of   132
    Conflict in India
    Gujarat   134
    Punjab   138
    Kashmir   140
    Hard Questions for the Women's Movement   142
    Recommendations   144

10 **Jamaica: The Search for Survival and Respect in**   145
    the Hostile World of the Inner City
    Herbert Gayle
    A Glimpse of the Problem of Violence   145
    Construction of the Problem   148
    Recommendations   154

11 **The Pacific: Gender Issues in Conflict and**   155
    Peacemaking
    Pamela Thomas
    The Causes of Conflict   156
    Pacific Women and Peacemaking   156
    Violence and the Media   158
    Domestic Violence and Male Control   158
    Recommendations   159

12 **Papua New Guinea: Women in Armed Conflict**   160
    Helen Hakena
    Brief Historical Background   160
    The Effect of the Crisis on Women in Bougainville   161
    Women and the Peace Process   163
    Challenges that Women Face   169
    Recommendations   170

13 **The Mano River Union Sub-region: The Role of**   171
    Women in Building Peace
    Christiana Solomon
    Women's Invisibility as Peace-builders   171
    The Mano River Union Sub-region: An Overview   172
    Women Building Peace in Sierra Leone   174
    Women Building Peace in Liberia   177
    The Mano River Women's Peace Network   177
    Obstacles to Women's Participation in Governance   178
    Recommendations   179

14 **Sierra Leone: Women in Conflict Resolution and**   181
    Post-conflict Reconstruction
    Kadi Sesay
    Women Taking the Lead   183
    Consultations with Civil Society   184
    Adopting a Regional Approach   186
    Women and Democracy   187
    Involving Women in Consolidating the Peace   189
    Recommendations   190

15 **Sri Lanka: Mother Politics and Women's Politics**   191
    Neloufer de Mel
    Background: The Reign of Terror   191

A Shift in Focus for Women's Groups 193
The Mothers' Front 195
Mother Culture 197
Legacy of the Mothers' Front 199
The Future of the Women's Movement in Sri Lanka ... 201
Recommendations 204

Bibliography

207

Appendices

I   Glossary 219
II   Extract from the Commonwealth Plan of Action for   222
     Gender Equality 2005–2015 on Gender, Democracy,
     Peace and Conflict

List of Contributors

230

Boxes

1   Definition of Gender Mainstreaming 8
2   The Focus of Commonwealth Activities in the Area   11
     of Gender, Democracy, Peace and Conflict
3   How Poverty and Unemployment Can Lead to   20
     Violence
4   Some Causes of Increased Domestic Violence   26
     During and Post-conflict
5   Various Theories of Peace-building 30
6   Different Views of Peace-building in Sierra Leone 32
7   Changes Women Experienced due to the Conflict in 41
     Sri Lanka
8   Women Finding Common Ground Across Ethnic   43
     Divisions
9   The Contribution of NGOs to UN Security Council   60
     Resolution 1325 on Women, Peace and Security
10   Lessons Learned from Successful Gender   66
     Mainstreaming in Timor-Leste
11   Gender Resource Package for Peacekeeping   68
     Operations
12   Protecting the Local Community during Peace   78
     Support Operations
13   Recommendations for Gender Mainstreaming in   86
     Post-conflict Reconstruction in Sierra Leone

14 Women Working Against Violence in Bangladesh   114
15 Why Women in Cyprus Want their Country United   127
16 The Deviant Responses of the Excluded   153
17 LNWDA and the Millennium Peace Prize   164
18 One Woman's Experience During the Reign of   192
    Terror in Sri Lanka

Figure
1   Construction of the Problem in Jamaica   149

Foreword

Gender Mainstreaming in Conflict Transformation: Building Sustainable Peace is the latest title in the Commonwealth Secretariat's series of publications which aim to influence gender mainstreaming policy and practice in critical development issues in the Commonwealth and globally.

Issues of socio-economic development, democracy and peace are inextricably linked to gender equality. The main argument of *Gender Mainstreaming in Conflict Transformation: Building Sustainable Peace* is that gender equality needs to be placed on the policy and programme agenda of the entire spectrum of peace and conflict-related initiatives and activities in order to achieve conflict transformation. These include conflict prevention and early warning mechanisms, peace negotiations and agreements; peace keeping, disarmament, demobilisation and reintegration; truth and reconciliation commissions; post-conflict reconstruction; peace building and peace education.

In the Commonwealth, as globally, unequal power relations, lack of access to resources, intolerance and lack of respect for individual rights and freedoms fuel armed and other forms of conflict within and between states. War is no longer fought mainly across international borders between professional soldiers in battlefields. Most of today's conflicts in the Commonwealth and globally take place within countries between different ethnic and socio-economic groups, with civilians being the main combatants and targets. Armed conflict has moved into the village, the community, the street and the home, resulting in a gendered distribution of suffering among women and girls, and men and boys. Deaths due to political violence tend to be overwhelmingly among men. Yet, civilians are the main victims of war, with women and children targeted for special forms of attack. Women and children are also increasingly participants in war, particularly as child soldiers, who are both boys and girls.

What is less well known, however, is that women have been making significant contributions to peace processes and rebuilding their societies in all phases of conflict. In recognition of this, in 2000 the United Nations Security Council made an urgent call in passing Resolution 1325 (UNSCR 1325), for "the equal participation and full involvement of women in all efforts for the maintenance and promotion of peace and security", and emphasised "the need to increase their role in decision-making with regard to conflict prevention and resolution".

Commonwealth Ministers Responsible for Women's/Gender Affairs in their new Plan of Action for Gender Equality 2005–2015 urged governments and member States to include women "at the highest levels of peace-building, peacekeeping, conflict mediation, resolution, and post-conflict reconciliation and reconstruction activities". They reaffirmed the 30 per cent target for women in peace initiatives which was endorsed by Heads of Government (CHOGM, Coolum, 2001), and encouraged member States to mainstream gender equality in all peace processes.

Gender Mainstreaming in Conflict Transformation: Building Sustainable Peace is intended as a contribution to the achievement of these goals. It grew out of a number of advocacy, capacity-building and policy development workshops held by the Commonwealth Secretariat in collaboration with other partners. Three regional workshops on 'Engendering Local Government' were hosted in Asia, the Caribbean and Southern Africa in collaboration with the Commonwealth Local Government Forum (CLGF) in 1996 to 1997. Four regional symposia on 'Gender, Politics, Peace, Conflict Prevention and Resolution' were held for Africa, Asia/Europe, the Caribbean and Pacific in collaboration with the Commonwealth Parliamentary Association (CPA) between 1997 and 2000, which culminated in Pan-Commonwealth workshops on 'Gender, Youth and Conflict Transformation' held in 2002, and 'Engendering Development and Democracy' held in the wings of the Commonwealth Heads of Government Meeting in Abuja in 2003. In addition, as part of the Secretariat's assistance to countries experiencing conflict, a national consultation was held in May 2001 in Sierra Leone on 'Women and Men in Partnership for Post-conflict Reconstruction', followed by a 'Women in Parliament' workshop in February 2002 which contributed to an increase in women's representation in parliament to 15 per cent in Sierra Leone's first post-conflict national elections held in May 2002.

These fora contributed a wealth of analysis and case studies that made it clear that women's participation in processes of democratisation, as well as in all phases of conflict in Commonwealth countries, were not just an ideal, but rather a reality that needs to be better understood by policy-makers and other political and social actors working in fields including democracy, development, peace and conflict. This book brings together this body of work into an advocacy, capacity-building and policy tool to contribute to gender mainstreaming in all processes of conflict transformation and in building sustainable peace.

The publication is divided into two sections. Part I, 'Gender, Peace and Conflict: Setting the Context', provides a gender analysis of conflict in the Commonwealth and globally. It includes chapters on 'Gender and Conflict Transformation in the Commonwealth'; 'Applying a Gender Lens to Armed Conflict, Violence and Conflict Transformation'; 'Achieving Gender Equality and Equity in Peace Processes'; 'Progress in Gender Mainstreaming in Peace Support Operations'; 'Gender Mainstreaming in Post-conflict Reconstruction'; and 'Creating an International Law of Peace'. Part II, 'National and Regional Experiences', documents case study experiences of gender and conflict in Commonwealth countries and sub-regions including Bangladesh, Cyprus, India, Jamaica, the Pacific, Papua New Guinea, the Mano River Union Sub-region, Sierra Leone and Sri Lanka.

We hope that *Gender Mainstreaming in Conflict Transformation: Building Sustainable Peace* will prove of interest and use to those working to achieve gender equality, peace, democracy and sustainable development, particularly in situations of armed and other forms of conflict.

Ann Keeling
Director

Rawwida Baksh
Head of Gender Section

Social Transformation Programmes Division
Commonwealth Secretariat

June 2005

Abbreviations

AFRC	Armed Forces Revolutionary Council (Sierra Leone)
BD	Bajrang Dal (India)
BPfA	Beijing Platform for Action
BJP	Bharatiya Janata Party (India)
BRA	Bougainville Revolutionary Army (Papua New Guinea)
CGG	Campaign for Good Governance (Sierra Leone)
CEDAW	Convention on the Elimination of All Forms of Discrimination against Women
CHOGM	Commonwealth Heads of Government Meeting
CHT	Chittagong Hill Tracts (Bangladesh)
CIVPOL	international civilian police
CMAG	Commonwealth Ministerial Action Group on the Harare Declaration
CPA	Commonwealth Parliamentary Association
CSW	Commission on the Status of Women (UN)
DDR	disarmament, demobilisation and reintegration
DFAIT	Department of Foreign Affairs and International Trade (Canada)
DFID	Department for International Development (UK)
DPKO	Department of Peacekeeping Operations (UN)
DRC	Democratic Republic of the Congo
ECA	Economic Commission for Africa
ECOMOG	ECOWAS Ceasefire Monitoring Group
ECOSOC	Economic and Social Council of the United Nations
ECOWAS	Economic Community of West African States
FAS	Femmes Africa Solidarité
FAWE	Forum for African Women Educationalists
GMS	Gender Management System
HAD	Hands Across the Divide (Cyprus)
HWF	Hill Women's Federation (Bangladesh)
IDP	internally displaced person
IGO	inter-governmental organisation
ILO	International Labour Organization
IPKF	Indian Peace Keeping Forces
IWDA	International Women's Development Agency (Australia)
JVP	Janatha Vimukthi Peramuna (Sri Lanka)

LNWDA	Leitana Nehan Women's Development Agency (Papua New Guinea)
LTTE	Liberation Tigers of Tamil Eelam (Sri Lanka)
LURD	Liberians United for Reconciliation and Democracy
LWI	Liberian Women's Initiative
MARWOPNET	Mano River Women's Peace Network
MDG	Millennium Development Goal
MDL	Mothers and Daughters of Lanka
MINUGUA	United Nations Verification Mission in Guatemala
MRU	Mano River Union
NCD	National Commission for Democracy (Sierra Leone)
NCDHR	National Commission for Democracy and Human Rights (Sierra Leone)
NGO	non-governmental organisation
NPRC	National Provisional Ruling Council (Sierra Leone)
NWM	national women's machinery
OECD	Organisation for Economic Co-operation and Development
OSCE	Organisation for Security and Co-operation in Europe
PCJSS	Parbatya Chattagram Jana Sanghati Samity (Bangladesh)
PNG	Papua New Guinea
PSO	Peace Support Operation
PWF	Progressive Women's Front (Sri Lanka)
RUF	Revolutionary United Front (Sierra Leone)
SLAUW	Sierra Leone Association of University Women
SLFP	Sri Lanka Freedom Party
SLWMP	Sierra Leone Women's Movement for Peace
STGM	Standard Generic Training Module (DPKO)
STI	sexually transmitted infection
UDHR	Universal Declaration of Human Rights
UNAIDS	Joint United Nations Programme on HIV/AIDS
UNAMSIL	United Nations Mission in Sierra Leone
UNDAW	United Nations Division for the Advancement of Women
UNDP	United Nations Development Programme
UNESCO	United Nations Educational, Scientific and Cultural Organization

UNFPA	United Nations Population Fund
UNHCR	United Nations High Commissioner for Refugees
UNICEF	United Nations Children's Fund
UNIFEM	United Nations Development Fund for Women
UNMISET	United Nations Mission of Support in East Timor
UNOCHA	United Nations Office for the Coordination of Humanitarian Affairs
UNP	United National Party (Sri Lanka)
UNSCR	United Nations Security Council Resolution
UNTAET	United Nations Transitional Administration in East Timor
UPDF	United People's Democratic Front (Bangladesh)
WAC	Women's Action Committee (Sri Lanka)
WCGJ	Women's Caucus for Gender Justice
WDF	Women's Development Foundation (Sri Lanka)
WHO	World Health Organization
WILPF	Women's International League for Peace and Freedom
YWCA	Young Women's Christian Association

PART ONE

Gender, Peace and Conflict:
Setting the Context

1 Gender and Conflict Transformation in the Commonwealth

Victor Pungong and Elsie Onubogu

The Commonwealth's Core Values and Principles

The Commonwealth today encompasses 53 sovereign States and some 1.6 billion people, making up almost a third of the world's population. Representing every region of the world, it is built on its member countries' shared commitment to core values and principles. These have been successively elaborated by leaders in Singapore (1971); Harare, Zimbabwe (1991); Millbrook, New Zealand (1995); Edinburgh, United Kingdom (1997); Fancourt, South Africa (1999); Coolum, Australia (2002); and Abuja, Nigeria (2003). In brief they are:

- respect for diversity and human dignity and resolute opposition to all forms of discrimination, whether rooted in race, ethnicity, creed or gender;

- adherence to democracy, the rule of law, good governance, freedom of expression and the protection of human rights;

- commitment to the elimination of poverty, the promotion of people-centred development and the progressive removal of the wide disparities in living standards among members; and

- commitment to equality between women and men and the empowerment of young people.

These values and principles are more likely to be realised where there is peace and stability. Conversely, armed conflict is more likely to arise when they are violated or neglected. The Commonwealth is therefore dedicated to the promotion of these values and principles as an essential factor in the prevention of conflicts and as fundamental to its work in reconciliation and peace-building in war-torn Commonwealth countries.

The Commonwealth has a long experience of upholding democracy and helping countries develop a stronger, more effective democratic culture. It is strategically placed to play an increasing role in helping to prevent and resolve conflicts ...

The Commonwealth is also committed to the fundamental values expressed in the Millennium Development Goals (MDGs), adopted by the world's Heads of Governments/States at a special United Nations Summit in 2000 and endorsed by Commonwealth Heads of Government in the Coolum Declaration of March 2002. The first MDG is to eradicate extreme poverty and hunger and the third MDG is to promote gender equality and empower women. As a disproportionate burden of poverty is borne by women and children, it is essential to address their needs in efforts to eradicate poverty. And as poverty is one of the factors leading to or exacerbating armed conflict, the empowerment of women is an important component in both poverty eradication and the prevention of armed violence. Peace is inextricably linked to equality between women and men. Commonwealth assistance to countries in post-conflict transition is therefore aimed at ensuring that processes of democratic institution-building are inclusive, and that gender issues in post-conflict reconciliation, rehabilitation and reconstruction are mainstreamed in peace support operations, peace negotiations and agreements.

The Commonwealth Approach to Preventing and Resolving Conflicts

The Commonwealth straddles every continent and region and every level of development. It includes countries of all sizes. It embraces virtually every race and every major religious group. It is therefore not a regional but a globally representative organisation. Its ability to fashion a sense of common purpose and unity out of such diversity is in itself a useful example of tolerance and peaceful co-existence.

The Commonwealth has a long experience of upholding democracy and helping countries develop a stronger, more effective democratic culture. It is strategically placed to play an increasing role in helping to prevent and resolve conflicts in its member countries as a result of its unique blend of attributes. These include:

- an established habit of decision-making by consensus;

- a common working language and shared traditions and institutions;

- informality of style;

- a core commitment to promoting unity in diversity and wide experience of plural societies; and

- a shared commitment at the highest political level to fundamental political values.

Broadly speaking, the Commonwealth has a two-pronged approach to conflict prevention and resolution: one is short term and problem solving and the other more long term, structural and preventive in character. The short-term approach is exercised through the good offices of the Secretary-General (see below) and seeks to resolve immediate or ongoing disputes or crises before they deteriorate into violent conflict. Over the long term, the Commonwealth approach is to address on a continuous basis the root causes of conflict within its member States through its political, economic, social and technical assistance programmes.

Both these approaches treat as important the Commonwealth principle that intervention in a member State can take place only at the request or with the concurrence of the Government in question. Such activities must also enjoy broad political support in the association as a whole. In this connection, Commonwealth and international assistance has been successfully mobilised in the past towards post-conflict reconstruction and capacity building.

The key to conflict prevention lies in persuading States to accept early international assistance aimed at promoting sustainable peace and defusing disputes and crises with the potential to cause violent conflict. Conflict resolution involves not only the signing of peace agreements but also long-term action to address the underlying causes of conflict.

Consensus-based associations like the Commonwealth appear less threatening and very often have a better understanding and feel for disputes in their member States. Thus they may be better placed for overcoming the inherent reluctance of States to accept early international interference in what are perceived to be purely domestic matters. This may give the Commonwealth a comparative advantage in the area of conflict prevention, which complements the primacy of the United Nations in peacekeeping and post-conflict peace-building. In both areas co-operation between all the relevant international players greatly enhances the prospects of success.

The Commonwealth Ministerial Action Group (CMAG)

At their meeting in Millbrook, New Zealand, in 1995, Heads of Government established a Commonwealth Ministerial Action Group on the Harare Declaration[2] (CMAG) as a standing mechanism to deal with serious and persistent violations of the Commonwealth's fundamental political values. Comprising the Foreign Ministers of eight Commonwealth countries, CMAG is charged with assessing the nature of the infringements and recommending measures for collective Commonwealth action aimed at the speedy restoration of democracy and constitutional rule. Measures that CMAG might take in response to such serious or persistent violations range from quiet diplomacy or good offices work and statements of concern to suspension from the Commonwealth.

CMAG initially confined its remit to the Commonwealth countries under military rule at the time of its creation: The Gambia, Nigeria and Sierra Leone. With Commonwealth as well as wider international support, all three countries made successful transitions from military rule to multiparty democracy.

At their meeting in Coolum, Australia, in March 2002, Commonwealth Heads of Government established a procedure for CMAG to deal with countries where there had not been a complete derogation of democracy and constitutional rule, but where there were nonetheless other serious or persistent violations of Commonwealth fundamental political values. In such circumstances, the Secretary-General would first seek to apply his/her good offices role to bring the country concerned back to full adherence to the Harare principles. However, if those efforts failed, the country concerned could be referred to CMAG.

The Secretary-General's Good Offices Role

The Secretary-General's good offices role is the Commonwealth's main preventive instrument for attempting to resolve situations before open conflict breaks out. If, in the course of monitoring political developments in member countries, the

Secretary-General deems that a particular situation is likely to deteriorate into a political crisis or armed conflict, he or she could apply their good offices either directly or through a special envoy to help defuse such a situation. The Secretary-General has, for example, appointed special envoys to Cameroon, Fiji Islands, Guyana and Tonga. This good offices role can also be applied to resolve conflict situations and to mobilise Commonwealth and international support towards post-conflict reconstruction.

A specific Good Offices Section was established in the Political Affairs Division of the Commonwealth Secretariat in 2003 to provide direct institutional support to the good offices work of the Secretary-General. With a stronger mandate to make more proactive use of the Secretary-General's good offices, the Commonwealth has reinforced its capacity to head off conflict and, where it does occur, to hasten reconstruction and assist with institutional mechanisms to promote stability and peace.

Gender Mainstreaming in the Commonwealth

The Commonwealth is committed to gender mainstreaming, that is, the process of bringing a gender equality perspective into the mainstream activities of government at the policy, programme and planning levels (see Box 1).[3] It has developed the Gender Management System (GMS) as a practical framework for doing this. Commonwealth Governments have agreed that a coherent multi-stakeholder approach, as called for in this framework, is necessary in order to sustain more equitable, people-centred development.

The 2002 Commonwealth Heads of Government Meeting (CHOGM) called for further efforts by Governments and the Secretariat to put gender mainstreaming at the centre of all policy and programme initiatives. More recently, the 7th Women's Affairs Ministers Meeting (Nadi, Fiji Islands, 30 May–2 June 2004) adopted a new Commonwealth Plan of Action for Gender Equality 2005–2015, which has as its aim to build on and deepen the gender mainstreaming approach, particularly when addressing persistent challenges such as gender-based violence and the achievement of women's full participation in

With a stronger mandate to make more proactive use of the Secretary-General's good offices, the Commonwealth has reinforced its capacity to head off conflict and, where it does occur, to hasten reconstruction and assist with institutional mechanisms to promote stability and peace.

Commonwealth Women's Affairs Ministers affirmed that the principles of democracy require women's equal political participation and representation for the achievement of gender equality and sustainable development.

leadership and decision-making. Commonwealth Women's Affairs Ministers affirmed that the principles of democracy require women's equal political participation and representation for the achievement of gender equality and sustainable development.

Box 1 Definition of Gender Mainstreaming

Mainstreaming a gender perspective is the process of assessing the implications for women and men of any planned action, including legislation, policies or programmes, in any area and at all levels. It is a strategy for making women's as well as men's concerns and experiences an integral dimension in the design, implementation, monitoring and evaluation of policies and programmes in all political, economic and social spheres so that women and men benefit equally and inequality is not perpetuated. The ultimate goal is to achieve gender equality.

Source: Agreed conclusions of the UN Economic and Social Council 1997/2

Through its leadership and catalytic role in gender mainstreaming, the Commonwealth Secretariat's Gender Section works in partnership with the Good Offices Section.

Gender Mainstreaming in Conflict Transformation in the Commonwealth

It has increasingly been recognised that women and men, girls and boys do not experience conflict in the same way and have different needs and priorities in its aftermath. For example, while young men and boys tend to play the role of 'protectors' of their communities and risk injury and death in combat, women and girls typically play the role of providers of everyday household needs and are at greater risk of being victims of human rights violations such as rape, sex slavery, abduction, trafficking and forced prostitution. Such gender-based differences require specific responses. Women also play a crucial role in maintaining and rebuilding the social fabric during and in the aftermath of conflicts. In Bougainville, for example, the Governor described women as the country's "unsung heroes".

Mainstreaming a gender perspective into all initiatives and efforts includes raising awareness of how being female or male influences vulnerabilities and defines capacities.

The 1995 Commonwealth Plan of Action on Gender and Development (PoA) and subsequent PoAs urged Governments to take vigorous action to promote and defend women's rights and promote women's participation in peace and democratic processes. The Commonwealth Secretariat was further mandated by the Durban CHOGM (1999) and the 5th and 6th Women's Affairs Ministers Meetings (Port of Spain, 1996; New Delhi, 2000) to promote the fundamental political values of the Commonwealth through increasing women's participation in political decision-making and peace processes at all levels. The Commonwealth Women's Affairs Ministers set a target of 30 per cent for women's participation in conflict mediation and resolution, peace-building, peacekeeping and post-conflict reconciliation and reconstruction initiatives. This target was subsequently endorsed by the 2001 CHOGM. Similarly, member States adopted United Nations Security Council Resolution 1325 (UNSCR 1325) on women, peace and security, urging Governments to ensure women's full and equal representation and participation in peace-building and conflict resolution processes.

The Commonwealth Secretariat hosted four regional symposia on Gender, Politics, Peace, Conflict Prevention and Resolution between 1997 and 2000 for Africa, Asia/Europe, the Caribbean and the Pacific. It also held a national consultation in Sierra Leone on 'Women and Men in Partnership for Post-conflict Reconstruction' in May 2001, following a decade of armed conflict that led to the virtual collapse of the country's social, economic, legal and political fabric. The consultation provided a platform for the people of Sierra Leone to share their experiences and views, and to define their own solutions so that women, men, girls and boys could work together to create a more democratic, equitable and prosperous society (see Chapter 5). A Pan-Commonwealth workshop on Gender, Youth and Conflict Transformation was subsequently held in London in 2002 to develop Commonwealth strategies for mainstreaming gender into all aspects of conflict prevention and resolution.

The Commonwealth Women's Affairs Ministers set a target of 30 per cent for women's participation in conflict mediation and resolution, peace-building, peacekeeping and post-conflict reconciliation and reconstruction initiatives. This target was subsequently endorsed by the 2001 CHOGM.

Election day in Sierra Leone (May 2002)
Ashley Barr/Carter Center

These fora took place within the framework of mandates, recommendations and commitments of Commonwealth and international meetings, including the Beijing Platform for Action in which Governments agreed that gender integration into democratic, conflict prevention and conflict resolution processes was a critical area of concern. The participants in the regional symposia recommended that:

- greater efforts must be made to increase the number of women in parliament and local government through constitutional, legal and electoral measures;

- political parties should encourage women to enter politics and should strive to ensure that high numbers of women candidates contest seats in elections;

- potential or actual women candidates should be given training and support; and

- the media should endeavour to present positive images of women as leaders and politicians.

Most recently, the Commonwealth Plan of Action for Gender Equality 2005–2015 (PoA) includes 'Gender, Democracy, Peace and Conflict' as one of the four critical areas for action over the next decade (see Box 2 and Appendix II).[4] The PoA states that:

> *The challenge now is to push beyond numbers and demonstrate the impact of women's contribution to democracy and peace in member countries; promote implementation and accountability for international legal instruments that Governments have ratified; harmonise national legislation with international standards as tools for promoting de-facto equality; encourage political parties to adopt the minimum 30 per cent target for women candidates; and ensure women's participation and representation in conflict prevention and resolution, peace-building and post-conflict reconstruction processes.*

... the Commonwealth Plan of Action for Gender Equality 2005–2015 (PoA) includes 'Gender, Democracy, Peace and Conflict' as one of the four critical areas for action over the next decade.

Box 2 The Focus of Commonwealth Activities in the Area of Gender, Democracy, Peace and Conflict

The Commonwealth Plan of Action for Gender Equality 2005–2015 (paragraph 3.12) states that activities in the area of gender, democracy, peace and conflict will focus on:

- Supporting the adoption, accession, ratification, implementation and monitoring of legal instruments and frameworks related to democracy, peace and conflict.

- Strengthening democratic and political systems through achievement of the Commonwealth target of at least 30 per cent of women in decision-making in the political, public and private sectors. This will require a strengthening of institutional capacity. Countries that have already reached 30 per cent should continue to strive for a higher target.

It is clear that efforts to prevent conflicts and rebuild war-torn societies can only achieve success through an integrated approach that is transparent, inclusive, accountable and ensures the equal participation of women, men and young persons.

Box 2 (continued)

- Supporting the development and mainstreaming of gender equality into early warning mechanisms, conflict prevention and resolution, peace agreements, peace-building, reconciliation, post-conflict reconstruction, and disarmament, demobilisation and reintegration processes.

- Promoting capacity-building and strengthening partnerships between governments, national women's machineries (NWMs), civil society, media, schools, institutions of higher education, religious organisations and other social institutions, regional and international bodies in the promotion of gender equality and tolerance of diversity.

- Ensuring the collection and dissemination of sex-disaggregated data and integrating gender analysis into policy-making, planning and programme implementation in conflict and post-conflict situations.

- Documenting and disseminating good practice in gender equality initiatives in the area of democracy, peace and conflict.

- Promoting the funding of programmes that will facilitate the gender-sensitive leadership of young people.

- Promoting attention to democracy, good governance, peace, security and the importance of gender issues in the school curriculum.

It is clear that efforts to prevent conflicts and rebuild war-torn societies can only achieve success through an integrated approach that is transparent, inclusive, accountable and ensures the equal participation of women, men and young persons. Such an approach has recorded positive (if sometimes temporary) results in countries including Papua New Guinea, Rwanda, Sierra Leone and South Africa. Following its experience in Sierra Leone, the Commonwealth Secretariat is now involved in assisting with gender mainstreaming in building a sustainable peace in Sri Lanka.

As the Commonwealth Secretary-General has stated:

When women and men are enabled to play their full part in the future of their country, when there is real debate about issues of collective concern – about education, health care, employment, social justice – extremist and violent ideologies are less likely to hold sway.

In line with its mandate, the Commonwealth Secretariat will continue to seek to head off conflicts before they occur, and develop and support initiatives with Governments and international partners to create institutional reforms that empower women and promote gender equality, peace and sustainable development.

How This Book Is Organised

The book is divided into two sections. Part I, 'Gender, Peace and Conflict: Setting the Context', provides an overview of some key issues concerning gender and conflict transformation. Following this first chapter focused on the Commonwealth and its approach to conflict prevention and resolution, Chapter 2 applies a gender lens to armed conflict, violence and conflict transformation. Chapter 3 then examines the progress made to date in achieving gender equality and equity in peace processes, while Chapter 4 focuses on gender mainstreaming in peace support operations, looking at international mandates for women's inclusion and at the current situation regarding gender and peacekeeping. In Chapter 5, the post-war situation in Sierra Leone is used as a case study of how gender can be mainstreamed in post-conflict reconstruction. Finally, Chapter 6 makes the case for creating an international law of peace.

Part II of the book, 'National and Regional Experiences', documents some of the ways in which specific conflict situations have affected women and men, and describes the work of women, in particular, in peace-building processes. Individual chapters focus on Bangladesh, Cyprus, India, Jamaica, the Pacific, Papua New Guinea, the Mano River Union subregion, Sierra Leone and Sri Lanka.

As the Commonwealth Secretary-General has stated: "When women and men are enabled to play their full part in the future of their country, when there is real debate about issues of collective concern – about education, health care, employment, social justice – extremist and violent ideologies are less likely to hold sway".

2 Applying a Gender Lens to Armed Conflict, Violence and Conflict Transformation

Linda Etchart and Rawwida Baksh

Armed conflict and violence, on a small or large scale, are profoundly gendered, though this fact is often obscured and gender is frequently thought to be irrelevant to the analysis of conflict.

Armed conflict and violence, on a small or large scale, are profoundly gendered, though this fact is often obscured and gender is frequently thought to be irrelevant to the analysis of conflict. Despite the fact that armed soldiers and the perpetrators of violence, armed or otherwise, have traditionally been men rather than women, there has until recently been little questioning of the role of particular constructions of masculinity and the characteristics of male culture and subcultures that are integral to armed conflict. As a result, efforts and campaigns to challenge and transform traditional gender roles have had insufficient impact within decision-making institutions.

This is not to say that male culture and subcultures are a *cause* of armed conflict. Armed conflicts arise and develop for particular reasons that will be different in every context, though they will usually be associated with unequal access to resources and lack of involvement in decision-making. However, the expressions of frustration – economic and social – in armed conflict take on forms that are gendered:

- in the mobilisation, training and deployment of troops;

- in the particular kinds of armed violence or armed reaction that troops and non-troops engage in; and

- in the way armed conflict is experienced by women and by men who are not combatants.

By applying a gender lens to armed conflict, that is, by disaggregating data according to gender and by examining women's and men's behaviour during armed conflict and how each is affected by conflict, it is possible to gain insights into the dynamics of armed conflict in all its aspects. Ways in which gender relations may change within a society affected by armed conflict can also be looked at, as well as the potential for a positive transformation of gender roles and gender expectations in societies attempting to transcend armed conflict. In addition, the connections between masculine identity and violence can be examined. Taking a holistic perspective – seeing violent conflict in the context of global economic conditions and global and local politics, and incorporating gender within that perspective – offers far greater possibilities for achieving the equitable and participatory forms of Government that are essential for sustainable development and lasting peace.

As affirmed in the statement of the UN Commission on the Status of Women (CSW) in 2004 on 'Women's equal participation in conflict prevention, management and conflict resolution and in post-conflict peace-building':[5]

> *To achieve sustainable and durable peace, the full and equal participation of women and girls and the integration of gender perspectives in all aspects of conflict prevention, management and conflict resolution and in post-conflict peace-building is essential.*
> (UNCSW, 2004, paragraph 6)

Armed conflict affects women and men differently, not just as victims but as perpetrators of violence against other communities.

The Impact of Armed Conflict on Gender Relations

Armed conflict affects women and men differently, not just as victims but as perpetrators of violence against other communities. In wartime, the different cultures of men and women may become polarised: militaries, particularly government militaries, have until recently been composed almost entirely of men. A strong and dominant form of masculinity will prevail in the armed forces, with one group of men dominating another group of men in a hierarchical system based around concepts of the ideal male.

The emphasis on manliness, courage and the goal of achieving the status of warrior hero may lead to an entrenchment of gender stereotyping and a clearly hierarchical gender division of labour, with women (as well as non-manly men) being relegated to what is perceived to be the inferior status of drivers, cooks and cleaners. If the greatest esteem is bestowed on the warrior hero in military and civil society, men within and outside the armed forces may be resistant to a blurring of gender divisions and a loss of status that might occur if they devote them-

The history of women's participation in liberation or revolutionary struggles in a number of conflict areas in the last 25 years has demonstrated that armed conflict may create opportunities for women's greater participation in decision-making within the family, within the community and on a national scale in a post-conflict country.

selves to home-making and childcare, even if only part-time.

In certain situations, those men who do *not* wish to participate in defending their communities by engaging in armed combat may not feel able to express their reluctance for fear of being regarded as cowards or traitors. Men and boys may find that the social and economic pressures to which they are subject are such that they are obliged to fight against their will to avoid being ostracised by their families and social group. Or they may find that taking up arms is their only means of gaining the respect of their peers, establishing an identity for themselves or merely surviving in situations of disadvantage where employment prospects are restricted.

The pressures on women to join armed forces, state and non-state, may be different from those of men, and there will be a range of factors influencing their recruitment that will differ according to context. Young girls may choose to join non-state forces or they may be kidnapped by rebels and forced into combat, as in the war in Sierra Leone where both kinds of recruitment occurred. Women in armed forces have necessarily found themselves having to adopt traditionally masculine characteristics in order to be effective, and they have learned to dress and behave like men in order to attain equality and take on combat roles. While they may achieve warrior status by exhibiting courage on the battlefield as combatants, and in this way challenge gender stereotyping and become empowered, the gender fluidity here is moving in one direction only and women's status at home as mother and carer is diminished, not enhanced.

Participation as combatants in armed conflict may change people's behaviour. They may gain confidence, be traumatised or become uncontrollable. Women's and men's socialisation prior to engaging in armed conflict will have an impact on subsequent behaviour, but the ways in which men and women behave to their own sex and to members of the other sex may change as a result of their experiences. Gender relations within the family and community may change temporarily or permanently. The history of women's participation in liberation or revolutionary struggles in a number of conflict areas in the last 25 years has demonstrated that armed conflict may create opportunities for women's greater participation in decision-making within the family, within the community and on a national scale in a post-conflict country. This has been the case in Mozambique, Namibia, Nicaragua and especially in South Africa, where women activists were able to ensure that gender equality was incorporated into the country's new Constitution.

On the other hand, gender inequality may increase in times of armed conflict and "the formations of dominant and violent military masculinities in conflict zones around the world create extreme forms of gender oppression" (UNDAW, 2003a). This oppression may take place within small groups or communities or against members of another community. Once gender oppression becomes the norm, it may continue after armed hostilities between enemy groups have ceased. Able-bodied men who have survived combat may find themselves in situations of greater power than previously relative to more vulnerable members of their own community, including women, and they may be outside the control of the Government. In situations of armed conflict, women and children, the elderly and the disabled are particularly vulnerable in the absence of law and order and the protection of community leaders.

The Beijing Declaration referred to the continued existence of "unequal power relationships between women and men in which women often did not have power to insist on safe and responsible sex practices". These unequal power relationships can become more unequal in times of armed conflict and in the aftermath, particularly in respect of women's being unable to avoid unsafe sex practices when threatened by violence.

Moreover, during armed conflict scarce resources may be devoted to defence in the form of recruitment and maintenance of combatants and the purchase and maintenance of weapons. This is likely to affect government budgets: there may be a reduction in investment in health and education services and in other benefits that impact more on women than on men. A reduction in services provided by the state may result in a greater burden being placed on carers, most of whom are women, and will therefore contribute to women's time poverty, itself an obstacle to women's empowerment.

... during armed conflict scarce resources may be devoted to defence in the form of recruitment and maintenance of combatants and the purchase and maintenance of weapons. This is likely to affect government budgets: there may be a reduction in investment in health and education services and in other benefits that impact more on women than on men.

Equating gender with so-called 'women's' issues and needs ignores the particular difficulties men face as men – in growing up, socialisation, relating to other men, finding an identity for themselves and gaining employment and status. This equation also ignores men's necessary involvement with women and children and the key role they play in ensuring women's well-being and therefore their own well-being and that of their children.

Masculine Identity and Violence

The achievement of gender equality is still to a large extent considered a women's issue despite a large body of research on men's gender identities and practices, masculinities and social relations. Some attention has been devoted to men and masculinity by a number of non-governmental organisations (NGOs) and inter-governmental organisations (IGOs), particularly in relation to men's contribution to combating the spread of HIV/AIDS, but issues surrounding the construction of masculine identity, male role models and the influence of perceptions of masculinity on violence and armed conflict have not been addressed fully by Governments and international organisations, and programmes on the ground aimed at the gender-sensitisation of boys and men require greater institutional support.

Equating gender with so-called 'women's' issues and needs ignores the particular difficulties men face as men – in growing up, socialisation, relating to other men, finding an identity for themselves and gaining employment and status. This equation also ignores men's necessary involvement with women and children and the key role they play in ensuring women's well-being and therefore their own well-being and that of their children. Men are often victims of personal and institutional violence, primarily at the hands of other men, so they have a great deal to gain from a reduction in levels of violence (UNDAW, 2003a: 12–13).

The socialisation of boys begins in the home and family and continues in the community, in the street and in the school. There may be peer pressure to reject all things viewed as 'feminine', and there is often an emphasis on masculine activities such as sport and fighting. Boys may be discouraged from engaging in home-making, housework and child care, all of which are often under-valued, and young men may seek respect from their peers by engaging in more 'manly' activities outside the home.

In terms of education, boys and young men may not value the more sedate activities – such as reading, an interest in the arts or academic or creative endeavours – if these are associated with girls and women. This can have a negative impact on their performance in schools and, in recent years, there is growing evidence that in some sectors young men in both developing and developed countries are beginning to fall behind their female counterparts in rates of educational enrolment and attainment. In Australia, Canada and the English-speaking Caribbean, there is an ever-smaller percentage of young men entering university. For example, in Jamaica the percentage of male graduates decreased from 70 per cent to 30 per cent between 1948 and 2000, and similar statistics have emerged elsewhere (Baksh-Soodeen, 2003).

Literacy is increasingly viewed as a 'feminine' subject, and in some countries the numbers of men entering primary teacher training programmes is decreasing, reducing the impact of young male teachers acting as role models for boys at school. A combination of lack of employment prospects and the support boys need to assist them in becoming responsible members of their communities has led vulnerable groups of young men into dropping out of school, if schools exist, and becoming alienated from society. In some cases they fall into high-risk activity such as drug-taking, drug dealing and violent crime that may result in early death. With widespread rural poverty in the developing world, young men and husbands may set out for the city to find employment and be disappointed. They may then turn to violence to survive (see Box 3).

In situations of armed conflict, or where armed conflict is coming to an end, the problems men face can be exacerbated by a lack of infrastructure, the disappearance of teachers and destruction of school buildings, internal displacement and disintegration of communities, poverty and unemployment, often combined with a proliferation of weapons and a culture of violence that may have begun many years earlier at the onset of armed conflict among hostile communities.

When peace agreements are on the table, and where demobilisation, disarmament and reintegration (DDR) programmes are being introduced, the education and re-training of ex-combatants is one of the most challenging tasks facing governments and peace support operations conducted with the support of IGOs and NGOs. Young men and young women in a number of countries, including Sierra Leone and Uganda, were kidnapped or coerced into becoming child soldiers. Where they have been child soldiers for their entire adolescence, they may have lost out almost entirely on their school education and have to start from the beginning.

Child soldiers in the Democratic Republic of Congo
Refugees International

Young men and young women in a number of countries, including Sierra Leone and Uganda, were kidnapped or coerced into becoming child soldiers. Where they have been child soldiers for their entire adolescence, they may have lost out almost entirely on their school education and have to start from the beginning.

... while it is often suggested that women are naturally non-violent, they have been active participants in modern warfare, especially in civil and liberation wars. Women combatants in the South West Africa People's Organisation ... occupied positions at all levels. In South Africa, women were also trained as cadres of Umkhonto We Sizwe, the armed wing of the African National Congress.

> **Box 3 How Poverty and Unemployment Can Lead to Violence**
>
> In Sierra Leone many young men were driven from their rural villages by poverty in the 1990s and went to the capital, Freetown, but were unable to find work there. These young men were then vulnerable to those recruiting for the Revolutionary United Front (RUF), who had begun to wage a civil war against the Government. Some became combatants as the only means of survival, as the RUF was able to provide subsistence and weapons. When the RUF was unable to pay them, the young men used the weapons as a means of providing subsistence. They began to threaten households in order to obtain food. Many of these 'volunteers' (and those who were kidnapped by the RUF) became rootless and unaccountable once no longer under "the authority of the extended family and their chief" (Forna, 2002). Some of them were then able to act with impunity during attacks on villages and on the capital, when so many girls and women were raped and thousands of women, children and men were mutilated.

Assessing Women's 'Natural Role' as Peacemakers

Any analysis of the relationship of women to armed conflict and peace must take care to avoid numerous pitfalls associated with this debate. Chief among these is the tendency to assume that 'women' can be treated and discussed as if their experiences everywhere were similar, regardless of other factors such as race, ethnicity, age or class. The diversity of experiences, identities and roles among women within the war-to-peace context is thus neither documented nor explained.

For example, while it is often suggested that women are naturally non-violent, they have been active participants in modern warfare, especially in civil and liberation wars. Women combatants in the South West Africa People's Organisation (SWAPO) occupied positions at all levels. In South Africa, women were also trained as cadres of Umkhonto We Sizwe, the armed wing of the African National Congress. In addition, women are not innocent of atrocities. In Sierra

Leone, for example, one example is that of Adama 'Cut-Hand', who earned her name from diligently cutting off the hands of her victims. Women commandos of the RUF also spearheaded attacks on villages and laid ambushes on highways linking major towns in the provinces.

At the same time, Gerard De Groot, an expert on women in the military, has noted that "Women … are not usually inclined toward violence. When they are violent, they tend to use their violence in a purposeful fashion, for instance to protect themselves or their children. Their aggression seldom rages out of control" (2002). Men, on the other hand, seem to be inherently more violent – committing the majority of violent crimes, for example – and this aggression is encouraged and developed in the military where, as noted earlier, men tend to be the majority of soldiers or combatants.

Both of these behaviours may be due to social conditioning – military training can teach women to be aggressive and men can be taught to be more peaceful and controlled. Feminist analyses of conflict challenge presumptions about 'natural' gender roles and instead reveal changes in women and men's traditional roles, identities and needs that are reflected in changes in household structures and marriage relationships, women's increasing economic role, fluid divisions of labour, etc.

Whether or not women have special or different perspectives, experiences and capacities that make them non-violent in orientation, however, "in a crisis, men and women, for whatever reason, [appear] to act differently … women tend to act more peacefully and are prone to seek conciliation. The presence of a man in a tense situation can be provocative, even if that man has no intention to provoke. On the other hand, the woman tends to calm stressful situations because she is expected to be peaceful" (De Groot, 2002). In addition, women are viewed as egalitarian, co-operative, nurturing and having an aversion to risk. These qualities, it is argued, have been largely ignored and under-utilised outside the family context but make women particularly effective as peacemakers.

Thus, though a minority of women have played a role in the conduct of hostilities for a variety of reasons, and to view them all as 'natural' peacemakers would be simplistic, many women have sought peace and taken an active role in mediation and conflict resolution initiatives (as the country experiences later

… though a minority of women have played a role in the conduct of hostilities for a variety of reasons, and to view them all as 'natural' peacemakers would be simplistic, many women have sought peace and taken an active role in mediation and conflict resolution initiatives …

As armed conflict has moved away from the battlefield into communities and into people's homes, women and children are now more likely to be the casualties of war. Whereas in the Second World War, 50 per cent of casualties were civilian, in more recent wars the figure is close to 90 per cent.

in this book make clear). In addition, the fact remains that women in armed conflict are more likely to be victims than perpetrators.

War, Women and Women's Bodies

The international community is now fully aware that rape and other forms of violence against women are systematically deployed, with the cruellest effect, as a weapon of war .... Discrimination and gender inequality are seeds that, during wartime, become a bitter fruit that destroys the fabric of communities and the lives of women and their families.

Noeleen Heyzer, Executive Director of UNIFEM[6]

As armed conflict has moved away from the battlefield into communities and into people's homes, women and children are now more likely to be the casualties of war. Whereas in the Second World War, 50 per cent of casualties were civilian, in more recent wars the figure is close to 90 per cent.

One consequence of this trend is that sexual violence against women – and sometimes against men – has increasingly become an instrument of war and a means through which military leaders seek to demonstrate their power and humiliate the women and men of an enemy community. Approximately 500,000 women were raped during the 1994 genocide in Rwanda, which involved the attempted destruction of enemy women's productive capacity and capacity to produce children. The Trial Chamber of the International Criminal Tribunal for Rwanda found that, "like torture, [rape was used for] intimidation, degradation, humiliation, discrimination, punishment, control or destruction of a person" (Prosecutor v. Akayesu. Case No. ICTR-96-4-T).[7]

In Bosnia, ethnic cleansing included the rape of Bosnian women as an act of contamination of their culture. An estimated 20,000 to 50,000 women were raped during five months in 1992 (NGO Working Group, 2002). The capture and desecration of Bosnian Muslim women by Serbian troops was part of military strategy, and women were imprisoned in hotels and other buildings specifically so that they could be raped by soldiers. The violation of women's bodies serves to undermine family cohesiveness and community stability and may serve as a motivation for violence as an act of revenge.

Violence, particularly sexual violence, against women during war also has to be seen in the context of violence against women in many societies in times of peace: for example, wife battering, rape, 'honour' killings and female genital mutilation. In some cases, the incidental rape of women in wartime that is not part of military strategy is an illustration of the destructive effects of certain aspects of the socialisation of boys in peace-time. Following a period of armed conflict, while new government structures and legal systems are being formed and consolidated and where communities and families have become refugees or moved into internally displaced persons (IDP) camps, women may continue to be as much at risk of gender-based violence as they were during the conflict itself. In IDP camps or in a post-conflict situation of scarce resources, women may also be coerced into providing sexual services in return for food or access to supplies.

Both incidental rape in war and rape as a military strategy will have similar consequences in the form of trauma, physical damage, pregnancies and the levels of sexually transmitted infections (STIs). These include HIV/AIDS (see below). Where a high value is placed on the chastity of women, the negative social consequences of rape in war may be grave for the women and their entire families. Male rape by enemy men may cause similar trauma and physical damage, but the social consequences are unlikely to be as significant.

The consequences for women of armed conflict are therefore multiple, different according to circumstances and different from those experienced by men. Some wars are now fought through women's bodies, and women's social status during and following armed conflict is affected by their status prior to the conflict. In addition, if the war changes their position in terms of their chastity or their status as married women (if their husbands are killed), women may lose economic power and the wherewithal to feed their families, children and dependents. Besides having to cope with the distress of losing parents, husbands, children and other relatives and friends, some women will find their lives spared at the cost of losing autonomy and control over their possessions. Women may indeed be deemed possessions in themselves and be claimed as war booty. The transfer of assets from losers to winners may include women *and* their productive labour and reproductive potential.

Violence, particularly sexual violence, against women during war also has to be seen in the context of violence against women in many societies in times of peace: for example, wife battering, rape, 'honour' killings and female genital mutilation.

By looking at armed conflict through a gender lens, women and men together can begin to question gender roles and gender stereotyping within and outside it. This involves taking a more holistic view of the relationship between violence against women in peacetime and violence against women in war.

Communities may fight to protect their women and may migrate to avoid their women being attacked. However, once women have been raped, they may no longer be considered assets of value that are worth protecting, and raped women may in some societies be at risk of being killed by members of their own families for the sake of family 'honour'. Even if raped women are welcomed back into their own *families*, they may still find themselves rejected by their *communities* as they are no longer 'chaste' and may not be considered marriageable. If they have lost their sons or are no longer able to bear children, they may also lose their value. A widow without sons may have land she has farmed with her husband expropriated by relatives. If her husband has disappeared but no body has been discovered or returned, a woman may also find that she is not allowed to remarry while her husband is missing and not accounted for.

The gender inequalities and different gender identities that precede conflict can be exacerbated by it. By looking at armed conflict through a gender lens, women and men together can begin to question gender roles and gender stereotyping within and outside it. This involves taking a more holistic view of the relationship between violence against women in peacetime and violence against women in war.

Gender-based violence within and outside armed conflict

Gender-based violence occurs at all times in all societies, causing damage to individuals, families and communities. It occurs in public places and in the home, and may be carried out by strangers or by members of the community or family. The damage done to individuals through gender-based violence denies them the right to security, liberty and development.

While gender-based violence affects women, men and children, women and girls are more vulnerable and constitute the majority of the victims. Although such violence cuts across status, class, religion, race and economic barriers, the social, cultural, economic and political realities in different regions will affect the forms it takes and the level of severity. Limited participation by women in decision-making positions and processes and discriminatory practices against them make them even more vulnerable.

Gender-based violence has been recognised at the international level as a violation of human rights, and most governments have endorsed and ratified a number of international human rights declarations and conventions with regard to the issue. The CEDAW Committee issued its General Resolution 12 on Violence Against Women in 1989. Governments agreed to take strategic action when they adopted the Beijing Platform for Action in 1995. The UN issued the Declaration on the Elimination of Violence against Women in 1993 and established the Trust Fund to Eliminate Violence against Women in 1997. In recent years, there have been concerted efforts by governments, NGOs, community-based organisations and international organisations, including the Commonwealth Secretariat, to address the problem and to take an integrated and multi-sectoral approach.

During times of armed conflict where, as noted above, violence against women's bodies may become an instrument of war, gender-based violence increases. There may be internal displacement of peoples, a disintegration of communities and a loss of stability and the rule of law provided by village elders and local and central government. Domestic violence may increase among refugees and IDPs as a way for men to express their feelings of frustration and powerlessness (WHO, 1997). A proliferation of light weapons and an increase in crime levels following armed conflict may also render women more vulnerable.

This raises an important question: how do women caught in the middle of violent conflict over issues of resources, identity and different kinds of political claims raise the question of violence within the home? In the hierarchy of violence that is inevitably set up in situations of conflict, violence within the four walls of the home acquires a lesser status than violence outside, and therefore it becomes a more than usually difficult issue to address.

Members of government forces and the police may also be involved in committing gender-based violence, which itself may escalate a conflict between one community and another. A breakdown in law and order in times of armed conflict reduces the security of whole communities, including women, and the recruitment of men and boys into armed forces may leave women and children alone and therefore less protected in their homes.

In the hierarchy of violence that is inevitably set up in situations of conflict, violence within the four walls of the home acquires a lesser status than violence outside, and therefore it becomes a more than usually difficult issue to address.

Girls and young women, as well as some young men, are vulnerable to sexual exploitation in times of armed conflict and post-conflict reconstruction, when they may be internally displaced and suffering economic hardship. Women may have to provide sex in return for protection, as for example in Sierra Leone, where this was demanded by rebels, soldiers, and Civil Defence Forces ....

The return of combat-traumatised men to their families after the end of hostilities may not necessarily mean that women's security increases, however, as levels of domestic violence may rise in a post-conflict environment (see Box 4). As pointed out by the Executive Director of UNIFEM, this frequently means that women are "forced to fight a private war when the public war is over".[8]

Box 4 Some Causes of Increased Domestic Violence During and Post-conflict

During and following the Bougainville crisis in Papua New Guinea, domestic violence became more prevalent and more brutal. The following reasons were suggested by the many women who were counselled and who were asked for explanations for their husbands and partners committing such offences:

- the easy availability of weapons;

- the violence their husbands or partners experienced or meted out as a result of the crisis; and

- lack of jobs, shelter and basic services.

Source: Helen Hakena

Sexual exploitation and HIV/AIDS

Girls and young women, as well as some young men, are vulnerable to sexual exploitation in times of armed conflict and post-conflict reconstruction, when they may be internally displaced and suffering economic hardship. Women may have to provide sex in return for protection, as for example in Sierra Leone, where this was demanded by rebels, soldiers, and Civil Defence Forces (Forster, 2002:145). Over 50 per cent of women experienced some form of sexual violence during the conflict there in 1999 (NGO Working Group, 2002). Where peace support operations are in place, a power imbalance is created between peacekeeping troops on a regular income and disadvantaged inhabitants of the host nation who are vulnerable to pressure to engage in unprotected sex (see Chapter 4).

In times of armed conflict the incidence of STIs, including HIV/AIDS, spirals and becomes a threat to whole communities. STI rates tend to be between two and five times greater in armed forces than in the rest of the population even during peacetime (Alex de Waal, 2002). In Uganda in 1997, for example, the national adult prevalence rate was 9.5 per cent, while among Ugandan soldiers it was 27 per cent (UNAIDS/ WHO, 2002). Over 60 per cent of the soldiers tested in Sierra Leone were reported to be HIV-positive (Forster, 2002: 151). Levels of infection may be even higher among non-state combatants (rebels and insurgents), who often lack military training and discipline and have no access to health information or services. Such groups have also been responsible for very high levels of rape and sexual abuse in many conflicts.

Gender, Conflict Transformation and Peace-building

Conflict transformation has been described by Johann Galtung as "co-operating to plug the holes in the boat we share rather than searching for the one who drilled the first hole" (Galtung et al, 2002). It is used as an alternative to the expression 'conflict resolution' and has a different meaning.

The difficulty with the term 'conflict resolution' is that it implies that conflict is a negative term and a state of human relations that must be avoided or suppressed, whereas it can be a dynamic and constructive force. In the area of war and peace 'conflict resolution' implies, or has been taken to imply, that conflict begins when people take up arms and ends when those people put down their weapons. The concept of 'conflict resolution' that is challenged here contains the view that armed conflicts can be 'resolved', with or without outside intervention or mediation, and that 'peace' in the form of an absence of or an end to violence is a desired outcome – the 'resolution' – when in practice a peace agreement is not usually accompanied by an instant reconciliation between previously hostile communities.

An anti-conflict approach to conflict resolution is one that attempts to achieve a military defeat or otherwise suppress the 'enemy', and subsequently uses force or the threat of force to keep one or more parties silent. Perpetrators of violence, particularly the leaders of armed groups, may be excluded from the

Conflict transformation has been described by Johann Galtung as "co-operating to plug the holes in the boat we share rather than searching for the one who drilled the first hole".

A creative-conflict approach enables all parties involved in violent conflict to be respected, to be enabled to speak out, to be listened to and to become involved in decision-making. Grievances and crimes committed on all sides may be expressed ... as part of the dialogue among opposing groups. This is part of 'conflict transformation', which takes a structural approach to conflict ...

peace table, captured, put on trial, convicted of war crimes and imprisoned as an example to others who may be thinking of engaging in similar acts of armed aggression. Though 'crimes against humanity' may have been committed – and though trials and convictions may be useful, appropriate and symbolically significant – if these processes lead to a suppression of what may be genuine grievances among particular sectors of a population they may only serve to exacerbate tensions that may erupt into violence at a later date.

A creative-conflict approach enables all parties involved in violent conflict to be respected, to be enabled to speak out, to be listened to and to become involved in decision-making. Grievances and crimes committed on all sides may be expressed, noted, documented and acknowledged as part of the dialogue among opposing groups. This is part of 'conflict transformation', which takes a structural approach to conflict and examines the outside forces that may have led peoples into conflict with each other, rather than wishing merely to identify wrongdoers and criminals. A conflict may arise and be sustained out of frustration at the lack of satisfaction of basic needs, and frustration may then lead to the creation of identity politics in disputes over resources or territory. The structural approach converts what has become a personal conflict – one group pitted against another and each group blaming the conflict on the other's behaviour and attitude – into a consensus among the parties that the conflict arises out of a deficient structure, that is, as a result of outside circumstances that have forced the parties to take certain opposing positions.

Once a consensus is reached that the blame lies elsewhere, then the parties can move beyond having to decide who is in the right, who has suffered the greatest injustices and who has committed the worst crimes. No longer is there a need to seek out one 'truth', an 'official version' of a conflict, with a view to identifying and distinguishing between 'perpetrators' and 'victims'. Rather, there is an acceptance that there are as many truths to tell as there are people to tell them, a multitude of truths with a multitude of people who can (re)write and be actors in their own history, both the past and into the future. These multitudes are made up of women as well as men. Here the importance of applying a gender lens becomes salient as in official histories of peoples and nations women have often been invisible – they have been hidden and their stories and activities left untold.

The recounting and interpretation of historical events such as the conquest of territories and the rise and fall of empires might be entirely different if told from the perspective of the family, the village, the dispossessed and the disenfranchised, or by those who were agents of change but whose actions went unnoticed. In applying a gender lens to state, regional or global politics and decision-making, what emerges is that the 'high' politics of parliaments, governments and regional and inter-national diplomacy have been performed and documented from a 'public', masculine perspective, and the 'low' politics of the private, the family and the community are left unexplored. The leaders' wishes are expressed and incorporated, identities are polarised and alternative visions are eclipsed.

In conflicts that spill over into violence, leaders may take up entrenched positions and use the media to pressure people to take on identities they may not previously have felt were theirs. In the interest of establishing parliamentary democracy and in order to create political parties and political identities, some people may find themselves being forced to take sides against their will and have to label themselves as belonging to a particular group, such as Tutsi or Hutu, Greek or Turkish, Serb or Croat, where they might have chosen another identity as their primary one or used multiple identities.

In the conflict transformation approach, different parties are enabled to envision their dreams for the future. As the aspira-tions of women and men may be different, the goals of women from different sides of a divide may have more in common with each other than they do with the visions of the men of their own side.

Conceptualising peace-building

Peace-building has become the buzzword in international policy as a key plank of post-Cold War global security. However, the concept is defined, interpreted and executed in a variety of ways and involves numerous different theoretical approaches and terms and a wide range of activities (see Box 5).

In the conflict transformation approach, different parties are enabled to envision their dreams for the future. As the aspirations of women and men may be different, the goals of women from different sides of a divide may have more in common with each other than they do with the visions of the men of their own side.

Box 5 Various Theories of Peace-building

Ernie Regehr has argued that peace-building:

> reflects a set of good intentions more than it does concrete programmes ... peace-building objectives have become defined in increasingly comprehensive terms, to the point that the term is in danger of simply duplicating the ideas and intentions of common security. (1995: 1, 3–8)

In contrast, Stephen Ryan views peace-building as:

> the struggle which most directly tries to reverse the destructive processes which accompany violence. This involves a shift of focus ... to the attitudes and socio-economic circumstances of ordinary people. Therefore, it tends to concentrate on the context of the conflict rather than on issues which divide the parties. (1990: 61)

This attention to the underlying conditions of deprivation and exclusion that can spark off violent conflict was re-affirmed by Lederach (1997). Others, like former Canadian Foreign Minister Lloyd Axworthy, equate peace-building with human security, defining it as "a package of measures to strengthen and solidify peace by building a sustainable infrastructure of human security. It's like a triage, the immediate reaction of the hospital staff when injured arrive" (1996). Within this context, the Canadian Peace-building Coordinating Committee has published a 'package of measures' that includes a wide variety of economic, political and security issues that they feel must be addressed in peace-building.

On the other hand, Roland Paris (1997) is highly critical of the current analysis and implementation of peace-building, claiming that it is a concept rooted in Western culture that is then replicated as a fairly uniform 'one-size-fits-all' programme in war-torn developing countries, most often in Africa, without careful adaptation.

While a precise definition does not seem possible, the focus suggested by Lederach (1997) on the underlying structural, relational and cultural roots of conflict is necessary for the sustainable transformation of societies. Peace-building must thus comprise all those multi-level strategies that seek to address the underlying causes of violent conflicts, either to prevent them from arising in the first place or to prevent a recurrence if they have already occurred.

Schoolgirls with placards urge peace in Freetown, Sierra Leone
Robert Knoth/Panos Pictures

Peace-building is also context specific as the issues that concern people in one country or sub-region will be similar to but distinct from those of people in other countries or regions. For example, a unifying issue in most women's peace-building is prevention of violence against women. Where the abduction and rape of women and girl-children is a focus of women's peace-building activities in the Mano River Union, gender and religion is thematic in Northern Nigeria. An example from Sierra Leone highlights the lack of precision about what constitutes peace and peace-building (see Box 6).

The re-constitution of the state in post-conflict societies provides an opportunity for women to challenge traditional gender roles, create spaces for new identities and imagine new possibilities for themselves (Baksh-Soodeen, 2003).

Box 6 Different Views of Peace-building in Sierra Leone

During the rebel war in Sierra Leone, peace was regarded as a single event. People would remark that "peace don kam", i.e., peace has come, after a peace agreement was signed and hostilities had ceased. Or they would say "de peace don pieces", meaning literally 'the peace is in pieces', to mark the resumption of hostilities. The focus was on the imposition of the peace that is not war and not on addressing the underlying structural inequities that led to the war. Major dissension occurred between civil society groups. Some viewed peace-building as developing relationships between conflicting groups. Others equated peace-building with military strength, arguing that military defeat of the rebel groups would secure lasting peace. A few believed peace-building mandated a structural approach and focused on issues of justice, reconciliation, rights and good governance issues. Eventually, convergence in perspectives occurred as groups learned that effective peace-building is a process that requires multi-faceted approaches.

Source: Christiana Solomon

Gender mainstreaming in post-conflict situations

The re-constitution of the state in post-conflict societies provides an opportunity for women to challenge traditional gender roles, create spaces for new identities and imagine new possibilities for themselves (Baksh-Soodeen, 2003). The drafting of new constitutions and the transformation of legal systems at the conclusion of a peace agreement provides opportunities for mainstreaming gender into all state institutions, including the executive, legislature, judiciary, security services and education system. In the formation of a new state or the transformation of an existing one, the teaching of civil and political rights is an essential component of participatory democracy. Citizens need to be aware of their social, economic and cultural rights, including their rights to property, inheritance, entering contracts and physical security. Failure to convey information to citizens about their rights, or to allow citizens to exercise these rights, is a cause for instability and may provoke a resurgence of armed conflict.

For the majority of countries (180 by end March 2005) that have ratified the Convention on the Elimination of All Forms of Discrimination against Women (CEDAW), there is a legal obligation for public authorities and institutions to inform women and men of women's rights under international humanitarian law. Under CEDAW, the state has an obligation to challenge discrimination against women and gender stereotyping (article 10(c)), and to encourage men to participate in raising their children. Article 5 (b) of CEDAW states that State parties shall take appropriate measures:

> To ensure that family education includes a proper understanding of maternity as a social function and the recognition of the common responsibility of men and women in the upbringing and development of their children ....

An important element in the retraining of ex-combatants in DDR programmes needs to be awareness-raising in the area of the rights of women to enter freely into marriage (16(b)) and women's equal rights to decide 'freely and responsibly on the number and spacing of their children' (16(e)).

In the interests of women's equal rights to hold public office in a participatory democracy, the educational sector has an obligation under CEDAW to contribute to the goal "to eliminate discrimination against women in the political and public life of the country" and to ensure that women can exercise the right to "be eligible for election to all publicly elected bodies; [and] ... to hold public office and perform all public functions at all levels of government" (article 7).

Sustainable peace is only attainable if all citizens, women and men, regardless of class or ethnicity, are able to vote in all elections and public referenda and be eligible for election to public posts.

Sustainable peace is only attainable if all citizens, women and men, regardless of class or ethnicity, are able to vote in all elections and public referenda and be eligible for election to public posts.

3 Achieving Gender Equality and Equity in Peace Processes

Elsie Onubogu and Linda Etchart

Growing realisation that the transition from conflict to post-conflict is an important opportunity for re-ordering society has highlighted women's traditional exclusion from policy- and decision-making about post-conflict reconstruction and led to increased demands for their inclusion.

The equal access and full participation of women in power structures and their full involvement in all efforts for the prevention and resolution of conflicts are essential for the maintenance and promotion of peace and security.

– Beijing Platform for Action, 1995

The absence of women in formally convened international meetings, including those for conflict resolution, is well documented (Charlesworth and Chinkin, 2000). Although the groundwork for gendered intervention should be laid at the peace negotiating table, the reality of peace processes is that the most attention is paid to the demands of those responsible for violence and bloodshed, and far less is given to alternative perspectives for peaceful reconstruction that might be offered by citizens who were caught up in the conflict. This has been attributed to the "tyranny of the emergency" (Mertus, 2000: xii). Growing realisation that the transition from conflict to post-conflict is an important opportunity for re-ordering society has highlighted women's traditional exclusion from policy- and decision-making about post-conflict reconstruction and led to increased demands for their inclusion. Women's non-governmental organisations (NGOs) have been active at the international level in seeking commitment to the inclusion of women in peace processes and the negotiation of peace agreements.

International Declarations and Resolutions

The need for gender mainstreaming in peace processes has been internationally recognised at least since the UN's Second World Conference on Women (Nairobi, 1985).[9] More specifically, the Platform for Action adopted at the Fourth World Conference on Women at Beijing in 1995 asserted that:

In addressing armed or other conflicts, an active and visible policy of mainstreaming a gender perspective into all policies and programmes should be promoted so that before decisions are taken an analysis is made of the effects on women and men, respectively. (Paragraph 141)

This policy goal translated into strategic objective E.1 requiring governments and international and regional institutions to:

Take action to promote equal participation of women and equal opportunities for women to participate in all forums and all peace activities at all levels, particularly at the decision-making level.

(Paragraph 142 (a))

And to:

Integrate a gender perspective in the resolution of armed or other conflicts. (Paragraph 142 (b))

Five years later, the Outcome Document of the Beijing +5 Special Session of the UN General Assembly again called for action at the international level to:

[e]nsure and support the participation of women at all levels of decision-making and implementation in development activities and peace processes ...

(United Nations, 2000a, paragraph 86 (b))

These statements in non-binding declarations and programmes for action were reiterated in the ground-breaking UN Security Council Resolution (UNSCR) 1325, October 2000 (see Chapter 4). This:

... calls upon all actors involved, when negotiating and implementing peace agreements to adopt a gender perspective, including, inter alia:

- *The special needs of women and girls during repatriation and resettlement and for rehabilitation, reintegration and post-conflict reconstruction;*

- *Measures that support local women's peace initiatives and indigenous processes for conflict resolution, and that involve women in all implementation mechanisms of the peace agreements; [and]*

Gender balance requires the inclusion of both women and men at all stages and in all roles within peace processes and social reconstruction, for example, as members of the parties' negotiating teams or as mediators.

- *Measures that ensure the protection of and respect for human rights of women and girls, particularly as they relate to the constitution, the electoral system, the police and the judiciary.*

UNSCR 1325 puts women's rights and gender equality squarely on the agenda for societal reconstruction and underlines the relevance of determining women's needs in a post-conflict settlement.

Gender Balance and Gender Mainstreaming

Two related concepts emerge from the international statements quoted above: gender balance and gender mainstreaming throughout the peace process and its subsequent implementation. Gender balance requires the inclusion of both women and men at all stages and in all roles within peace processes and social reconstruction, for example, as members of the parties' negotiating teams or as mediators. The expert group meeting on 'Peace agreements as a means of promoting gender equality and ensuring participation of women – A framework of model provisions', held in Ottawa, Canada, from 10–13 November 2003 in preparation for the 2004 meeting of the Commission on the Status of Women (CSW), provides recommendations in this regard (UNDAW, 2003b).

The participation of more women directly or indirectly in a peace process, however, does not of itself ensure the inclusion of women's concerns in the substance of any agreement reached. Gender balance in participation must be accompanied by gender mainstreaming. Women and men may have different needs and priorities in the reconstruction process and may face different obstacles to achieving their objectives. Women may also have different perceptions of the causes of the conflict and thus of the appropriate concessions for bringing it to an end. Highly relevant to a gendered analysis of the conflict is the social, economic and political position of women before and during the conflict, as well as in what might be called the transition to post-conflict. These are not a series of unconnected events but rather patterns and forms of behaviour that reveal mindsets and obstacles.

The very concepts of 'post-conflict', 'reconstruction' and 'rehabilitation' may be problematic. Just as women and men experience war differently, so are their experiences of post-conflict gendered. There can be no assumption that the violence stops for women with a formal ceasefire. Rather, as seen in Chapter 2, the forms and locations of gender-based violence change. Women's relations with war-traumatised children, family members and former fighters all place gendered demands on them. Demographic changes flowing from the conflict – in particular the disproportionate number of women – impact on issues such as access to land, housing and social benefits, and return after internal or international displacement. Priority in social and health services may be given to those (primarily males) who fought in the conflict, contributing to hardship and poverty for those with social responsibility for the care of others. A focus on addressing ethnic or religious difference that fuelled the conflict can obscure continued gender-based discrimination. In turn, the intersections of ethnic or religious discrimination with gender-based discrimination should be identified and considered.

Not only is 'post-conflict' a misnomer for women, so too are the notions of reconstruction and rehabilitation. Both concepts assume an element of going back, restoring to a position or capacity that previously existed. But this is not necessarily what women want. Emerging from situations of armed conflict, women may not want to return to the status quo before the conflict and may seek full citizenship, social justice and empowerment based on respect for their human dignity and human rights. The goal is societal transformation rather than restored dependence and subordination. If women are excluded from decision-making in the drafting of peace agreements, as has been the case historically, their interests may not be taken into consideration. If only men are involved in the implementation of those agreements, again women's interests may be sidelined.

In many post-conflict situations there is a three-way relationship among the designated leaders, the population and international agencies. Where the presence of UN or regional, military or civilian personnel is envisaged, their level of involvement and mandates must also be determined. The presence of international agencies may help further women's interests post-conflict. Members of the international institutions may be allies for women against local communities resistant to women's empowerment and may be able to assist in accessing resources and in identifying leaders. However, they may also be an obstacle. A bureaucrat who is not versed in gender matters

Emerging from situations of armed conflict, women may not want to return to the status quo before the conflict and may seek full citizenship, social justice and empowerment based on respect for standards of women's human dignity and human rights. The goal is societal transformation rather than restored dependence and subordination.

*Conflict Resolution
Workshop in Sri Lanka*
Sumede Lyanage/Voluntary
Service Overseas

*UNSCR 1325
calls for women's
involvement ...
in ... peace
agreements,
post-conflict
reconstruction
and in the
drafting of new
laws, yet in
several instances
of nation-building
in the last years
of the twentieth
century,
opportunities for
including gender
equality in new
constitutions
were lost.*

may prove an additional hurdle for local women to overcome in presenting issues and concerns. International agencies may be ignorant of local initiatives and programmes and make no attempt to find out what is happening on the ground. Members of international agencies can even be positively harmful to women, as when peacekeepers become involved in sexual abuse and trafficking (see Chapter 4).

UNSCR 1325 calls for women's involvement at the peace table and in decision-making bodies involved in the formulation of peace agreements, post-conflict reconstruction and in the drafting of new laws, yet in several instances of nation-building in the last years of the twentieth century, opportunities for including gender equality in new constitutions were lost. The end of armed conflict provides the possibility for gender relations and identities to be renegotiated, and for women to increase their participation in public life. In practice, however, women have had to shout very loud for their voices to be heard.

Obstacles to Women's Participation in Peace Talks

Since the inclusion of women in peace processes has traditionally been so limited, in reality achieving gender balance means seeking ways of bringing women into these processes. Similarly, long-standing failure of those negotiating such agreements to take account of the separate and distinctive needs of women in the reconstituted society means that gender mainstreaming must be directed towards addressing this deficit.

This means identifying the obstacles to women's participation in peace talks and considering the difference it might make to post-conflict reconstruction if women were included. Some obstacles to participation can be readily identified:

1   Far fewer women have wielded the guns, and the allocation of power envisaged in peace agreements is limited to those who have been fighting for it.

2   Even when women have fought and been part of the fighting units, they become invisible again at peace talks, on the assumption that what men from the community want is what women also want.

3   Negotiating teams are usually drawn from government, diplomatic or military echelons. Women are largely absent

from all these existing national power structures and thus are not considered for inclusion in international negotiations or in international roles.

4   Women may be excluded from public life by local custom and tradition.

5   Even where women are not deliberately excluded, their activities are not seen as political. Stereotyped assumptions about women's roles means that the work they do to ensure their family's and community's survival and building networks throughout the conflict is simply not perceived by those conducting negotiations as relevant to organisation and leadership in the post-conflict society. Women who engage in manifestly political and conciliatory roles in a society experiencing conflict, including the provision of care and education to victims of conflict, are often not encouraged to see their work as political or even as directly engaging in public welfare as such.

6   Logistical and security issues also tend to exclude women, for example, the practice of holding peace negotiations far from the local community. Especially where women have been targeted throughout the conflict and there has been a high incidence of sexual violence, women may have security concerns about attending any negotiations.

7   Other constraints might be inability to access resources to attend or women's caring commitments.

International negotiators must change their biased mindsets about the roles people are performing in society to look holistically and from a critical gender perspective at the contributions of all sections of the community. Those responsible for the organisation of peace talks should ensure that women leaders and peace-builders are identified, that visible and effective security arrangements for women are put in place and that provision is made for their needs.

Why Women Must be Included in Peace Processes

It may be questioned why it is important to ensure the participation of women in peace processes, that is, to query whether gender balance matters and whether international and national

Those responsible for the organisation of peace talks should ensure that women leaders and peace-builders are identified, that visible and effective security arrangements for women are put in place and that provision is made for their needs.

An effective peace process should be built on the widest base of experience and therefore must take account of local women's lived experiences during the conflict and their enormous responsibilities post-conflict. Gender balance does not mean the inclusion of a few highly placed international women but listening and responding to the diverse experiences of women who have lived through the conflict.

negotiators cannot be relied on to ensure gender mainstreaming. There is controversy over whether women negotiate differently from men, whether they speak with a "different voice" (Gilligan, 1982) that is inherently better suited to building relationships and connections and commonalities among warring parties and, even if this is so, whether they can bring these skills to the peace table. It is often asserted that women have a special relationship to peace, that those who give life reject violent means of ending it. These claims are also rejected on the basis that they are empirically and theoretically unsustainable (see also Chapter 2).

There are other reasons for supporting women's claims to participation in the processes of societal reconstruction.

First, human rights standards of equality and fairness require women's participation in public life. As noted earlier, the majority of States have adopted the Convention on the Elimination of All Forms of Discrimination against Women, Article 8 of which requires the need "to ensure to women, on equal terms with men and without discrimination, the opportunity to represent their governments at the international level". No State has made a reservation to this provision. There has been little attempt to apply it in the context of peace processes, but failure to include women in policy- and decision-making about state and institution-building legitimises their subsequent exclusion from such positions within the state and its institutions.

Second, conflict is highly gendered. Women's different experiences during conflict are likely to be central to their determination of their post-conflict priorities and needs. It is therefore essential that these experiences are fed directly into all stages of the process and taken into account. In modern forms of conflict civilians – overwhelmingly women, children and elderly persons – are deliberately targeted for abuse and violations. The gendered impact of conflict continues after the ceasefire. Since most of the fighting is among men, there is typically a demographic shift to women making up the majority of the population, many as female single parents and de facto carers of others displaced by conflict. An effective peace process should be built on the widest base of experience and therefore must take account of local women's lived experiences during the conflict and their enormous responsibilities post-conflict. Gender balance does not mean the inclusion of a few highly placed international women but listening and responding to the diverse experiences of women who have lived through the conflict (see Box 7).

Box 7 Changes Women Experienced due to the Conflict in Sri Lanka

Sweneetha: My husband worked at a sawmill [but] he was at home for a day as he had hurt his leg. Villagers informed the army that he had been shot. The army took him away that night. When my mother-in-law, four children and I went to the camp the next day, I was told that he was never brought to the camp. Later we found out that he had been killed. I was 24 and he was 29. Before my husband was taken away I used to be very backward, never stepped out of the house at night. But now I have the strength to face anything, even step out at night and fight someone. I am not scared of anyone.

Leela: I lost my 14-year-old son, abducted on his way to school. To date I have no news of him. I joined the Mothers' Front in November 1989. Before this I was not involved in any organisation and was confined to my home. There was no necessity for me to take part in community activities. But with the disappearance of my son and my joining the movement, I have become self-confident and now I can go alone to police stations and courts and move with people. This is the strength I have gained through my pain and sorrow.

Udula: When I lost my husband during the insurgency I was only 26 years old with two small children. The unexpected loss of my husband left me with many responsibilities. Gradually I learnt how to cope on my own. The inaugural rally of the Mothers' Front was a turning point in my life. Although I knew many women had met the same fate as mine, I did not expect to see such a large crowd. At the meeting an Executive Committee was elected and I was elected Vice-President.

Source: Neloufer de Mel

Women can come together in their own parallel process to draw up their demands for post-conflict reconstruction, as in the meeting of Afghan women at the Summit for Democracy held in Brussels, 4–5 December 2001, simultaneously with the UN Talks on Afghanistan held in Bonn.

Finally, as Box 7 also illustrates, it is important for women to move from being perceived solely as victims of conflict to agents for transformation and empowerment. What is obvious from all conflict zones are the many movements, initiatives and networks that women build up and operate throughout its duration (see next section). The local conditions, the factors promoting and inhibiting peace, are well known to local women and they can bring that knowledge to the peace table. Failure to include these views and ideas can lead to an impoverished understanding of peace and security that focuses on militarism and power supported by force.

Accepting the importance of ensuring the participation of women in talks for post-conflict reconstruction opens up other contested issues – for example, determining who speaks on behalf of local women and ensuring that representatives are able to give a comprehensive overview of the needs of all women in the conflict zone. Women would have had widely different experiences throughout the conflict, and their post-conflict situations will also vary. Strategies must be devised to ensure that as many voices as possible are heard. For example:

- Women can come together in their own parallel process to draw up their demands for post-conflict reconstruction, as in the meeting of Afghan women at the Summit for Democracy held in Brussels, 4–5 December 2001, simultaneously with the UN Talks on Afghanistan held in Bonn.

- Local women can be informed about the peace talks by sending observers to the process who can report back to women's groups and through local networks such as churches. Such observers must be carefully chosen and given training in their task. They should also be supported in the feedback process.

- There can be a broad consultative process throughout the state, as was the case with the South Africa constitution-making process.

The United Nations, the Commonwealth, the Organisation for Security and Co-operation in Europe (OSCE) and many other government organisations, IGOs and NGOs have made significant strides in promoting and implementing gender mainstreaming in conflict transformation.

Women in Peace Movements and as Leaders

Examples from Bangladesh, Cyprus, Papua New Guinea, Sierra Leone and Sri Lanka demonstrate the power of women's collective efforts in supporting women's rights and gender equality in times of armed conflict, in forming protest movements against government policies and in demanding the inclusion of women in decision-making and for policy changes (see Part Two). Such movements often start with the humanitarian and practical – seeking shared means of acquiring food and water to feed the family for example, or creating informal schooling programmes. Other initiatives may be more overtly political such as forming groups to demand information about disappeared male relatives.

Women's groups have provided support for women who have lost their husbands, restoring their self-confidence and bringing them in to the public sphere, sometimes for the first time. Women also occupy positions and take on roles previously filled by the men who are absent. They have brought individual women and women's groups together in campaigns for minority and women's rights. They have succeeded in crossing ethnic divides and national borders, which demands courage and tenacity in the face of obstacles (see Box 8).

Box 8 Women Finding Common Ground Across Ethnic Divisions

When a group of Greek Cypriot and Turkish Cypriot women from different NGOs overcame the ban on bi-communal contact and met for a workshop in London in February 2002, differences in ideological positions and needs as well as visions emerged. However, the women formed close alliances and developed a joint agenda in support of reunification: "No matter what political leaders are saying or doing, we are continuing the journey to peace although some may not be ready to go through all that peace entails". As trust and openness to the others' viewpoints increased, the women addressed what they had in common as women regarding Greek-Turkish-Cyprus relations. They agreed to reinforce each other's efforts for peace-building and for women's increased representation in public life.

Source: Maria Hadjipavlou

Examples from Bangladesh, Cyprus, Papua New Guinea, Sierra Leone and Sri Lanka demonstrate the power of women's collective efforts in supporting women's rights and gender equality in times of armed conflict, in forming protest movements against government policies and in making demands for the inclusion of women in decision-making and for policy changes.

Women's involvement in support groups and peace movements may introduce them into public life for the first time and enable them to think of themselves as potential leaders. By taking on leadership positions in local and central government and joining with other women to form lobby groups, women activists have succeeded in bringing about constitutional changes with regard to women's rights in several post-conflict countries ...

Support among women's movements worldwide and from the international community – from international NGOs and governments of third countries – can be important in maintaining morale and raising the profile of quiet voices that might otherwise be lost in the cacophony of propaganda that often accompanies violent conflict between communities.

Women's peace movements have to create strategic alliances with other members of society, in particular the political elites. Gender issues that concern women and men, but that women's groups campaign around – such as reproductive rights and women's equality with regard to marriage, child custody and property inheritance – may be eclipsed by more pressing issues in a situation of armed conflict. It is essential that these issues are highlighted in the process of creating new constitutions as part of a peace-building and post-conflict reconstruction process.

Women's involvement in support groups and peace movements may introduce them into public life for the first time and enable them to think of themselves as potential leaders. By taking on leadership positions in local and central government and joining with other women to form lobby groups, women activists have succeeded in bringing about constitutional changes with regard to women's rights in several post-conflict countries – including Afghanistan, Namibia, South Africa and Timor-Leste – that provide models for other countries emerging from conflict. Women's activism, supported by national women's machineries (NWMs), IGOs and NGOs, has brought about a large increase in the percentage of women in local and national government. For example, in the 2004 local elections in Namibia, women gained 123 of 283 seats countrywide – up to 43.4 per cent from 41.3 per cent during the previous elections.

Through participation in government in a critical mass, women parliamentarians, with the support of male parliamentarians, can introduce and promote legislation to enable women to gain access to education and knowledge of their rights, inherit property, increase their rights over their own bodies and protect themselves and their children against violence and discrimination.

A Framework for Gender Mainstreaming in Post-conflict Reconstruction[10]

Gender mainstreaming is not just a matter of procedures and processes. There are also substantive concerns that must be addressed. In a post-conflict situation, certain issues have particular significance for women. A gendered framework for post-conflict reconstruction should address women's physical security, their economic security and their legal security (all of which overlap). Local conditions must be taken into account. Some of these issues are appropriate for inclusion in an agreement while others must be undertaken by those in positions of responsibility within the area.

Human rights guarantees

Human rights standards underpin physical, economic and legal security. Their inclusion, including equality provisions, in post-conflict arrangements has become accepted. International human rights instruments may be listed in a peace agreement as binding on the parties (for example, in the General Framework Agreement for Peace in Bosnia and Herzegovina), annexed to the agreement and/or incorporated into constitutional frameworks, for example through a Bill of Rights. Human rights institutions and localised implementation mechanisms might be included, as with the Human Rights Chamber in Bosnia.

Inclusion of human rights instruments, however, is insufficient to guarantee to women the same protection of their rights as men. There must be full understanding of the concept of women's human rights and a commitment to their implementation. At a minimum, if the State is not a party to CEDAW, provision should be made for assistance to it to ratify or accede to the Convention and for the submission of its first report to the Committee on the Elimination of Discrimination against Women. If the State is already a party, technical and practical assistance might be offered for fulfilment of its obligations.

Attention should also be given to how a human rights culture can be developed and the role of civil society, including the media, in achieving this. Article 5 (a) of CEDAW requires States to:

A gendered framework for post-conflict reconstruction should address women's physical security, their economic security and their legal security (all of which overlap). Local conditions must be taken into account. Some of these issues are appropriate for inclusion in an agreement while others must be undertaken by those in positions of responsibility within the area.

Post-conflict, women face particular threats to their security, in particular gender-based violence .... Violence against women undermines their autonomy, citizenship status and human dignity. It is both a direct violation of women's human rights and causes violations of other rights.

modify the social and cultural patterns of conduct of men and women, with a view to achieving the elimination of prejudices and customary and all other practices which are based on the idea of the inferiority or the superiority of either of the sexes or on stereotyped roles for men and women.

The guarantee of economic and social rights has been considered especially significant for women's pursuit of citizenship on a basis of equality with men. Accordingly, a rights-based approach should be taken towards the provision of needs, especially access to appropriate and affordable health care and education. Programmes should be developed to address issues – such as forced or early marriage or gender-based violence – that may prevent women and girls from accessing services.

Physical security

Post-conflict, women face particular threats to their security, in particular gender-based violence (see Chapter 2). Violence against women undermines their autonomy, citizenship status and human dignity. It is both a direct violation of women's human rights and causes violations of other rights. Such conditions are antithetical to any real concept of democracy and steps must be taken to deal with both violence against women that occurred during the conflict as well as gender-based violence that is likely to continue in ways still connected to the conflict. This includes violence committed by those suffering from post-traumatic stress, by men returning to households headed by women during the war and by men facing dislocation and unemployment on return.

States should expressly accept their obligation to prevent, punish and eradicate violence against women – for example, by incorporating into national law the principles and recommended measures contained in the 1993 General Assembly Declaration on the Elimination of Violence against Women (GA Res. 48/104, 20 December 1993). For ongoing violence, measures such as safe places for reporting violence, secure refuges and training of police officers, the judiciary, those offering social aid, housing officials and health personnel in dealing with violence against women should be given priority. Women should be appointed to all such positions. There must be an insistence that cultural traditions can never justify violence, while drawing on local expertise to determine ways in which it can be addressed. A women's protection officer might be designated within the UN administration (or elsewhere) to play a co-ordinating role.

The presence of UN and other institutional military and civilian forces can provide a safe space for the civilian population in place of the conflict and fear of attack that preceded their mobilisation. Nevertheless, the presence of large numbers of unattached men in itself creates physical security concerns for women, especially when the men have comparatively large amounts of money available (see Chapter 4).

Economic security

In many countries, women are excluded from full participation in economic life through unequal access to land and property, which in turn denies them the means of subsistence and security for obtaining mortgages, credit and loans. In agricultural communities this also denies women food security. Land-holding systems are complex and highly specialised, especially where they depend on a mix of legislation and customary law, and of communal and personal property rights. In many systems women suffer through both legal discrimination and traditional attitudes and customs that deny them property rights, including inheritance. The position of women with respect to land and property ownership is exacerbated by conflict, which destroys existing structures (already prejudicial to women) and causes massive displacement.

The situation does not ease post-conflict. For example, women who have been able to move on to unoccupied land during the war may be evicted by returning owners. In customary land ownership, where proof of title is through possession and occupation, the land becomes subject to competing claims between displaced persons and new occupiers. Women whose male relatives have died or disappeared and have no recognised capacity to inherit remain permanently dispossessed. Beyani (2001) argues that state intervention through legislation, enforceable through the courts, is needed to provide women with full access to land, property and inheritance rights, informed by a human rights approach that addresses

The position of women with respect to land and property ownership is exacerbated by conflict, which destroys existing structures (already prejudicial to women) and causes massive displacement …. The situation does not ease post-conflict.

Judges may be unwilling to give effect to the new laws and fall back on applying custom that is disadvantageous to women. Tradition may still exclude women from local land management. Legislation must therefore be coupled with a comprehensive package of legal advice ... and a public awareness campaign around the disadvantages suffered by women through lack of access to land.

their unequal position within the traditional family structure. Such legislation must be informed by a prior gender audit, in which local women have been consulted, of the existing legal and de facto situation.

Even where such legislation is passed, its implementation is not likely to be effective without additional measures. People have no legal security where they are ignorant of, or can make little use of, their existing or new rights. The court structures may be weak, financially out of reach or unavailable in rural areas. Judges may be unwilling to give effect to the new laws and fall back on applying custom that is disadvantageous to women. Tradition may still exclude women from local land management. Legislation must therefore be coupled with a comprehensive package of legal advice and assistance, practical steps to facilitate access to the law, judicial education, education of those administering land rights and a public awareness campaign around the disadvantages suffered by women through lack of access to land.

Structural issues

Structural issues that should be addressed as integral to the post-conflict presence of the international community include:

- The participation of women at all levels and in all functions of the international agencies present in the post-conflict zone. This means overcoming the male predominance and bias of international institutions, as it is extremely difficult to urge gender equality in national institution building if there is no example from the international bodies implementing the agreement.

- Ensuring attention to gender equality throughout the administrative structures of an international administration.

- Facilitating support for local women from the international community and establishing genuine partnership among local NGOs and agencies and administrators. Channels for communication between local women and the international agencies must be established.

- Ensuring budgetary allocation for gender programmes in the reconstruction process and ensuring that promises of resources that are made by the international community are kept in a timely and non-bureaucratic manner.

- Considering how gender intersects with other identities such as ethnicity and religion, ensuring that quotas (for example, quotas on the basis of ethnicity for positions of power within the state institutions) do not exclude gender balance.

- Identifying short-, medium- and long-term objectives. There may have to be immediate attention to essentials such as security, shelter, health care and provision of food and water. The work of UNHCR in identifying gender concerns in refugee camps might provide some useful analogies for this.

Gender, Justice and Reconciliation

International Criminal Tribunals and the International Criminal Court

The role of the international community is also to establish international norms of human rights and justice, providing an ethical dimension to peace. No longer is there simply victors' justice when hostilities cease. There has been a paradigm shift in attitudes, and now accountability and justice are considered an essential part of building peace in post-violence societies.

To this end, a landmark decision was made 1993 when the UN Security Council decided to set up the International Criminal Tribunal for the Former Yugoslavia (ICTY) to prosecute those accused of war crimes and crimes against humanity. This was followed by the setting up of the International Criminal Tribunal for Rwanda (ICTR). Under their provisions, *individuals* were to be held responsible at the international level for their actions, even if these were committed under orders.

In addition, for the first time in the history of international law, the ICTY recognised sexual violence by a man against a woman as a war crime, which is itself a symbolic step in the process of recognition that violence against women will not be tolerated. The trial chamber found that acts of kidnapping and sexual violence against women and the girls satisfied the requirements of enslavement as a crime against humanity. And at the ICTR, sexual violence against women was designated as

... for the first time in the history of international law, the ICTY recognised sexual violence by a man against a woman as a war crime .... The trial chamber found that acts of kidnapping and sexual violence ... satisfied the requirements of enslavement as a crime against humanity. And at the ICTR, sexual violence against women was designated as an act of genocide. These decisions were groundbreaking in international law with regard to gender-based violence.

Due in large part to intense lobbying ... by women's organisations under the umbrella grouping of the Women's Caucus for Gender Justice, a broad range of sex crimes are included within the jurisdiction of the ICC, including sexual slavery, enforced prostitution, forced pregnancy, enforced sterilisation and other forms of sexual violence "of comparable gravity".... [T]he Court is expected to hear its first case soon.

an act of genocide. These decisions were groundbreaking in international law with regard to gender-based violence.

A permanent International Criminal Court (ICC) has now been set up in The Hague, the Netherlands. The Rome Statute of the ICC was adopted in July 1998 and has been signed to date by 139 States and ratified by 99. It entered into force in July 2002. Due in large part to intense lobbying and advocacy by women's organisations under the umbrella grouping of the Women's Caucus for Gender Justice, a broad range of sex crimes are included within the jurisdiction of the ICC, including sexual slavery, enforced prostitution, forced pregnancy, enforced sterilisation and other forms of sexual violence "of comparable gravity". The judges and Prosecutor have been chosen and the Court is expected to hear its first case soon. This will probably relate either to the Democratic Republic of the Congo or Northern Uganda (Brandon and du Plessis, 2005).

These international courts all deal only with the most serious crimes, since it is not possible to prosecute everyone responsible for human rights abuses – whether in international or in local courts. There will never be infinite resources available, so 'absolute justice' will never be achieved. However, they have the advantage of showing to the world that even in a war situation where there is a breakdown of law and order, those engaging in criminal activities or considering doing so, may have to pay the price later. Their impunity is not guaranteed, and they may suddenly find the eyes of the world upon them. These courts send out a message to all those who know about them that certain types of behaviour are considered by the majority of people to be unacceptable and that those who commit crimes are liable to prosecution.

Truth and Reconciliation Commissions (TRCs)

Truth and Reconciliation Commissions (TRCs) provide an opportunity for those who have been the victims of crimes that have gone unnoticed or unpunished to have those crimes recorded and remembered, documented and published for posterity so that those who come after can learn from them. TRCs have been criticised on a number of counts, including being inadequate and contradictory. In South Africa, the TRC was regarded by some as a charter for impunity, as in most cases those who had committed crimes were not brought to justice. But even if justice is not achieved, there is a need for understanding of the past and a need for truth. The past has to be acknowledged for any healing to take place.

TRCs also provide an opportunity for those who were perpetrators – sometimes victims are also perpetrators – to tell their stories, and perhaps to engage in self-reflection and to think about the meaning of their actions. By acknowledging wrongdoing, by asking forgiveness, there is a possibility of reconciliation, so that those who have committed crimes have a chance of being accepted and reintegrated into society, even if they are not forgiven.

TRCs give a chance to the voiceless, those who have remained silent, to tell their story. As internal wars are now fought through the bodies of women as well as by men and women as combatants, it is the women's stories which contribute to the making of history: their testimonies are themselves history. No one likes to testify, but it has been found that women who do testify particularly about sexual violence tend to grow stronger in the stand. Finally they realise the guilty person is not them, the guilty person is sitting on the other side of the room, now with no power over them.

In South Africa, the mandate of the Truth and Reconciliation Commission was:

> ... to establish as complete a picture as possible of the cases, nature and extent of the gross violations of human rights which were committed during the period March 1960 and December 1993. The antecedents, circumstances, factors and the contexts of such violations, as well as the motives of such violations, as well as the perspectives of the persons responsible for committing such violations should be established.

This mandate raises a number of questions when viewed in the context of gender relations and women's status in South Africa and indeed in all communities. Human rights abuses committed in times of armed conflict have to be seen in the context of gender-based violence that occurs in peacetime, in the public and private spheres. Looking at the motives and perspectives of such violations is useful in planning legal and educational mechanisms to assist in changing attitudes towards women's rights in the post-conflict reconstruction process.

TRCs give a chance to the voiceless ... to tell their story. As internal wars are now fought through the bodies of women as well as by men and women as combatants, it is the women's stories which contribute to the making of history .... No one likes to testify, but ... women who do testify particularly about sexual violence tend to grow stronger in the stand.

... special TRC sessions for women were held without the presence of men, and gender training workshops were conducted to assist those engaged in hearing testimonies from women. This was repeated in Sierra Leone in 2003, when a series of workshops were organised with the support of UNIFEM to strengthen the capacity of local NGOs to deal with the gender dimensions of the peace and reconciliation process ....

In August 1996, in response to a submission prepared following a workshop on Gender and the TRC, the South African TRC accepted a set of recommendations regarding the human rights abuse of women and how it should deal with these. The recommendations, which were adopted, included the following:

- Women should receive special hearings;
- The TRC should be sensitive to cultural norms in specific communities in relation to gender issues;
- Women need to be encouraged to speak out;
- Preparatory workshops, especially for rural women, should be held especially about how to deal with the media.
- Women can tell stories on behalf of others, and women could come together to tell their stories as a collective;
- Hearings could be held in camera;
- Commissioners should be trained in gender-related issues;
- Reparations policy should not be gender blind.

As a result of these recommendations, special TRC sessions for women were held without the presence of men, and gender training workshops were conducted to assist those engaged in hearing testimonies from women. This was repeated in Sierra Leone in 2003, when a series of workshops were organised with the support of UNIFEM to strengthen the capacity of local NGOs to deal with the gender dimensions of the peace and reconciliation process (see Chapter 5).

The Role of Men and Boys in Achieving Gender Equality

In the Beijing Declaration, governments expressed their determination to encourage men to participate in all actions towards gender equality (paragraph 25). A new emphasis on men and boys led the CSW in 2004 to focus as one of its two themes on 'The role of men and boys in achieving gender equality'.[11] This was preceded by an Expert Group Meeting on the same topic in October 2003 in Brasilia, Brazil, organised by the UN Division for the Advancement of Women (UNDAW), in collaboration with the Joint United Nations Programme on HIV/AIDS (UNAIDS), the International Labour Organization (ILO) and the United Nations Development Programme (UNDP).

The report of the meeting noted that men and boys can and do play an important role in promoting women's empowerment in the home, the community, the labour market and the workplace. "A better understanding of gender roles and relations, and related structural inequalities, increases opportunities for effective policy measures and actions for overcoming inequalities" (UNDAW, 2003a: 3). It is only if men in government, in the community, in the workplace and at home have an understanding of gender roles and relations that they will be able to challenge unequal power relationships and take and support initiatives to achieve greater gender equality.

The report also made reference to the statement in the Millennium Declaration of September 2000, adopted by the Member States of the UN, that the promotion of gender equality is essential for the eradication of poverty and hunger and the promotion of sustainable development. As poverty and competition for scarce resources are major factors in causing armed conflict between different communities and States, gender equality is an important element in achieving social justice and sustainable peace. Education of boys in gender relations is essential to the achievement of more equal power relationships, and this is highlighted in the report.

The Expert Group's analysis, conclusions and recommendations, which resulted in a set of seven conclusions and recommendations agreed by the CSW, are important for the work of governments, IGOs and NGOs in the area of conflict prevention and resolution and post-conflict reconstruction and peacebuilding. They also have implications, directly and indirectly, for governments and intergovernmental institutions involved in military activity and peace support operations in war-torn countries.

The recommendations called for the education of boys and young men to involve a questioning of traditional gender roles and for enhancing awareness and knowledge among men of their roles as parents, legal guardians and caregivers and of the importance of sharing family responsibilities. Fathers as well as

A Mozambican soldier spends time with his baby son before returning to the front line.
Jenny Matthews

Men and boys have a vital role to play in disseminating information about women's rights ... and encouraging women to take up positions of leadership .... Men's support ... [is] needed to enable women to fulfil their ambitions as part of a programme to achieve the Commonwealth goals of democracy ..., the protection of human rights, and equitable and sustainable development.

mothers can be included in programmes that teach infant childcare development (UNCSW, 2004: 6 (c)). It is essential that school curricula, textbooks and other information used in schools and elsewhere promote gender equality, that they do not encourage boys to engage in high-risk activities that include armed combat, and that they promote images of men as parents and carers as well as farmers, employers, employees and holders of public office.

Men and boys have a vital role to play in disseminating information about women's rights, respecting those rights and encouraging women to take up positions of leadership in the government, judiciary, police and armed forces. Men's support and encouragement are needed to enable women to fulfil their ambitions as part of a programme to achieve the Commonwealth goals of democracy, the rule of law, good governance, freedom of expression, the protection of human rights, and equitable and sustainable development.

It is important to recognise that men as well as women participate in peace movements and that cross-community alliances are not limited to women-to-women exchanges. Initial suspicion from male colleagues towards a women's group can be overcome by overtures towards inclusion, and divisions between men and women can develop into co-operative partnerships. Reducing gender inequality gives greater scope for women and men to work together to achieve social justice and sustainable peace. Greater gender equality contributes to sustainable development and prosperity that provide the conditions for peace among communities and States.

By means of gender awareness programmes, men often come to understand that they too can gain from greater gender equality. Successful gender training as part of gender mainstreaming has to convey the message that men and women are not in competition with one another in a zero-sum game but are equal partners in a project that will benefit all communities and help to create a more just society.

Recommendations for Involving Men and Boys and Addressing Their Concerns

- The special needs of marginalised and alienated young men should be recognised.

- The well-being of men as well as women must be seen as a legitimate aim of measures designed to achieve gender equality.

- Men also need to be seen as victims of violence by other men.

- Men and boys must be encouraged to challenge notions that boys derive their identity only from physical strength.

- Analysis of armed conflict must incorporate an understanding of the role of the social construction of masculinity.

- Men need to gain an understanding of gender, including the social construction of masculinity.

- The active involvement of men and boys in promoting gender equality must be seen as a critical factor in peacekeeping, peace-building and post-conflict reconstruction.

- Men must not be constantly portrayed in a negative way as perpetrators of violence against women, but shown as partners and allies in building a more gender-responsive and just society.

- Male responsibilities in family life must be included in the education of boys from the earliest stages.

- Boys must be encouraged to train in the caring professions such as that of primary school teacher or nurse.

- Police forces and the military must be encouraged to introduce gender-sensitisation as part of their training.

- Training in CEDAW and international humanitarian law as it relates to women's and men's rights needs to become mandatory for peacekeeping forces.

4 Progress in Gender Mainstreaming in Peace Support Operations

Linda Etchart

... international recognition of the importance of gender mainstreaming in peace processes can be found in numerous UN declarations and resolutions. The need for ... gender mainstreaming in UN Peace-keeping Support Operations ... has also been widely acknowledged.

International Calls for Women's Inclusion

Chapter 3 pointed out that international recognition of the importance of gender mainstreaming in peace processes can be found in numerous UN declarations and resolutions. The need for women to have equal representation in decision-making positions related to conflict resolution and for gender main-streaming in UN Peacekeeping Support Operations (PSOs) has also been widely acknowledged. The Beijing Platform for Action (BPfA) of 1995 stated that:

> *Although women have begun to play an important role in con-flict resolution, peacekeeping and defence and foreign affairs mechanisms, they are still under-represented in decision-making positions. If women are to play an equal part in securing and maintaining peace, they must be empowered politically and eco-nomically and represented adequately at all levels of decision-making.* (Paragraph 134)

The following year, Graça Machel's influential report on the impact of armed conflict on children (presented by the UN Secretary-General to the 51st General Assembly) noted that:

> *While women's roles in protecting and sustaining children and families are well recognised, their participation in the economic, political and security arenas is less well acknowledged and sup-ported. Women have been active agents of peace-building and conflict resolution at the local level and their participation at the national, regional and international levels should be increased.* (Paragraph 309)

In 2000, the outcome document of the 23rd Special Session of the UN General Assembly entitled *Women 2000: Gender*

Equality, Development and Peace for the twenty-first century (Beijing +5) states that:

> The under-representation, at all levels, of women in decision-making positions, such as special envoys or special representatives of the Secretary-General, in peacekeeping, peace-building, post-conflict reconciliation and reconstruction, as well as lack of gender awareness in these areas, presents serious obstacles. (Paragraph 16)

'Actions to be taken' at the national level by governments include:

> To ensure and support the full participation of women at all levels of decision-making and implementation in development activities and peace processes, including … peacekeeping and peace-building …. (Paragraph 86b)

Within the Organisation for Security and Co-operation in Europe (OSCE) and the European Council, the importance of gender mainstreaming in PSOs has also been recognised.

The Windhoek Declaration and the Namibia Plan of Action

The Lessons Learned Unit of UN Department of Peacekeeping Operations (DPKO) held a seminar from 29–31 May 2000 on 'Mainstreaming a Gender Perspective in Multidimensional Peace Support Operations', hosted by the Government of Namibia. The resulting Windhoek Declaration and Namibia Plan of Action called for "the principles of gender equality" to permeate entire peace missions to ensure the "participation of women and men as equal partners and beneficiaries in all aspects of the peace process – from peacekeeping, reconciliation and peace-building, towards a situation of political stability in which women and men play an equal part in the political, economic and social development of their country".

The Plan of Action recommended the following measures:

- Equal access and participation by women and men should be ensured … at all levels and stages of the peace process; and

- In negotiations for a ceasefire and/or peace agreement, women should be an integral part of the negotiating team

The resulting Windhoek Declaration and Namibia Plan of Action called for "the principles of gender equality" to permeate entire peace missions to ensure the "participation of women and men as equal partners and beneficiaries in all aspects of the peace process … towards a situation of political stability in which women and men play an equal part in the political, economic and social development of their country".

The [Namibia] Plan contained provisions regarding a 50 per cent target for women in leadership positions in PSOs and for greater efforts to be made to increase the number of women ... in ... police forces involved in PSOs. It called for gender mainstreaming training for PSOs ... and for obligatory induction training in gender issues to be given to all UN personnel on arrival in mission areas.

and process. The negotiating team and/or facilitators should ensure that gender issues are placed on the agenda and that those issues are addressed fully in the agreement.

It requested that UN peace support operations should incorporate a mandate on gender mainstreaming that should refer to the provisions of the Convention on the Elimination of All Forms of Discrimination against Women as well as other legal instruments. It also requested that mechanisms be established to enable PSOs to mainstream gender into post-conflict reconstruction. The Plan contained provisions regarding a 50 per cent target for women in leadership positions in PSOs and for greater efforts to be made to increase the number of women trained and deployed in military and civilian police forces involved in PSOs. It called for gender mainstreaming training for PSOs, for gender awareness guidelines and materials to be made available to UN Member States contributing peace support personnel and for obligatory induction training in gender issues to be given to all UN personnel on arrival in mission areas.

In order for these changes to be implemented, the Plan set out a list of posts and required procedures and stipulated that mechanisms would have to be put in place to ensure monitoring, evaluation and accountability.

The Brahimi Report and the UN Secretary-General's response

The Windhoek Declaration and Namibia Plan of Action came at an important moment in the history of peacekeeping missions, when their past and future roles and actions were being questioned and assessed in the wake of perceived failures in Rwanda and the former Yugoslavia. In March 2000 UN Secretary-General Kofi Annan appointed a 10-member panel on UN peace operations, led by Ambassador Lakhdar Brahimi of Algeria, to make frank, specific and realistic recommendations for change in UN peace operations. The Brahimi Report, which appeared in August 2000, included an investigation into the expanding role of the UN into the areas of peace-building and state-building, including its involvement in the establishment of legal systems and the recruitment of both judicial and security personnel such as the armed forces and the police.

There are gender implications in all these areas but, apart from brief references to the need for equitable gender distribution of UN personnel, the Brahimi Report is almost gender blind. This was surprising since there had been so much development in this area before its release, including the Namibia Plan of Action discussed above and the strengthened mandate for integrating gender perspectives into peacekeeping support operations provided by Beijing +5, which had taken place in June of the same year.

The October 2000 Report of the UN Secretary-General on the implementation of the Brahimi Report was, however, more far-reaching in promoting gender equality. It highlighted the importance of maintaining a gender perspective (III.B.1.43 (b)) and gender expertise (2.29) in PSOs. It stated that UN law enforcement and criminal procedures should be standardised to take into account CEDAW, among other conventions (III.3.32). It also recommended designated experts in integrated mission task forces in areas including "gender equality issues" (2.54).

The Secretary-General's Report recognised a role for the UN in "electoral and governance assistance, including to national human rights institutions and national machineries for the advancement of women" (B.1.42). It called on Member States "to redouble efforts to identify female civilian police candidates (and in fact females candidates in all other areas)" (4.97). It acknowledged that more than gender balance and gender sensitivity were needed to integrate gender perspectives into peacekeeping operations, and duly proposed the creation of a Gender Unit in the Office of the Under-Secretary General/ DPKO (5.142), as had been proposed in the Namibia Plan of Action.

However, there was resistance to the establishment of a Gender Unit from the UN Advisory Committee on Administrative and Budgetary Questions, and the Special Representative of the Secretary-General decided instead to appoint two senior gender advisers: one in Civil Affairs (Governance and Public Administration) and another in the Human Rights Unit.

Despite this setback, as well as the failure to adopt several of the other Namibia recommendations, progress was made in establishing the instruments for implementing the Plan of

... the Brahimi Report is almost gender blind. This was surprising since there had been so much development in this area before its release, including the Namibia Plan of Action discussed above and the strengthened mandate for integrating gender perspectives into peacekeeping support operations provided by Beijing +5, which had taken place in June of the same year.

UNSCR 1325 on women, peace and security … was the first Resolution ever passed by the UN Security Council to specifically address the impact of war on women and women's contributions to conflict resolution and sustainable peace.

Action. On International Women's Day in 2000 Ambassador Chowdhury of Bangladesh issued a Presidential Statement on behalf of the UN Security Council, affirming that the "equal access and full participation of women in power structures and their full involvement in all efforts for the prevention and resolution of conflicts are essential for the maintenance and promotion of peace and security". Soon afterwards, and encouraged by Ambassador Chowdhury, the NGO Working Group on Women, Peace and Security came together to push the Security Council to hold a thematic debate on the role of women in international peace and security. After holding an Arria Formula meeting[12] with NGOs and an open debate (see Box 9), the Council under the Namibian Presidency passed UN Security Council Resolution (UNSCR) 1325 on women, peace and security on 31 October 2000. This was the first Resolution ever passed by the UN Security Council to specifically address the impact of war on women and women's contributions to conflict resolution and sustainable peace.

Box 9 The Contribution of NGOs to UN Security Council Resolution 1325 on Women, Peace and Security

The Arria Formula meeting held on 23 October 2000 prior to the open session of the UN Security Council on Women, Peace and Security gave representatives of women's NGOs from Guatemala, Sierra Leone, Somalia and Tanzania a chance to explain their work, demonstrate their competence and submit their recommendations on a large number of issues. The NGO Working Group on Women, Peace and Security presented thirty-two recommendations to the Arria Formula meeting on the need for increased women personnel at senior levels in all UN departments and missions, indicating that information on women should appear in reports prepared by the Secretariat and submitted by the Secretary-General.

Source: Hill, 2002

UN Security Council Resolution (UNSCR) 1325 on women, peace and security (2000)

Most of the recommendations listed in the Namibia Plan of Action were integrated in some form into UNSCR 1325, the text of which reaffirms the important role of women in the prevention and resolution of conflicts and in peace-building and the need to increase their role in decision-making in this regard. It recognises the urgent need to mainstream a gender perspective into peacekeeping operations and calls on Member States to take action to achieve these aims.

Among other things, UNSCR 1325:

- calls on the UN Secretary General to implement the existing Plan of Action (A/49/587) calling for an increase in the participation of women at decision-making levels in conflict resolution and peace processes;

- urges the UN Secretary-General to appoint more women as special representatives; and

- requests the UN Secretary-General to provide Member States with training guidelines and materials on the protection, rights and particular needs of women, as well on as the importance of involving women in all peacekeeping and peace-building measures.

UNSCR 1325 does not call for obligatory gender training for UN personnel arriving at mission areas, as is proposed in the Namibia Plan of Action. However, it does invite Member States to incorporate gender training in the form stated above into national training programmes for military and civilian personnel in preparation for deployment on PSOs.

Item 8 of the Resolution calls on all actors involved in negotiating and implementing peace agreements to adopt a gender perspective. In addition, item 17 requests the Secretary-General, where appropriate, to include progress on gender mainstreaming throughout peacekeeping missions in his reporting to the Security Council.

With regard to CEDAW, UNSCR 1325 does not follow the Namibia Plan's request and require that all mandates for PSOs should refer to the provisions of the Convention and other relevant international legal instruments, nor does it call for

... UNSCR 1325 ... reaffirms the important role of women in the prevention and resolution of conflicts and in peace-building and the need to increase their role in decision-making in this regard. It recognises the urgent need to mainstream a gender perspective into peacekeeping operations and calls on Member States to take action to achieve these aims.

obligatory training on CEDAW for peacekeeping personnel. However, it does call on all parties to armed conflict to fully respect international law including CEDAW (1979) and its Optional Protocol of 1999.

The Resolution invited the Secretary-General to carry out a study into the impact of armed conflict on women and girls, the role of women in peace-building and the gender dimension of peace processes and conflict resolution, and to submit a report to the Security Council on the results of this study. This was duly carried out.

The 2002 report of the UN Secretary-General on women, peace and security

The Inter-agency Task Force on Women, Peace and Security, co-ordinated by Angela King, Assistant Secretary-General and Special Adviser to the Secretary-General on Gender Issues and the Advancement of Women, prepared the UN study, *Report of the Secretary-General on women, peace and security* (S/2002/1154), published on 16 October 2002. It was then submitted to the UN Security Council, which discussed the report and issued a Presidential Statement stressing the importance of the representation of women in all aspects of peace operations and of a gender-sensitive approach.

The Report comments that violence and discrimination against women are increased by conflict, and that the proliferation of small arms increases the risk of domestic violence, which often continues after a conflict has ended. It also refers to the increased risk of contracting HIV/AIDS as a result of armed conflict and the extra burden that this places on family carers, including those who look after orphans. It notes that the extra responsibilities placed on women in these circumstances may push them into engaging in illegal or dangerous activities in order to survive.

With regard to UN peacekeeping operations, the UN Secretary-General's Report recommended the following three actions:

- Incorporate gender perspectives explicitly into the mandates of all peacekeeping missions, including provisions to systematically address this issue in all reports to the Security Council;

- Require that data collected in research, assessments, appraisals, monitoring, evaluation and reporting on peace operations are systematically disaggregated by gender and age, and that specific data on the situation of women and girls and the impact of interventions on them are provided; and

- Ensure necessary financial and human resources for gender mainstreaming, including the establishment of gender advisers/units in multidimensional peacekeeping operations and capacity-building activities, as well as targeted projects for women and girls as part of approved mission budgets.

The Report goes on to stress the need for the protection of women and girls in internally displaced persons (IDP) camps, where they "face the risk of violence at the hands of those who are in a position to facilitate their passage, determine their refugee status or issue their identity cards .... Women may also be forced to engage in prostitution in exchange for food or other essential goods and services" (Section VI.50). It also states that "Women should be fully involved in the management of refugee camps, including in decision-making" (VI.51).

Implementation of Recommended Actions

Incorporating a gender perspective

Although a Gender Unit at DPKO headquarters was not immediately established, guidelines for gender mainstreaming in peacekeeping missions were adopted and integrated into DPKO in 2002/3. Efforts were made to integrate gender into the following UN activities:

- The code of conduct for peacekeepers;

- Mandates for peacekeeping missions;

- Procedures for the International Criminal Court;

- Training materials for peacekeepers; and

- UN Assessment Missions.[13]

The NGO Working Group on Women, Peace and Security published a report, 'One Year On', in July 2002, commenting

Efforts were made to integrate gender into the following UN activities: the code of conduct for peacekeepers; mandates for peacekeeping missions; procedures for the International Criminal Court; training materials for peacekeepers; and UN Assessment Missions.

Ten of the current 17 peacekeeping operations now have a dedicated gender advisory capacity – which could mean either a formalised unit or a gender advisor: Afghanistan, Burundi, Côte d'Ivoire, the Democratic Republic of the Congo, Kosovo, Haiti, Liberia, Sierra Leone, Sudan and Timor-Leste.

on the success of individual UN Senior Gender Advisers in the DRC, Kosovo and Timor-Leste, but regretting what it perceived as a lack of institutional support. At the UN Security Council debate in October 2002, Noeleen Heyzer, Executive Director of UNIFEM, echoed the Working Group's findings in indicating that, despite the successes mentioned, a gender perspective had still not been sufficiently incorporated into peacekeeping operations elsewhere. She commented that effort in gender mainstreaming had been isolated in the form of a single staff person or small unit lacking sufficient seniority and resources. Moreover, local women often had little contact with missions and believed that their needs had been largely ignored. She reiterated that gender expertise must shape all aspects of UN mission planning.

Following these discussions, a DPKO Gender Advisors' Workshop for all field-based gender advisors and focal points was held from 24–31 October 2002. It discussed the development and implementation of training materials, including the second phase of the 'Gender Mainstreaming in Peacekeeping Operations' project, which had been placed under the mandate of the Best Practices Unit of DPKO (see below).

The post of Gender Adviser at DPKO Headquarters to support gender mainstreaming efforts in the field was set up as a temporary position in October 2003. This was permanently filled in August 2004. Ten of the current 17 peacekeeping operations now have a dedicated gender advisory capacity – which could mean either a formalised unit or a gender advisor: Afghanistan, Burundi, Côte d'Ivoire, the Democratic Republic of the Congo, Kosovo, Haiti, Liberia, Sierra Leone, Sudan and Timor-Leste.

Collecting sex-disaggregated data

There is still a need for sex-disaggregated statistics. For example, the UN Secretary-General's Report 2003 on Sierra Leone (S/2003/663) provided statistics on the numbers of recruits (592) who graduated from police training school in Freetown in 2002, but these were not broken down by gender.

Training courses and materials

DPKO drew on and adapted training courses created by the Canadian Department of Foreign Affairs and International Trade (DFAIT) and the United Kingdom's Department for International Development (DFID) to use in training military personnel and civilian police participating in UN peacekeeping operations. The materials were to be used for pre-deployment training and induction courses at mission level. Gender training was field-tested in Bosnia, Eritrea and Timor-Leste and was then used in the Democratic Republic of the Congo (DRC) and in Sierra Leone in 2001.

National Police of Timor-Leste officers and UNPOL officers at a handover ceremony in 2003
Robel Mockonen/UN Mission in Support of East Timor

In Timor-Leste, the UN Department of Governance and Public Administration had the task of setting up an entire public administration system, which gave the UN Gender Affairs Unit, under Sherrill Whittington, a unique opportunity to mainstream gender at an early stage within and outside the UN Transitional Administration in East Timor (UNTAET).[14] Basing its work around UN mandates as well as the East Timorese women's Platform for Action adopted in June 2000, the Gender Unit, through advocacy, consultation, information exchange and the provision of technical assistance, and in

Basing its work around UN mandates as well as the East Timorese women's Platform for Action adopted in June 2000, the Gender Unit … contributed to gender mainstreaming in a range of sectors … including in the drafting of legal instruments in the areas of the Constitution, criminal law, prisons, police procedures, conditions of employment, health, property and education.

> **Box 10 Lessons Learned from Successful Gender Mainstreaming in Timor-Leste**
>
> Significant gains were made in mainstreaming gender in political processes in Timor-Leste as a result of women's activism, coupled with affirmative action measures introduced by UNTAET leading up the first free election of 31 August 2001. Several lessons learned could be applied to other peacekeeping operations with similar mandates:
>
> - If constructive partnerships are to be established to enable women's full participation, there must be a dedicated mechanism within the mission, such as a Gender Unit, to prepare for, oversee and facilitate this process.
>
> - The Office of the Special Representative of the Secretary-General (SRSG) must promote measures for the equal participation of women in at all levels. Rhetoric supported by committed action must be the standard.
>
> - The mission Office of Communications and Public Information (OCPI) should be fully utilised and involved to inform both rural and urban populations of women's right to political participation, with female candidates given equal media coverage and air time.
>
> - Partnerships with other UN and international entities and women's civil society organisations are essential, with all supporting the goals of women for full and equal participation.
>
> - Support should also be given to the development of local organisations to promote the participation of women candidates.
>
> *Source:* Whittington, 2004

collaboration with Rede Feto (the East Timorese Women's Network), contributed to gender mainstreaming in a range of sectors, including in the drafting of legal instruments in the areas of the Constitution, criminal law, prisons, police procedures, conditions of employment, health, property and education. The Gender Unit facilitated a substantial increase in the number of women in decision-making positions at the local and national level. It offered training workshops for potential women candidates in elections, and the number of women rose to 27 per cent in the Timor-Leste Constituent Assembly (one of the highest in the Asia-Pacific region and globally) and 50 per cent in the Village Development Councils. The percentage of women in the police force also rose to 30 per cent.

Gender and Peacekeeping was subsequently introduced as one of the Standard Generic Training Modules of DPKO, with the Human Rights module also containing references to the elimination of discrimination against women and to CEDAW. In April 2003, the United Nations Mission in Sierra Leone (UNAMSIL) acted as the facilitator in an exercise to field-test the DPKO gender training materials. Gender training has been delivered to peacekeepers and international civilian police (CIVPOL) officers. UNAMSIL also began training members of the Family Support Units of the Sierra Leone police, which have the mandate to deal with offences against women, children and vulnerable groups.

A DPKO *Handbook on UN Multidimensional Peace Operations*, published in December 2003, contains a chapter specifically on gender mainstreaming.[15] It states that peacekeeping operations "must seek to protect women's rights and to ensure that they are integrated into all actions promoting peace, implementing peace agreements, resolving conflict and reconstructing war-torn societies" and that "it is crucial that their activities and policies uphold the principles of gender equality and non-discrimination" (p 115). With regard to missions mandated to provide technical assistance in institution building and the development of national legislation, the chapter emphasises the importance of including gender equality in all national institutions and domestic laws, including laws concerning inheritance, marital property, domestic violence, political participation, employment and social security. The handbook states that a "clear commitment to promoting gender equality throughout the entire mission is required from the beginning" (p 121).

In 2004 the Peacekeeping Best Practices Unit of DPKO produced the *Gender Resource Package for Peacekeeping Operations* (see Box 11). Launched at a panel discussion on 'Gender and

In April 2003, the United Nations Mission in Sierra Leone acted as the facilitator in an exercise to field-test the DPKO gender training materials. Gender training has been delivered to peacekeepers and international civilian police officers. UNAMSIL also began training members of the Family Support Units of the Sierra Leone police, which have the mandate to deal with offences against women, children and vulnerable groups.

A woman soldier from Nepal takes part in a UN peacekeeping operation

Peacekeeping: Practical Tools for Change' at the UN, the package consists of a book and a CD-ROM and includes numerous additional resources. One panellist[16] suggested that the role of States includes not only to promote mainstreaming of gender perspectives in peace operations, but also to:

- Foster partnership approaches and exchange best practices on action plans and training;

- Contribute to best practices; and

- Nominate women in the composition of national peace-keeping contingents.

Box 11 Gender Resource Package for Peace-keeping Operations

Intended for use by all peacekeeping personnel – gender specialists and non-specialists alike – the *Gender Resource Package* offers concrete guidelines on how to identify gender issues and how to mainstream gender equality into all aspects of peacekeeping. The package provides guidance on mainstreaming gender at the planning stage as well as after the establishment of a peacekeeping operation, with separate chapters on a range of topics from gender and HIV/AIDS, to gender and electoral assistance, to gender and the legal and judicial system. It includes a number of practical tools, such as a gender assessment checklist for planning and guides to implementation. It also contains a guide on gender-based violence and scenarios covering prohibited acts. According to DPKO, there will be an active strategy in the field to make certain that the package is put to use by, for example, managers to ensure that they are key advocates.

The Composition of Peacekeeping Missions

There is no evidence that women make better peacekeepers, but a great deal of evidence to suggest that the presence of women improves an operation's chances of success. A better gender balance means that the operation more closely resembles civilian society. Its members are therefore more likely to observe social conventions that define civilised behaviour (De Groot, 2002).

The gender composition of the DPKO executive, as well as the nature of the tasks to which DPKO personnel have been assigned, has meant a degree of scepticism regarding gender mainstreaming within the Department itself. Peacekeeping missions were, and still are, conducted overwhelmingly by military and police personnel. While women peacekeepers have made an important contribution to the success of a small number of individual peacekeeping missions in the past, as in Guatemala and Namibia, they still constitute a minute proportion of the total number of peacekeepers worldwide.

For example, at the end of 2002 there were almost 40,000 military and civilian police and fewer than 4,000 civilian personnel from 89 countries serving in peacekeeping operations around the world (DPKO, 2004). At the end of 2003, men constituted 98.5 per cent of the military personnel engaged in PSOs and 96 per cent of the police. In the same year, even among the non-military personnel engaged in peace support operations, 75 per cent of the professional employees were male (with 51 per cent of the general service staff being female). Of the 17 current peacekeeping missions, two women have been appointed head of mission, or Special Representative (in Burundi and Georgia). In contrast, the UN Office for the Coordination of Humanitarian Affairs (OCHA) had 35 per cent of its decision-making positions occupied by women in 2003 (ibid).

Canada and the USA have the highest percentage of women (12 per cent) in their armed forces compared with the rest of the world, but the percentages of women assigned to peacekeeping operations in 2002 were low: 5 per cent of Canadian and 8 per cent of US military peacekeepers were women. Despite these low numbers, the Canadian Government has been at the forefront of gender mainstreaming in peacekeeping operations.

The fact that the teams involved in peacekeeping are composed almost entirely of men poses particular problems for PSOs in terms of their obligations to achieve gender equality in the reconstruction of institutions in war-torn societies:

There is no evidence that women make better peacekeepers, but a great deal of evidence to suggest that the presence of women improves an operation's chances of success. A better gender balance means that the operation more closely resembles civilian society. Its members are therefore more likely to observe social conventions that define civilised behaviour (De Groot, 2002).

... military life and military culture have traditionally been centred around a clear separation of the public and the private ... and extreme forms of gender stereotyping that lead to the development of a cult of 'hypermasculinity' that promotes a greater subordination of women ... than exists in the civilian world. This can lead to the consumption of pornographic material ... that denigrate women by portraying them as "sexual objects and commodities" (UNCSW, 2004).

- They have the task of achieving gender equality within the peacekeeping institutions themselves, which is not an easy task in overwhelmingly male institutions based around particular conceptions of manliness; and

- A traditionally male institution (the military) may be given the task of promoting gender equality in the reconstruction of institutions in a society where there may have been a high degree of gender inequality prior to the armed conflict.

As noted in Chapter 2, military life and military culture have traditionally been centred around a clear separation of the public and the private, a gender division of labour in terms of family and caring responsibilities and extreme forms of gender stereotyping that lead to the development of a cult of 'hypermasculinity' that promotes a greater subordination of women and suppression of the feminine than exists in the civilian world. This can lead to the consumption of pornographic material, including videos and images from the Internet, that denigrate women by portraying them as "sexual objects and commodities" (UNCSW, 2004). The Committee on the Status of Women (CSW) recommended in March 2004 that action be taken by governments and others to combat the use of pornography in the media as well as the use of information and communications technologies for harassment, sexual exploitation and trafficking in women and girls. The question of combating the use of pornography is one of particular relevance with regard to military culture and its impact on gender equality.

The presence of a few women is unlikely to have much impact on military culture, though they may have a higher profile than their numbers might suggest and therefore a powerful symbolic presence. A 1995 study for UNDAW found that there were significantly fewer incidents of rape and prostitution with just a token female presence (De Groot, 2002). The reconstruction of a post-conflict society provides opportunities for mainstreaming gender equality into peace agreements, new constitutions, democratisation processes and the legal system. When the people entrusted with these monumental tasks are predominantly men in a male-oriented culture, they will need special training in gender awareness and gender sensitivity if these opportunities are not to be wasted.

A female member of the Swedish Infantry Battalion attached to the UN peacekeeping operation in Cyprus
UN Department of Public Information

The Role of Gender Training in Peace-building

Considering the difficulties of recruiting women into peace-keeping operations, and into the armed forces in general in countries with a voluntary intake of recruits, the best that can be hoped for in the foreseeable future is that gender training programmes for all peacekeepers, men and women, contribute to the safety of host populations and to the success of peace-building initiatives.

Gender training enables peacekeepers to deal more sensitively with local people whom they are paid to protect (though military peacekeepers may not always have much contact with their host population, and in some cases may not be permitted

Gender training enables peacekeepers to deal more sensitively with local people whom they are paid to protect ...

Some peacekeeping operations ... have ... achieved success in gender mainstreaming sufficient to be held up as examples of good practice. Central to their success have been programmes to involve local women in ... the political process in their countries. Half of the civilian peacekeepers in Namibia were women and they played an important role in reaching out to Namibian rural women ...

to do so by their commanding officers). It is notable that as part of the Eritrea/Ethiopia UN peacekeeping operation, peacekeepers were obliged to enrol for gender training sessions that were open to the general public. Angela Mackay, who developed gender training materials for military and civilian peacekeepers at DPKO, New York over 2001–2002, noted that these training sessions were often "the first time that military peacekeepers had actually spoken to the local people or heard their perspectives" (Mazurana, 2002: 48).

Militaries have the capacity to engage in awareness-raising on gender relations and to contribute to positive social change. In order for them to do this, however, there needs to be a much broader understanding of gender issues within the military establishment, as well as commitment to gender equality on the part of government advisers.

Some peacekeeping operations, influenced by the efforts of particular individuals working within the UN, have demonstrated commitment to gender equality in peace-building and achieved success in gender mainstreaming sufficient to be held up as examples of good practice. Central to their success have been programmes to involve local women in decision-making and in the political process in their countries. Half of the civilian peacekeepers in Namibia were women and they played an important role in reaching out to Namibian rural women, who were not familiar with mechanisms for popular participation in government, and encouraging them to vote. The operation was considered successful in its objective of strengthening participatory democracy and in promoting women's entry into political decision-making.

The Potential Negative Impacts of Peacekeepers

Several peacekeeping operations in the 1990s were less successful in contributing to women's empowerment within the host communities; indeed in Cambodia and Sierra Leone they have come under severe criticism for their negative impact on the civilian female population.

Increase in sex work and prostitution

In post-conflict societies – where women have been widowed, children orphaned and whole communities impoverished by war – marriage to, cohabitation with or the sale of sexual services to peacekeepers and others may be the only means of survival. Military as well as non-military peacekeepers and some humanitarian workers have become accustomed to buying sexual services in the absence of their wives and girlfriends. The number of women working in prostitution in Cambodia increased from 6,000 in 1992 to 25,000 in 1994, coinciding with the presence of an international peacekeeping force made up entirely of men (Enloe, 2000: 99).

Peacekeepers may be well paid in comparison with the earnings or subsistence level of most of the local population. In Sierra Leone in 2002, for example, there was a contingent of around 17,500 UN peacekeeping troops in a population of around 4 million of whom many had lost their families, farms and livelihoods. Some women and girls were able to find a means of survival through consensual relations with soldiers.

Some military personnel are said to follow what is known as the '500 km rule', which allows them to engage in relations with members of the opposite sex other than their spouses if they are more than 500 km away from home (Bratt, 2002: 59, 79). A survey carried out on members of the Netherlands armed forces on a five-month foreign assignment indicated that 45 per cent of them had had sexual contact with sex-workers and other local people during their tour (Tripodi and Patel, 2002: 59).

Militaries engaged in peacekeeping made it known in the 1990s that it was unrealistic to imagine that their men might forgo sexual relations when on missions. However, in the UN *Peacekeeping Handbook for Junior Ranks*, troops are "forewarned of facing long sexual abstinence" and told not to involve themselves in "any sexual relationship which may create long-lasting complications for you and others. Do not involve yourself with a sexual affair with any member of the local population" (Spees, 2004). There is no guidance, however, with regard to legal responsibilities with regard to consensual sexual relations if they do occur. There is a clear need for governments and others, not least military leaders, to examine and

In post-conflict societies – where women have been widowed, children orphaned and whole communities impoverished by war – marriage to, cohabitation with or the sale of sexual services to peacekeepers and others may be the only means of survival.

Peacekeeping forces may already carry high levels of HIV infection in parity with the rest of the population of their country, or higher levels, since STI rates tend to be greater among the military .... Peacekeepers are among the most mobile populations in the world, and a range of factors contributes to their being one of the communities most vulnerable to HIV/AIDS.

confront responsibilities towards women and men, soldiers and civilians, especially young people, involved in relationships as a result of the stationing of peacekeeping troops (Cockburn and Zarkov, 2002: 112).

Fatherless children

One of these responsibilities is the question of 'UN children' fathered by military and civilian peacekeepers serving away from home. Estimates of the numbers of such children vary, but figures have been given of 25,000 'UN children' in Cambodia and 6,600 in Liberia (War and Children Identity Project, 2001). As the abandonment of children is a violation of the Convention on the Rights of the Child, the UN is obliged to hold those who conceive while on mission, financially and legally responsible for their children, and to ensure their co-operation with the local court if the person responsible falls under its jurisdiction, which he may do under the particular country's Status-of-Forces Agreement.[17] If the contributing State has exclusive jurisdiction over its nationals, as is often the case, then it is likely that no action will be taken, particularly as the Member States are not accountable to the UN as to how they deal with allegations of violations by peacekeeping personnel (Spees, 2004) (see also section below on 'Human rights violations').

The spread of STIs and HIV/AIDS

If peacekeepers engage in unprotected sex that may result in unwanted pregnancies, they also run the risk of contracting sexually transmitted infections (STIs) and HIV/AIDS. Peacekeeping forces may already carry high levels of HIV infection in parity with the rest of the population of their country, or higher levels, since STI rates tend to be greater among the military (see Chapter 3). Peacekeepers are among the most mobile populations in the world, and a range of factors contributes to their being one of the communities most vulnerable to HIV/AIDS.

First, HIV/AIDS spreads fastest in conditions of poverty, powerlessness and social instability that are often associated with armed conflict and areas where peacekeepers are deployed.

One Government participating in the Cambodia operation reported that 25 per cent of its peacekeepers returned home HIV positive, carrying the potential to destroy their own families and communities (DeGroot, 2001).

Second, soldiers tend to be healthy, young men isolated from their partners and suffering from occupational stress. Not only is the army one of the most sexually active segments of the population (Bratt, 2002:60), but soldiers in the ranks are sometimes among the most bored groups, as they spend a great deal of their time exercising, drilling and waiting, with few opportunities for combat. Boredom and isolation encourage them to 'sight-see' through close encounters with local people without taking precautionary measures. Moreover, members of some military forces have a tendency to engage in excessive alcohol consumption, which can lead to engaging in high-risk activities such as unprotected sex (Beevor, 1991).

When this is combined with relatively high UN rates of pay that are awarded to those posted to areas affected by conflict and poverty, UN bases will tend to attract local people, female and male, who are vulnerable to risk-taking in highly insecure circumstances. Moreover, IDPs, with whom peacekeepers often come into contact, are themselves a particularly marginalised and vulnerable group, with women IDPs six times more likely to become infected with HIV/AIDS than the rest of the population (WHO, 2000).

Human rights violations

In 1996 the Graça Machel report on children in armed conflict noted a rapid rise in child prostitution with the arrival of peacekeeping forces (United Nations, 1996). Other reports of human rights violations committed by peacekeepers emerged from 1997 onwards, starting with Somalia, and investigations revealed allegations of abuses, including sexual violence against women, in the course of a number of peacekeeping missions (De Groot in Olsson, 2001: 34; Crossette, 1999).

In 2002 a study conducted by Save the Children Fund UK and the UN High Commissioner for Refugees (UNHCR) documented allegations of widespread sexual exploitation and abuse by aid workers, including UN agency personnel serving in PSOs in West Africa (Spees, 2004: 2122). No reference to

In 2002 a study conducted by Save the Children Fund UK and the UN High Commissioner for Refugees (UNHCR) documented allegations of widespread sexual exploitation and abuse by aid workers, including UN agency personnel serving in PSOs in West Africa (Spees, 2004).

The involvement of humanitarian workers and UN personnel in organised prostitution ... came to the attention of the world in the late 1990s. By 2000 the Head of the UN Commission on Human Rights in Sarajevo, Bosnia and Herzegovina acknowledged that although "a small number of women were brought into Bosnia and Herzegovina for the purpose of sexual exploitation before 1995 ... the real problem started with the arrival of peace-keepers in 1995" ....

these was made in the Brahimi Report, however. "Sexual violence against women around any military culture is not new ... [but] the causes for such violence on the part of peacekeeping troops have not been fully explored", nor its connection to the "prevalence of racist attitudes and beliefs among troops when deployed to communities about which they have little knowledge or understanding" (WCGJ, 2004).

When violations of human rights and of international humanitarian law take place, difficulties can arise with regard to jurisdiction. As noted above, UN military and civilian police personnel usually come under the jurisdiction of their sending States, which are not accountable to the UN as to how they prosecute such cases. Where there is joint jurisdiction, host States may be reluctant to prosecute those who provide them with security. There have been a number of allegations of human rights abuses committed by peacekeepers, but few prosecutions either in host States or in countries of origin in view of the complexities. There is the added obstacle of peacekeepers from States that are not party to the Rome Statute being granted immunity from the International Criminal Court, as well as the deployment as part of peacekeeping missions of employees of private security companies, who are not subject to the same degree of training and accountability (Spees, 2004:26).

Human trafficking and UN peacekeeping

The involvement of humanitarian workers and UN personnel in organised prostitution, including the trafficking of young girls from country to country, came to the attention of the world in the late 1990s. By 2000 the Head of the UN Commission on Human Rights in Sarajevo, Bosnia and Herzegovina acknowledged that although "a small number of women were brought into Bosnia and Herzegovina for the purpose of sexual exploitation before 1995 ... the real problem started with the arrival of peacekeepers in 1995" (quoted in Spees, 2004: 26). The former UN Under-Secretary General and Special Rapporteur on Violence Against Women, addressing the UN Human Rights Commission in 2001, also referred to Bosnia and Herzegovina and Kosovo, where she said there had been reports of a "vast increase in trafficking activity" (Coomaraswamy, 2001).

In Bosnia, the Dayton Accord of 1995 brought in 50,000 international personnel, the vast majority of them men. The US, for example, which has the highest ratio of women to men in its armed forces, sent a contingent of 91 per cent men. It was in that year that trafficked women began to be brought in from Moldova, Romania and Ukraine. Preliminary surveys showed that 30–50 per cent of those purchasing sexual services in Bosnia were from the international community, and that they were providing 80 per cent of the revenue derived from such services (Rees in Cockburn, 2002: 63).

Addressing the Negative Impacts of Peacekeepers

The UN Standard Generic Training Module for peacekeepers, dedicated to the subject of gender and peacekeeping, confronts the question of the negative effects of the presence of peace-keepers in a post-conflict environment. It explains women's vulnerability to prostitution where they may have lost peace-time jobs and pensions, and the relative power peacekeepers have in relation to the local population in the form of "money, mobility, access to food, water and other goods, and force" (p 14). The module also states that organised crime, including trafficking of women, tends to move into a post-conflict society where there is a lack of law enforcement.

Despite the scarcity of information with regard to peace-keepers' vulnerability to HIV/AIDS in the two UN reports on peacekeeping of October 2000, in March 2000 DPKO had already decided to distribute one condom a day to each soldier deployed on missions, and UN Security Council Resolution 1308 (2000) expressed concern over the possibility of peace-keeping troops spreading the disease. Subsequently, HIV/AIDS training courses were completed in Accra, Ghana; Pretoria, South Africa; and Harare, Zimbabwe (Bratt 2002: 75). In 2001 a memorandum of understanding between DPKO and UNAIDS was signed, the first outcome of which was the issu-ing of HIV/AIDS awareness cards to peacekeepers in Sierra Leone in 2001. Further, a commitment was made that by 2003 HIV/AIDS training for peacekeeping forces would be manda-tory, following a joint UNAIDS/UNIFEM initiative signed in May 2001 to strengthen the global response to the epidemic through developing gender-sensitive manuals for peacekeepers.

In 2001 a memorandum of understanding between DPKO and UNAIDS was signed, the first outcome of which was the issuing of HIV/AIDS awareness cards to peacekeepers in Sierra Leone in 2001. Further, a commitment was made that by 2003 HIV/AIDS training for peacekeeping forces would be mandatory ....

> ### *Box 12* **Protecting the Local Community during Peace Support Operations**
>
> Safeguards that should be put in place to protect the local community from the possible negative impacts of peacekeepers include:
>
> - checks against recruitment of personnel with criminal records of violent behaviour or sexual harassment, including instances when recruitment is carried out through private agencies;
>
> - the recruitment of more women into peacekeeping and civilian police forces;
>
> - the provision of appropriate and regular training in gender relations and cultural mores, including awareness of the potential for social exclusion of women who suffer sexual abuse or have sexual relations with foreign men;
>
> - acceptance of codes of conduct for international personnel, which codes are seen to be monitored and to lead to appropriate disciplinary action when violated;
>
> - removal of immunity from criminal procedure in local courts for those accused of criminal activity, including sexual violence; and
>
> - safeguards against the re-deployment elsewhere on another international mission of anyone who has been dismissed for violations of the code of conduct.

In March 2003, DPKO and the United Nations Population Fund (UNFPA) launched a new HIV/AIDS prevention, gender awareness and women's rights training initiative for the 15,000 peacekeeping personnel stationed in Sierra Leone. A press release issued by UNFPA on 6 March stressed the role the peacekeepers would be able to play "to educate communities and prevent HIV infection" in the future, and acknowledged that "it is crucial that peacekeepers have the knowledge to protect themselves and the communities they serve".

The UN has made efforts to address the problem of trafficking through, for example, the Special Trafficking Operations Programme in Bosnia and the Trafficking and Prostitution Investigation Unit in Kosovo (Spees, 2004). In view of the perceived and documented problem of peacekeepers' involvement in creating a market for human traffickers, in March 2004 DPKO issued a Policy Paper on 'Human Trafficking and United Nations Peacekeeping'. The document refers to peacekeepers being seen as "more part of the problem than the solution" to trafficking (p 1), and notes that the issue of trafficking is not being taken seriously by peacekeeping institutions.

The document also states that "allegations and incidences of peacekeeper involvement with trafficking run counter to UN principles" (p 1). It sets out a Programme of Activity to ensure that UN peacekeepers at least 'Do No Harm' (p 2) and that they assist others in anti-trafficking efforts. At the same time it recognises that "peacekeeping is not intrinsically well suited to dealing with the complexities of human trafficking" (p 2). It recommends that DPKO and UN missions "prevent, minimise and punish peacekeeper involvement in sexual exploitation and abuse" (p 2).

The document notes that, while it may be difficult to differentiate between trafficking victims and local prostitution, the use of prostitutes by UN personnel in an environment where "vulnerable individuals in local populations … have had to resort to prostitution for income", and where UN staff members are in a position of disproportionate power, is an "exploitative activity" and therefore to be discouraged "even where prostitution is not a crime" (p 7).

The Secretary General's *Bulletin on Sexual Exploitation and Abuse* has adopted a stance of zero tolerance on prostitution as well as human trafficking. This will require strong commitment from DPKO senior management, Member States and UN Mission senior personnel. Its three programmes of activity are:

1 Awareness and training;

2 Discipline, accountability and community relations; and

3 Support to anti-trafficking activities.

Work plans have been established for each of these programmes, which will need to be mainstreamed into the work of DPKO and missions.

The Secretary General's Bulletin on Sexual Exploitation and Abuse *has adopted a stance of zero tolerance on prostitution as well as human trafficking. This will require strong commitment from DPKO senior management, Member States and UN Mission senior personnel.*

A United Nations peacekeeping soldier accompanied by a group of local children in Timor-Leste
Eskinder Debebe/
UN Department of Public Information

The DPKO document noted that additional capacity is needed to monitor behaviour, report complaints, undertake investigations and address breaches of discipline. It also recommends activities to address problems in mission-community relations. DPKO also said that it would develop a "substantial set of tools for dealing with the problem of human trafficking" to be introduced into its training modules, including a guidance package of materials to be maintained by the Peacekeeping Best Practices Unit.[18]

Next Steps

There has been a sea-change in attitudes towards gender mainstreaming within DPKO since 2000. The efforts of particular individuals and bodies, both inside and outside the UN, in arguing for the necessity of gender mainstreaming for the achievement of just and equitable sustainable peace – and the positive response of both the UN Under-Secretary-General for Peacekeeping Operations, Jean-Marie Guéhenno, and the UN Secretary-General, Kofi Annan – have been instrumental in bringing about this transformation. Gender-awareness and gender mainstreaming are now an integral part of peacekeeper training materials available to contributing States, and gender units and advisers in particular peacekeeping missions have been successful in contributing to mainstreaming gender equality into new constitutions, the judiciary and other state and non-state institutions and bodies.

It now remains for the UN Secretary-General and the UN Security Council to ensure that gender is mainstreamed into the initial planning stages of a PSO and at all stages of a peace process, and for contributing States to ensure that their peacekeepers receive training in human rights, including women's rights, and are accountable for any exploitation of and violations against local citizens.

It now remains … for contributing States to ensure that their peacekeepers receive training in human rights, including women's rights, and are accountable for any exploitation of and violations against local citizens.

Recommendations to Facilitate Gender Mainstreaming in Peace Support Operations[19]

• A gender equality perspective must be brought to bear in the elaboration of ceasefire agreements and peace accords;

• Militaries must endeavour to recruit equal numbers of women and men in peace support operations at all levels;

• Sex-disaggregated statistics should be collected for all aspects of peacekeeping operations;

• Efforts must be made to maintain family life for personnel in peacekeeping operations: this may include 'accompanied' tours with husbands, wives and children being kept together, where possible;

• Gender and human rights training must be supplied to military personnel in peace support operations;

• Gender sensitisation modules should be introduced in the initial stages of police and military training; and

• Disciplinary action and effective accountability mechanisms need to be established to prevent impunity for violations of human rights by peacekeeping personnel.

5 Gender Mainstreaming in Post-conflict Reconstruction

Rawwida Baksh

... analyses of 'post-modern' conflicts – which identify the protagonists and beneficiaries of war as agents of the state, rebel groups, warlords, mercenaries ... have usually failed to take account of the gender dimension .... Analysing a conflict through a gender lens will thus contribute important insights into how to undertake the ... reconstruction process to the benefit of the society as a whole.

As discussed in Chapter 2, war is inherently gendered, not least because the armed forces in any conflict, be they government or rebel, tend to be made up predominantly or even exclusively of men, and because notions of masculinity will affect the conduct of individuals and groups within those forces. In addition, women and men, girls and boys, are affected differently by war. However, analyses of 'post-modern' conflicts – which identify the protagonists and beneficiaries of war as agents of the state, rebel groups, warlords, mercenaries, or all of these – have usually failed to take account of the gender dimension in either the causes of armed conflict, the way in which it is conducted or its impacts. Analysing a conflict through a gender lens will thus contribute important insights into how to undertake the post-conflict reconstruction process to the benefit of the society as a whole. This chapter seeks to do such an analysis, using Sierra Leone as a case study.

The war in Sierra Leone (1991–2001) damaged the entire fabric of society, including the political, legal, economic and social spheres, and affected every individual. A range of factors have been identified as contributing to the outbreak of the war, including ethnic and class divisions and disparities between urban and rural development – which were framed during the colonial period and played out under post-independence regimes. Rationales of both greed and grievance, or combinations of both, have also been put forward. In general, the following causes and functions of the armed conflict have been identified:

- The felt need to overthrow a corrupt and repressive government and create greater social justice;

- The overcentralisation of power in the capital and the consequent neglect of the rural population, many of whom were not able to access educational and employment opportunities;

- Individuals' wish to gain power and control over the country's resources, particularly the diamond mines;

- The physical and economic insecurity of predominantly young men, which led them to join either government or rebel armed forces for protection and the wherewithal to survive.

An analysis of poverty, one of the contributing factors of the conflict, also has to take into account gender differences. In the 'geography of gender' mapped out by Naila Kabeer (2003), the regions with the lower social and economic indicators are predominantly those where women are least economically active and have least access to education and training opportunities, credit, ownership of land and political leadership.

Gender inequality intersects with economic deprivation to produce more intensified forms of poverty for women than men. Gender inequality is part and parcel of the process of causing and deepening poverty in a society and [addressing this] must therefore constitute part and parcel of measures to eradicate poverty (Kabeer, 2003: xiii).

If the burden of poverty falls on women and children, then the provision of opportunities for the economic empowerment of women will be a factor in reducing levels of poverty. The achievement of gender equality is a key factor in development and in achieving the Millennium Development Goals, which will benefit both women and men.

In Sierra Leone, the lack of gender equality can be regarded as a contributory factor not only to women's poverty but to that of men and boys also, which has been identified as a key cause of the war.

Women and men, girls and boys, experienced the war differently as perpetrators, victims and emerging leaders ...

The Gender Dimensions of the War in Sierra Leone

Women and men, girls and boys, experienced the war differently as perpetrators, victims and emerging leaders, in the following kinds of ways:

- The majority of the perpetrators of human rights abuses, including rape and other forms of gender-based violence, were men.

Men and boys, both combatants and civilians, experienced trauma and post-traumatic stress. Many civilian men had experienced the horror of their wives and daughters being raped, mutilated and killed in their presence, and being powerless to defend them.

- Women and girls were more likely to have been targeted for sexual abuse, resulting in the birth of babies, the transmission of sexually transmitted infections (STIs), and the spread of HIV/AIDS. It is estimated that around 250,000 women and girls were raped during the armed conflict (UNIFEM, 2005).

- While it was mainly marginalised and disenfranchised young men who joined the rebel forces for security or economic gain, they were joined voluntarily by a number of women who were able to benefit from their participation (see Chapter 13).

- A great number of girls were kidnapped and enslaved by the rebels against their will, and others felt compelled to join armed groups for their own safety. It is estimated that of around 50,000 child soldiers, up to 12,000 were girls (UNIFEM, 2004).

- Women had less education and training than men and therefore fewer opportunities for productive economic activity. There was an increase in prostitution, also linked to the presence of large numbers of peacekeepers (see Chapter 4).

- Men and boys, both combatants and civilians, experienced trauma and post-traumatic stress. Many civilian men had experienced the horror of their wives and daughters being

Return of the first group of over 500 child soldiers by the RUF to the UN in Makeni, Sierra Leone
Gwynne Roberts/
Commonwealth Secretariat

raped, mutilated and killed in their presence, and being powerless to defend them.

- By participating in peace initiatives and women's demonstrations, some women were able to gain confidence in their abilities and skills in leadership, and raise their expectations for their future lives.

In the post-conflict environment, it was also apparent that women/girls and men/boys were affected, and also took advantage of the oportunities that presented themselves, in different ways:

- Women constituted the majority of those living in internally displaced people's camps or settlements, where they often lacked protection and access to basic necessities.

- The resettlement programmes offered to ex-combatants and civilians were unequal. There was a perception that male perpetrators of the war received a greater 'peace dividend' than women, with regard to, for example, housing and employment.

- Many women had lost their spouses and became heads of households. Without land titles they were liable to be evicted from their homes.

- The widespread destruction of hospitals and health clinics has had serious consequences for women, particularly in areas of natal/maternal care and child health. Sierra Leone has the highest incidence of maternal mortality in the world – 1,800 per 100,000 live births (UNFPA, nd).

- Women have encountered greater opportunities for education, training and political participation and leadership in the post-war environment and post-conflict reconstruction programme.

- In defining the post-conflict reconstruction process, women did not wish to return to the status quo as it was before the armed conflict and sought opportunities for social transformation: full citizenship, social justice, empowerment based on respect for their human dignity and human rights.

- As in the majority of countries emerging from conflict, women have also increased their representation in national parliaments and local government.

Towards the end of the conflict, at the beginning of the process of disarmament and the reintegration of ex-combatants, the Gender Section of the Commonwealth Secretariat facilitated a national consultation on 'Women and Men in Partnership for Post-conflict Reconstruction' ...

... the Report of the National Consultation, Freetown, Sierra Leone, published by the Commonwealth Secretariat (Baksh-Soodeen and Etchart, 2002), identified a number of gender equality objectives as essential for the reconstruction of the political, legal, economic and social spheres ....

The May 2001 National Consultation

Towards the end of the conflict, at the beginning of the process of disarmament and the reintegration of ex-combatants, the Gender Section of the Commonwealth Secretariat facilitated a national consultation on 'Women and Men in Partnership for Post-conflict Reconstruction' which was held in Freetown in May 2001 in collaboration with the Sierra Leone Ministry of Social Welfare, Gender and Children's Affairs and other partners, including the British Council, the United Nations Development Programme (UNDP) and the United Nations Children's Fund (UNICEF).

The consultation brought together women, men and young people from a range of national organisations and institutions, governmental and non-governmental, to engage in dialogue and to define their own solutions so that they could work together to create a more equitable, stable and prosperous future.

The papers, recommendations and national plan of action in the Report of the National Consultation, Freetown, Sierra Leone, published by the Commonwealth Secretariat (Baksh-Soodeen and Etchart, 2002), identified a number of gender equality objectives as essential for the reconstruction of the political, legal, economic and social spheres (see Box 13).

> ### *Box 13* Recommendations for Gender Mainstreaming in Post-conflict Reconstruction in Sierra Leone
>
> The national consultation identified the need for gender equality to be mainstreamed in all post-conflict reconstruction processes, including the political, legal, economic and social. Recommendations included the need for:
>
> - The Government to take concrete steps to implement the UN and Commonwealth targets of 30 per cent of women in parliament, local government and public decision-making through legislation and the electoral process.
>
> - A government, parliament, judiciary and legal system that enshrines the promotion and protection of women's rights.

Box 13 (continued)

- Legal reform to change laws weighted against women relating to property and inheritance rights, divorce and violence against women.

- Zero tolerance of violence against women and children and support for programmes in this area.

- Training and sensitisation of the police to address sexual violence.

- An examination of traditional practices that discriminate against women with a view to instituting laws to end these practices, e.g. female genital mutilation.

- Effective education, counselling and information campaigns, in local languages, to enable women to be aware of their rights under the law, to have control over their own lives and bodies and to enable them to participate equally in the prevention and treatment of HIV/AIDS and STIs.

- Increased access to education and skills training for women.

- Social protection for women and children.

- Special programmes for child ex-combatants and young drug addicts.

- The creation of new social values through public awareness and education to improve the status of women.

- Raising gender awareness and sensitivity among men and boys.

- Consulting and engaging young people – female and male – in the development of their communities, for whom they are a key constituency and resource.

- Representation of the disabled in consultative groups, district committees, etc.

It became clear from the consultation that Sierra Leoneans of all ages felt that the social values they shared should be upheld by the political, legal, economic and social institutions, and participants expressed a desire for more equitable and accountable systems than had existed previously.

Several speakers and participants in the consultation questioned some of the traditional practices in the country that were harmful to women and which served to curtail their participation in public life. It was noted that many women lacked the training and skills necessary to contribute to the reconstruction process and that efforts were required to enable them to gain those skills. The consultation endorsed international conventions that seek to protect women and young people and to enhance their status in society. Women were encouraged to come forward, to speak out and to contribute to promoting women's empowerment and gender equity.

The national consultation demonstrated the importance of women, men and young people engaging in dialogue on the way forward. It is through such partnerships, through women and men creating alliances, that changes in beliefs and practices that prevent women's equal entry into political, peace and development processes at all levels will come about.

It became clear from the consultation that Sierra Leoneans of all ages felt that the social values they shared should be upheld by the political, legal, economic and social institutions, and participants expressed a desire for more equitable and accountable systems than had existed previously.

Gender Equality in Political and Public Decision-Making

For most of the post-independence period, and particularly after 1967, Sierra Leone had been governed by a single-party political system interspersed with military rule. Political violence that marred the post-independence period was superseded by unprecedented violence and abuse of rights during the war, further excluding women from genuine participation in the political process.

One of the key recommendations of the May 2001 consultation was that women should be represented in decision-making bodies, including in parliament and local government, in line with UN and Commonwealth mandates.

To this end a 'Women in Parliament' training workshop was held in February 2002, facilitated by the Commonwealth Secretariat and Commonwealth Parliamentary Association, in collaboration with the Ministry of Social Welfare, Gender and

Children's Affairs, the Ministry of Development and Economic Planning, the British Council and the National Democratic Institute. Taking place a few months prior to the first post-conflict national elections in May 2002, its aims were to seek the commitment of leaders of political parties to include at least 30 per cent of women in their lists of candidates, and to develop the campaigning and leadership skills of potential women candidates. The workshop was followed by strenuous efforts by other organisations – including the 50/50 Group, which advocated gender parity in political representation, the National Democratic Institute and the Task Force for Women in Politics – to encourage and train women from all parties as parliamentary candidates.

These initiatives contributed to a significant increase – to 15 per cent – in the representation of women in the parliament elected in May 2002. The number of women holding key cabinet positions has increased by 60 per cent. The local government elections in May 2004 resulted in greater inclusion of women in all districts across the country.

Gender Equality in Human Rights and Legal Reform

Although the Convention on the Elimination of All Forms of Discrimination against Women was ratified by the Government of Sierra Leone in 1988, no report on the progress of its implementation has yet been submitted. In late October 2004 a nine-member group of experts from the CEDAW Committee met with government representatives to discuss the implementation of the Convention. Among those meeting with the expert team were the Gender Affairs Minister, the Attorney General and representatives of the Health, Education, Economic Development and Planning Ministries.

The United Nations Mission in Sierra Leone (UNAMSIL), in collaboration with its partners, has raised the profile of women's rights in the country through sustained training and awareness-raising programmes. The newly established Law Reform Commission is working with the Ministry of Social Welfare, Gender and Children's Affairs to ensure that discriminatory laws against women are reviewed and brought into line

... these initiatives contributed to a significant increase – to 15 per cent – in the representation of women in the [Sierra Leone] parliament elected in May 2002. The number of women holding key cabinet positions has increased by 60 per cent. The local government elections in May 2004 resulted in greater inclusion of women in all districts across the country.

All armed groups had carried out human rights violations against women and girls, the TRC report found. These included killings, rape and other sexual violence, ... amputation, forced pregnancy, disembowelment of pregnant women, torture, trafficking, mutilation, theft and the destruction of property. While forced conscription was used mainly – but not solely – against males, rape and sexual slavery were committed almost exclusively against females.

with CEDAW. In the meantime, the establishment of family support units in all district police stations has brought about additional protection and support for the victims of gender-based violence and has enabled more women to report cases of sexual abuse. The performance of the justice system is also improving in this regard, as evidenced by an increase in the number of convictions and the imposition of prison sentences for gender-based violence and related offences.

According to a report by Refugees International (2005), UNAMSIL has had many successes, including increased stability, the establishment of the Special Court for Sierra Leone and the return of refugees from Liberia and Guinea. The report noted, however, that vital elements necessary for Sierra Leone's long-term stability included "notably strengthening the justice system and continued training for government officials and security personnel in the areas of human rights and gender issues".

Gender and the Truth and Reconciliation Commission (TRC)

The Truth and Reconciliation Commission's 1,500-page report, released in October 2004, provides an excruciatingly thorough and detailed account of the atrocities carried out in the war, which officially ended in January 2002. Out of the 10,002 adult victims that the Commission was able to identify, 33.5 per cent were female. Among the 1,427 child victims, that proportion rose to 44.9 per cent.

All armed groups had carried out human rights violations against women and girls, the TRC report found. These included killings, rape and other sexual violence, sexual slavery, slave labour, abduction, assault, amputation, forced pregnancy, disembowelment of pregnant women, torture, trafficking, mutilation, theft and the destruction of property. While forced conscription was used mainly – but not solely – against males, rape and sexual slavery were committed almost exclusively against females.

Woman and child amputee in Freetown
Gwynne Roberts/Commonwealth Secretariat

UNIFEM support to the TRC

Many women were reluctant to come forward to relate their experiences. Overcoming such hurdles posed a challenge to officials of the TRC, many of whom were men. The Commission's mandate included looking specifically at crimes against women, but its personnel admitted at the outset that they had little knowledge or experience of eliciting testimony from women or conducting interviews with a gender perspective.

The United Nations Development Fund for Women (UNIFEM) made a commitment to support capacity-building in this area and gave assistance throughout the TRC process. UNIFEM and the Nairobi-based Urgent Action Fund for Women's Human Rights conducted a training workshop on gender-based human rights violations at the time of the hearings in 2003. The workshop focused on the impact of armed conflict on women and children, promoting gender sensitivity in handling female victims' testimonies and building the skills necessary to deal with victims and witnesses.

According to Betty Murungi of the Urgent Action Fund, "From our early experience with the Arusha tribunal [International Criminal Tribunal for Rwanda], it became quite clear that if these issues of sexual abuse that happen during wartime and internal conflict are left to the devices of officials … matters that relate to crimes committed against women are

Woman police officer, May 2001, Freetown
Gwynne Roberts/
Commonwealth Secretariat

often ignored, mischaracterised, or completely under-investigated" (quoted in *Africa Renewal*, 2005).

Sometimes traditional power relations threatened to impede the collection of information. "One commissioner said he went to a community where he was leading a team of recorders that were collecting testimonies. The women did not come out, only the men came", according to Florence Butegwa, UNIFEM representative for West Africa. "When they were asked why, the men said 'We can speak for the women'" (ibid).

Addressing structural inequalities

Hoping to avert similar crimes in the future, the TRC recommended numerous measures to help those women who suffered directly from the war, as well as to enhance the status of women more generally.

For women affected by the war, the TRC called on communities "to make special efforts to encourage acceptance of the survivors of rape and sexual violence as they reintegrate into society". It recommended that the Ministry of Gender Affairs establish a directory of donors and service providers where women could obtain information and help. The Government should provide free psychological support and reproductive health services to these women, while relief agencies should aid women ex-combatants with skills training and other assistance to advance their social reintegration.

The Commission urged reforms in the legal, judicial and police systems to make it easier for women to report cases of sexual and domestic violence. It called for the repeal of all statutory and customary laws that discriminate against women, including in marriage, inheritance, divorce and property ownership. It also recommended that the Government address the customary practice whereby a victim of rape was obliged to marry the rapist.

Gender-Based Crimes in the Special Court

In an advance towards accountability for atrocities and recognising women's rights, the Statute of the Special Court for Sierra Leone included rape, sexual slavery, enforced prostitution, and forced pregnancy as crimes against humanity. The

Statute also expressly considered "rape, enforced prostitution and any form of indecent assault" as violations of humanitarian law.

The Trial Chamber of the Special Court approved the addition of 'forced marriage' to the counts contained in an indictment against six defendants accused of leading the former Armed Forces Revolutionary Council (AFRC) and the Revolutionary United Front (RUF). The Trial Chamber's decision marks the first time that a court has recognised forced marriage as a crime against humanity under international law. The Court includes the new allegation under the category of 'sexual violence' within the larger category of crimes against humanity.

At the Conference on Gender Justice in Post-conflict Situations, organised by UNIFEM and the International Legal Assistance Consortium (ILAC) in September 2004, concerns were expressed at the discrimination still suffered by women under common, Islamic, customary and traditional systems of law in Sierra Leone, particularly in relation to marriage, rape, sexual violence, inheritance and ownership of land. It was recommended that the Government, in addition to introducing changes to existing laws in collaboration with agencies and women's groups, undertake educational programmes in the area of gender-based violence (Sooka, in UNIFEM and ILAC, 2004: 12).

... the Statute of the Special Court for Sierra Leone included rape, sexual slavery, enforced prostitution, and forced pregnancy as crimes against humanity. The Statute also expressly considered "rape, enforced prostitution and any form of indecent assault" as violations of humanitarian law.

Gender Issues in Poverty Eradication and Economic Empowerment

Poverty in Sierra Leone, mainly attributed to years of bad governance and economic mismanagement, is endemic and pervasive. The country has systematically ranked at the bottom of the Human Development Index since 1990. The conflict exacerbated the severity of poverty. Internal and external displacement of people further impoverished vulnerable groups, especially women, who are disproportionately represented among the poor. Women account for 51 per cent of the population and contribute to most of the household food requirements, including carrying out domestic chores and caring for the aged and children. Despite this, women remain marginal-

Many lost their homes in Sierra Leone
Gwynne Roberts/
Commonwealth Secretariat

ised in society and lack adequate access to productive assets including land, credit and technology.

As part of the post-conflict reconstruction process the Government of Sierra Leone drew up an interim Poverty Reduction Strategy Paper (I-PRSP), which was completed in 2001. The view of the World Bank was that while the I-PRSP provided a good analysis of poverty in Sierra Leone, it needed to be strengthened by including gender inequality (clearly articulated under the description of the non-income aspects of poverty) in the causes of poverty. A strategy was therefore adopted that focused on gendered analysis, advocacy on gender, monitoring and capacity building. The Gender Sensitisation and Training Strategy (GSTS) elaborated by the advisory team on gender was regarded as a vitally important tool for gender mainstreaming and for an engendered PRSP.

The consultants concluded that the exercise of gender mainstreaming would require a pool of local gender focal points and policy-makers, as well as a pool of professionals in the private sector, in NGOs and among community and local leaders, who were not only gender sensitive but also had gender technical skills and knowledge for the success of planning, monitoring and implementing the PRSP.

The overall objective of the GSTS was to:

- create awareness of gender issues;

- train men and women to recognise and deal with gender issues at home, in the work place and in society; and

- put in place a pool of gender focal points both in the public and private sector.

The Commonwealth Secretariat assisted in engendering the full PRSP by providing a long-term gender expert to the Government. The PRSP was completed and approved by the World Bank in May 2005.

Gender Equality in Education, Training and Employment

The education sector was particularly hard hit by the conflict, with some 80 per cent of educational infrastructure country-wide destroyed, and teaching/learning materials and equipment vandalised. Migration to safe areas of the country by people fleeing the war increased the pressure on educational facilities in these areas, with schooling taking place in double shifts and in makeshift structures such as Camp Schools.

The consultation pointed to the high illiteracy rate among the population, especially among women, and recommended that substantial resource allocation should be made for the

The Commonwealth Secretariat assisted in engendering the full PRSP by providing a long-term gender expert to the Government. The PRSP was completed and approved by the World Bank in May 2005.

Rebuilding lives: girls at the FAWE Centre, Freetown
Gwynne Roberts/Commonwealth Secretariat

Young women and men participating in the Commonwealth Secretariat's national consultation expressed the view that the existing situation in Sierra Leone did not provide an adequate foundation for their optimum development socially, economically, politically and culturally, leading to feelings of frustration and marginalisation among young people.

provision of functional literacy programmes throughout the country and that adult learning and teaching methods/techniques should be included in the teacher-training curriculum.

Other recommendations included the setting up of special schools for the blind, deaf and mentally challenged; the sharing of limited resources between formal and non-formal educational programmes; and the launching of community level programmes throughout the country to address the special educational and training needs of school drop outs. The Government has since introduced a new Education Act that contains a number of provisions to assist young people, especially girls, in returning to school.

The Role of Young Women and Men in Post-conflict Reconstruction

Young women and men participating in the Commonwealth Secretariat's national consultation expressed the view that the existing situation in Sierra Leone did not provide an adequate foundation for their optimum development socially, economically, politically and culturally, leading to feelings of frustration and marginalisation among young people. The consultation stressed the importance of engaging young women and men, who form a key constituency and resource in the country. Recommendations made by the young people included:

- The need for free access to education and training opportunities at all levels, taking into account the culture of peace, democracy and positive change;

- Better co-ordination between line ministries and NGOs to provide job-oriented training; and

- A vigorous nationwide campaign run by the Government to eradicate drug abuse.

Young women and men at the consultation called for the development of a National Youth Policy to ensure the participation and representation of all youths, especially the most marginalised, and to serve as a mouthpiece for young people.

With the support of intergovernmental organisations and NGOs, the Government of Sierra Leone subsequently estab-

GENDER MAINSTREAMING IN POST-CONFLICT RECONSTRUCTION

lished a new Ministry of Youth and Sports in 2003. One of the goals of the Ministry's revised National Youth Policy is "to enhance the empowerment of young women by incorporating gender sensitivity into all aspects of the youth policy and programmes".

Challenges Remaining

While there have been a series of initiatives on the part of Government, the Commonwealth Secretariat, the UN (including UNAMSIL and UNIFEM) and many national and international organisations and agencies to facilitate gender mainstreaming in the post-conflict reconstruction process, there are still tremendous challenges facing the Sierra Leonean people in their efforts to achieve women's empowerment and gender equality, including women's equal participation in decision-making at all levels. The PRSP has been engendered, and the Human Development Index shows an appreciable increase in access to education and retention of girls in schools. Progress has been slow, however, in introducing essential legal reforms with regard to women's rights in marriage, property ownership and inheritance.

Gender cuts across all aspects of post-conflict reconstruction initiatives, including security, political representation, community governance, human rights and legal reform, health and education, housing infrastructure and livelihoods. The experience of war in Sierra Leone illustrates its differential impacts on women, men, girls and boys. The need to mainstream gender in all post-conflict reconstruction efforts is essential to creating an inclusive, democratic society and to building a lasting and sustainable peace.

Gender cuts across all aspects of post-conflict reconstruction initiatives, including security, political representation, community governance, human rights and legal reform, health and education, housing infrastructure and livelihoods.

Vision of the Women of Sierra Leone
(articulated at the May 2001 National Consultation)

- We want to live in a country that is at peace.

- We want to bring up our children so that they respect peace, democracy, the rule of law and equality between women and men.

- We want to live in a country where the economy is stable, goods and services are affordable, skills training and financial, business and other opportunities are provided, so that we are economically empowered.

- We want to live in a country where we walk with pride and participate fully at the highest levels of politics and public service without fear or harassment.

- We want to live in a country where every woman is safe from all forms of abuse, all forms of violence including rape, sexual and other forms of abuse.

- We want to live in a country that practises zero tolerance of violence against women.

- We want to live in a country where every woman is an educated woman and every woman is a healthy woman.

- We want to live in a country where every woman is aware of her legal and human rights and where the Government, judiciary and legal systems promote and protect these rights.

- We want to live in a country where there are gender-sensitive health, social and other programmes which effectively address the spiralling incidence of HIV/AIDS and STIs, bearing in mind the special needs and problems of women, boys and girls of the armed forces.

- We want to live in a country that provides a stable, secure and safe environment for young women and men to actualise their potentials, and where they are encouraged and empowered to participate in decision-making at all levels.

6 Creating an International Law of Peace

Christine Chinkin

At present there is an *ad hoc* political approach to peace processes and post-conflict reconstruction. Yet although the context of every conflict is different, there are commonalities. In particular, while there may be situations where gender issues are especially highlighted throughout the conflict, gender relations are fundamental to every conflict and its aftermath. Traditional accounts of conflict resolution and post-conflict reconstruction, however, do not capture the relevance of gender.

International law has historically been divided into the laws of war and the laws of peace. From their origins the laws of war have been subject to codification, updating and reformulation. The laws of peace, on the other hand, have been assumed to comprise the rest of international law – that is, the body of international law that is not particular to a state of international or internal armed conflict. The time appears to be ripe for a more specific 'law of peace' that encompasses the settlement of disputes and post-conflict reconstruction.

Formulating a law of peace would clarify the continuum of conflict prevention, resolution (and attempted resolution) and post-conflict reconstruction to develop an international legal framework that identifies the legal obligations and duties of the diverse actors. It could form an international legal counterpart to the understandings generated by work in international relations, peace studies and development studies on complex emergencies and 'new' wars. In addition, advocates for the centrality of gender equality can and must play an important role in crafting this law.

Formulating a law of peace would clarify the continuum of conflict prevention, resolution ... and post-conflict reconstruction to develop an international legal framework that identifies the legal obligations and duties of the diverse actors .... In addition, advocates for the centrality of gender equality can and must play an important role in crafting this law.

Sources of the New Law

This body of law would not only look at the processes but also pay attention to their transformative potential. One authority and source for its creation, and for the centrality of gender relations, derives from UN Security Council Resolution (UNSCR) 1325 (see Chapter 4). The law might include:

- issues of gender justice and equality in reconstruction;

- principles of inclusive participation;

- concepts of international crimes and responses to them;

- the emerging concept of a responsibility to protect through humanitarian assistance and obligations;

- economic and social rights as part of sustainable development through a rights-based approach to post-conflict reconstruction;

- analysis of the principles of non-intervention, identifying a broad construct of intervention and restraints on it, including an understanding that intervention in conflict denotes a duty to ensure appropriate reconstruction;

- practices and policies derived from international dispute resolution;

- accountability and responsibility for non-compliance; and

- interaction of national and international law through constitution-making informed by international human rights standards, and the legal incorporation of those standards through national judicial and administrative bodies.

There has been much criticism of international administration, including of the failure to incorporate gender at all stages. Development of a coherent body of law requires independent critical analysis of the practices of States and international agencies and the building up of a body of best practices. This would enable such practices to be followed as a matter of obligation rather than their being dependent on the goodwill or gender sensitivity of particular officials.

A second source is the entitlement of everyone, under the 1948 Universal Declaration of Human Rights (UDHR), "to a social and international order in which the rights and freedoms" in the Declaration can be "fully realised" (article 28). This builds on the commitment in its preamble to national and international measures to secure the universal recognition and enforcement of the rights it contains – economic, social and cultural and civil and political. By using the language of entitlement, the UDHR makes it the duty of all international actors – not just States – to act for the achievement of these rights. Intervention by the international community – bilateral, institutional and non-governmental – is explicit through peace processes and subsequent reconstruction. To determine a package of international obligations in the context of post-conflict reconstruction, centred on the people of the territory in the terms of article 28, would be a significant development in international law.

A third source consists of the initiatives of non-state actors, including: (a) the practice of the humanitarian, human rights and development NGOs that are now the inevitable accompaniment to any conflict situation; and (b) the activities of multinational companies. This includes not only what is actually done in the field but also the host of instruments that direct their behaviour such as resolutions, codes of practice, memoranda of understanding, policy statements and guidelines for their practice.

Benefits of an International Law of Peace

As this review of potential sources suggests, development of an international law of peace requires the bringing together of principles from what are currently distinct branches of international law:

- human rights, including commitment to the rule of law and democratisation;

- international humanitarian law;

- prohibition of the use of force in international relations;

- the right to sustainable development;

- the obligation for the peaceful settlement of disputes;

- the emerging law of transitional justice; and

- refugee law.

In that it derives from existing international law, it is binding on all actors – including those that have tended to remain

A recognised international legal framework that covered post-conflict reconstruction ... would provide important protections to women and offer a tool and a language for their empowerment.

aloof from legal obligations and prefer to see their activities as development or aid, notably the international financial institutions. It commences with the 'minimalist' mandate to 'do no harm'.

A recognised international legal framework that covered post-conflict reconstruction would determine what civilian populations might expect from an international dispute resolution process and its outcomes, taking account of the differing expectations of women and men. It would provide important protections to women and offer a tool and a language for their empowerment. It would also create an expectation that the UN Security Council would include these obligations in context-specific resolutions and that peace agreements would also incorporate these matters. Indeed, if they were not explicitly included, they could be read in as obligations of international law.

Recognising post-conflict reconstruction as an integrated and coherent body of law would also have implications for integrated financing of the different stages of the various operations, rather than the current *ad hoc* approach of looking to different budgets and methods of financing. In addition, it would impose obligations on international facilitators and mediators to take account of gender throughout the negotiations, to bring gender experts into the process or undertake appropriate training for themselves, to be receptive to requests for participation by appropriately identified women – or to initiate this if no such request is forthcoming – and to ensure that all aspects of any agreement reached are subject to a gender audit.

Recommendations

- The settlement of disputes and post-conflict reconstruction should be governed by a coherent and integrated body of law – a Law of Peace – in which gender equality and equity is an integral part.

- A body of best practice in gender mainstreaming in the legal aspects of post-conflict reconstruction needs to be developed and followed as an obligation rather than as a result of good will.

- Economic, social rights and cultural rights, as well as civil and political rights, should be secured and enforced by international actors, state and private, in the context of post-conflict reconstruction.

- All peace agreements should be subject to a gender audit.

PART TWO

National and Regional Experiences

7 Bangladesh: Women and Minorities in Conflict Resolution

Amena Mohsin

Bangladesh is a society that has experienced violence in all possible forms, including war, flood, famine and state-induced violence. In fact the very emergence of Bangladesh as an independent state was a violent one. The nine-month long war of liberation, which began with the Pakistan military's crackdown on the Bengalis of then East Pakistan on the night of 25 March 1971, left three million dead and 20 million raped.

Reconstruction of such a war-ravaged society was a Herculean job that required the co-operation of all segments of society. However, a society that experiences violence internalises that violence, and Bangladesh has been no exception. The state became increasingly authoritarian: in 1974 an emergency was declared and a Special Powers Act was passed that gave extraordinary powers to the police. Political dissidence, instead of being accommodated, was suppressed, and in 1975 the country moved from a multi-party democracy to a one-party system.

In August 1975 Sheikh Mujibur Rahman, along with his family members, were assassinated by a group of young majors. From then until 1990 the country was under military and quasi-military rule. During this period various political parties and civil society groups led movements for the restoration of democracy. Many of these turned violent. In December 1990 retired General Ershad had to resign in the face of a massive popular upsurge against him. Since then the country has been under civilian rule. But the culture of protest has remained a culture of violence.

Since 1991 Bangladesh has had three parliaments, yet they have failed to play an effective role because they have been constantly boycotted by the major political parties under one pretext or another. *Hartals* (shutdowns) have become a regular feature. These totally disrupt the normal activities of ordinary

> *Bangladesh is a society that has experienced violence in all possible forms, including war, flood, famine and state-induced violence.*

The process of nation- and state-building in Bangladesh has impacted negatively on indigenous women. During conflict and periods of instability it is women who are most affected and are the most vulnerable group.

citizens. More importantly they became increasingly violent, and ordinary citizens were frequently killed in the cross-fire and bomb explosions of the rival parties. This led, in 2000, to the passing of the Public Safety Act, which authorised the police to arrest people on suspicion and hold them without trial or bail. The military has also again become a factor in Bangladeshi politics. Thus, despite being a multi-party democracy, the country has evolved a violent and undemocratic political system.

Ethnic and Religious Differences

Bangladesh is home to about 45 ethnic communities. The desire of the people of the Chittagong Hill Tracts (CHT) to remain separate from and not integrate themselves into the Bengali nation led to an armed insurgency in the Hills in the early 1970s. The ethnic minorities of the plains are also resentful because the state has not fulfilled its obligations regarding the land rights of indigenous peoples. The Constitution of Bangladesh gives no recognition to its minorities, although special laws have been enacted for their protection.

The religious minorities also feel discriminated against because the state in 1978 dropped secularism as one of its planks and replaced it with absolute faith in Allah. In 1988 the Constitution made Islam the state religion, with the provision that other communities would have full freedom to observe their religious practices. The state's identification with one community, that is, the dominant Bengali Muslim community, has placed the other ethnic and religious communities at a disadvantage. A 'we' versus 'them' divide is thus created, despite the fact that Bangladesh came into being on a secular plank and all the communities – irrespective of their religious and ethnic backgrounds – had participated in its formation.

Minority Women and the State

The process of nation- and state-building in Bangladesh has impacted negatively on indigenous women. During conflict and periods of instability it is women who are most affected and are the most vulnerable group. Minority women are addition-

*Chakma Tribe, Chittagong
Hills, Bangladesh*
Mark McEvoy/Panos Pictures

ally vulnerable because they also fall outside the 'we' paradigm. The terms 'minority people' and 'minority women' can only be understood in relation to the modern state. They denote 'other-ness' or 'being out of the mainstream'. Those who live, or choose to live, outside the mainstream population are marginal-ised. The failure of the state to accommodate its indigenous peoples is a result of its built-in limitations. Its institutions are not conducive to accommodation; rather they are built on an ethos and values that celebrate and emphasise the values of autonomy, competition and control associated with power and domination. At the conceptual level the state predicates itself on the ideology of nationalism, which is exclusionary rather than inclusive. It emphasises uniformity and homogeneity rather than diversity and plurality.

The above formation of the state both at the institutional and conceptual levels makes the situation of minority/indige-nous peoples quite problematic and precarious. Indigenous peoples continue to live according to their own socio-economic and cultural practices, and often within their own

While the indigenous population is vulnerable within the structures and ideals of a modern state, indigenous women are more vulnerable than men ...

political structures. These practices and structures tend to be at variance with those of the dominant population.

While the indigenous population is vulnerable within the structures and ideals of a modern state, indigenous women are more vulnerable than men and suffer from insecurity in two major ways:

- they are less privileged as women members of the state, which is based on patriarchal values that privilege men and masculinity; and

- they are vulnerable as members of an indigenous community as their lived experiences, insecurities, struggles and perceptions of empowerment may not necessarily be similar to those of women belonging to the dominant group.

Development, Displacement and Insecurity

The development aims of the state are often in conflict with the interests and values of indigenous peoples. The former regards the resources of land – and land itself – as commodities that need to be exploited for profit, while for the latter these may be sacrosanct. For indigenous peoples, the land is the abode of their ancestors and their spirits. State development endeavours have often led to the displacement of indigenous peoples from their land, which violates them both physically and psychologically and is a major factor behind their insecurity, particularly that of women.

In terms of survival, forests constitute an integral part of the lives of the indigenous peoples of the CHT and of the Garo community of the plains, who regard themselves as the children of the forest. Women use the forest resources for the needs of everyday life and for economic activity. The state has taken over vast tracts of forest as Reserve Forests, as well as leased out forest for commercial purposes. This has displaced the indigenous peoples from their habitat as well as depriving women in particular of their source of livelihood without providing alternative sources of income. It has not only increased the burden on women but has altered their social status. Among the Garos, for example, women enjoyed a privileged position in a matrilocal society. However, the removal of their source of income has forced them into working as housemaids and in the beauty parlours of Dhaka city, which is both distressing for them and disruptive of the community's social structure. Many of them are marrying Bengali men primarily to ensure their own security. The Garos regard this as a process by which their ethnic group is being extinguished.

Loss of status has been accompanied by sexual violence against women resulting from displacement and from development-induced poverty. The extreme poverty of the Mahali women in Dinajpur, for example, has left them vulnerable to the predations of contractors employed in the Government forestry programmes (*Muktokantho*, 6 December 1999). In the Birishiri thana, where 80 per cent of the Garo families are dependent on the forest for survival, the Government forest development projects have rendered them homeless. However, the women continue to enter the forest to collect wood and fuel, where they are vulnerable to members of the Bangladesh Rifles – and to the Border Security Forces of India if they happen to cross the frontier (*Banglabazar Patrika*, 5 December 1999).

In the CHT, too, the forest development projects have led to displacement of the population. The Kheyang, a forest-living and forest-dependent people, have been barred from entering the forests where they had been living for generations. Since the state acquired the forests as Forest Reserves, cases have been filed against many of the Kheyang as illegal squatters. This has placed the women in a disadvantageous position: as the men are afraid to go out, the women have to go to market as well as do the domestic chores. Many other Hill people are living as internally displaced persons (IDPs) following state acquisition of forests.

Among the Garos ... women enjoyed a privileged position in a matrilocal society. However, the removal of their source of income has forced them into working as housemaids and in the beauty parlours of Dhaka city, which is both distressing for them and disruptive of the community's social structure.

Militarisation and Insecurity

The country witnessed an armed insurgency in the CHT for over two decades – it began in the mid-1970s and ended with the signing of a peace accord on 2 December 1997. The accord, however, left many of the crucial issues – such as land, property rights and the issue of Bengali settlers – quite ambiguous. Though a Task Force was created, no special provision was made for women-headed households. Full powers have also not been devolved to the local bodies. Due to the ambiguities and non-implementation of the accord, the situation in the CHT

The conflict/ insurgency in the CHT has led to the intense politicisation of women. From the beginning, women have been associated with the political struggle for the emancipation and autonomy of the Hill people and for women's rights. In February 1975 a Mohila Parishad (Women's Council) was formed by the political arm of the autonomy movement ...

is far from peaceful today. It appears that the region has entered into a second stage of conflict as polarisations have appeared among the Hill people themselves, and they are divided into pro-accord and anti-accord groups.

During the insurgency period and in the period following the peace accord, women in the CHT endured both physical and psychological insecurity. This was caused by the armed conflict as well as by the continued presence of the state and its military apparatus. With the men no longer able to do so, women were forced to take on jobs in the public sphere. According to a report of the Chittagong Hill Tracts Commission, between 1991 and 1993 over 94 per cent of the rapes of Hill women were committed by Bengali security personnel, many against girls under 18 years of age (CHT Commission, 1997).

Both boys and girls were at risk of abduction during the period of armed conflict. Hill students at Dhaka University dared not visit their homes. The Organising Secretary of the Hill Women's Federation, Kalpana Chakma, was abducted in 1996 on the eve of the general elections and was never seen again. Since the peace accord was signed, out of the 50,000 people displaced by the conflict, it is the many women heading households who have been reluctant to return to their homes out of fear for their own security.

The armed insurgency itself led to an internalisation of violence and a militarisation that has created a masculinised ethos. Women's vulnerability has increased since the accord was signed due to the presence of weapons and drugs and a corresponding increase in violence and criminality. With the influx of Bengali settlers and the presence of security personnel, 'eve-teasing' (sexual harassment), previously unknown in the Hills, has spread to the Hill people.

Women as Agents of Change and Conflict Resolution

The conflict/insurgency in the CHT has led to the intense politicisation of women. From the beginning, women have been associated with the political struggle for the emancipation and autonomy of the Hill people and for women's rights. In February 1975 a *Mohila Parishad* (Women's Council) was formed by the political arm of the autonomy movement, and auxiliary organs were created in almost all the villages of the Hill Tracts. Later each village also constituted a *Mohila Panchayet*, restricted to women only, which took up issues of oppression and violence against women as well as undertaking political awareness-raising programmes.

The Hill Women's Federation (HWF) also played a crucial role in the movement of the Hill People. They took up cases of rape of Hill women by security personnel and raised them in public fora, and pursued the cause of the Hill women through networking with Bengali women's organisations. In 2000 the HWF and the United People's Democratic Front (UPDF), the anti-accord group in the CHT, published a book titled *Paharer Ruddho Kontho* (*Silenced Voices of Women*), narrating the lived experiences of trauma, fear and insecurities of the Hill women during the insurgency. In June 2001 the same coalition published the diary of Kalpana Chakma, who has become a symbol of the Hill people's struggles and sacrifices.

Despite the Hill women playing an active role during the insurgency and having endured great suffering, women were not included in the peace process on either the Hill people's side or on that of the Government. The peace accord signed between the Government of Bangladesh and the Parbatya Chattagram Jana Sanghati Samity (PCJSS) makes no reference to the sufferings of the Hill women nor does it provide compensation or rehabilitation to rape victims and war widows.

The CHT women's movement, and other indigenous groups such as the Garos through their student forum (Bagachash), have networked with mainstream organisations and joined them in demonstrations against sexual harassment, rape, acid-throwing, slum and brothel-clearance, and against the Government's policies on oil drilling and other environmental issues. In this way, groups previously concerned with ethnic discrimination have been widening their horizons to encompass broader issues that strengthen their democratic participation in the national body politic.

Despite variations in party ideologies and state identification with one community and religion, Bangladesh is a secular society. This provides civil society with a broad platform and framework for conflict management and resolution. This is not to suggest that polarisations do not exist within civil society, but women's organisations have united over issues of human and

Despite the Hill women playing an active role during the insurgency and having endured great suffering, women were not included in the peace process on either the Hill people's side or on that of the Government.

[Women] have a long history of intervention to maintain inter-community harmony and provide succour and relief to victims at the community level. This happened during Hindu-Muslim riots in 1964 in Pakistan, in 1992 in the wake of incidents in India following the destruction of the Babri Masjid in Ayodhya, and again in post-election violence against Hindu minorities in October 2001.

women's security. They have always played an effective role in conflict-associated activities. In the immediate aftermath of independence, they were involved in rehabilitation programmes, providing work and capacity-building for rape victims, many of whom were not accepted by their families. They have a long history of intervention to maintain inter-community harmony and provide succour and relief to victims at the community level. This happened during Hindu-Muslim riots in 1964 in Pakistan, in 1992 in the wake of incidents in India following the destruction of the Babri Masjid in Ayodhya, and again in post-election violence against Hindu minorities in October 2001.

Box 14 Women Working Against Violence in Bangladesh

The women's movement in Bangladesh first came together against violence against women in the 1980s. These protests led to the formation of Shommilita Nari Shomaj (United Women's Front), a coalition of women's organisations. Women's organisations have actively solicited the co-operation of the mass media, resulting in published material related to violence against women, malpractice in health care and family planning. They have also campaigned intensively for legal measures for violations against women, enactment of a uniform family code to replace the various personal laws perpetuating gender inequality within the family in various religious communities and the implementation of CEDAW. The strategies they adopted have included:

- Awareness raising;
- Dissemination of information through posters, folk songs and street theatre;
- Rallies, workshops and seminars;
- Networking;
- Protests;
- Confidence-building measures; and
- Publications.

Civil society in Bangladesh (and in particular women's organisations) has been advocating for women's rights and women's political participation for a long time (see Box 14). They need to unite across gender, class, religious and ethnic lines. Ways must be found to move beyond the divisions resulting from post-independence nation-building and development policies to create greater human security and sustainable peace.

Recommendations

- The culture of violence surrounding political activity in Bangladesh needs to be addressed.

- In order to ensure the rights of ethnic communities, it is desirable that the state recognises their cultural distinctiveness and respects and recognises the pluralist reality of Bangladesh through constitutional amendments. These require a two-thirds majority in Parliament and may therefore need the support of both government and opposition parties.

- Women from indigenous communities are particularly vulnerable to violence and require greater physical and economic security in order to be able to remain in their ancestral lands.

- Increased political representation for women. Women's organisations have been campaigning for an increase in reserved seats from 30 to 64 to 150 with the provision of direct elections. This would give a voice to women MPs, who otherwise have little voice and credibility because they are accountable to the party rather than to any constituency. In order for women to make an impact at the national level, they must have representation in parliament, the centre of political decision-making. It is imperative that minority women are included in the process and that a certain number of seats are reserved for them.

Civil society in Bangladesh (and in particular women's organisations) has been advocating for women's rights and women's political participation for a long time (see Box 14). They need to unite across gender, class, religious and ethnic lines. Ways must be found to move beyond the divisions resulting from post-independence nation-building and development policies to create greater human security and sustainable peace.

Recommendations (continued)

• Women must be included in peace processes.

• Sensitisation on gender and minority issues needs to be included in the academic curriculum. The mainstream orientation of the present academic curriculum is not sensitive to the history and culture of minorities. Although gender and women's studies have made inroads at the university level, this needs to be extended to primary and high school education for two reasons: first, in order to sensitise children to gender and a pluralist culture at a formative stage; and second, because few people attain university level.

8 Cyprus: Peace Is Too Precious to Be Left to Men Alone

Maria Hadjipavlou

'Choose Your Side!'

Our birthplace is split in two and we
Are caught on barbed wire – hybrids
Turk and Greek alike

"Is it December is it July
Choose your Side
Are you Turkish or Greek
There's no Purgatory in between"

We cannot be from both Sides
Because we are two, one and the other
You refused to believe in:
We are loneliness itself.

(From *Yashin*, 2000)

As the poet tells us, a dividing line has split Cyprus into two. This decades-old line is some 112 miles long, stretching across the island and separating the country into North and South. According to one's positioning in politics and historical moments, it is referred to as 'the green line', 'the ceasefire line', 'the dead zone', 'the demarcation line', 'the partitioning line', 'the Attila line', 'the no-man's land' or 'the border'.

These different designations form part of the collective historical, ideological and political experiences of Cypriot communities. The view that 'it is us who suffered more' prevails on both sides. Each side's pain and war memories are filled with selective representations and each lacks self-reflection. There is mutual denial of each other's pain, grievances and loss. Remembering and not-forgetting are significant aspects of national narratives that are filled with martyrs, heroes, monu-

Divided societies need a gendered understanding and analysis of their conflict experience in order to gain new insights into the kinds of accommodation that would address both sides' fears, needs, concerns and hopes, and where women's and men's perspectives and contributions would be valued equally.

ments, statues, public representations and bravery, all leading to a patriarchal sense of 'our exclusive national identity and family' and rarely allowing a space for shared responsibility.

The conflict culture as it is constructed and defined by masculine, militaristic politics excludes women from the issues of war and peace. The socialisation into the 'enemy image' in deeply divided societies like Cyprus is highly patriarchal and exclusionary, and is contrary to the feminist discourse around inclusion, conflict reduction and conflict resolution. The feminist discussion of the concept of power has also been relevant to conflict resolution, warning against the use of coercion in peace negotiations. Feminism, like other social reform movements, emphasises equality as a shared value among all human beings. Conflict resolution addresses equality through its recognition of basic human needs. Divided societies need a gendered understanding and analysis of their conflict experience in order to gain new insights into the kinds of accommodation that would address both sides' fears, needs, concerns and hopes, and where women's and men's perspectives and contributions would be valued equally.

War, and specifically inter-communal strife, acts as a catalyst in bringing to the surface unaddressed trauma, past grievances and instincts for survival, creating patterns of behaviour in everyday life that aim to reinforce the badness of the other side (Evans and Lunn, 1997). Communities in conflict view their differences as irreconcilable and are thus unable to craft a joint language to dialogue around other possibilities. In such a heavily loaded context it is necessary to use unofficial third parties to help groups from across the divide to meet face-to-face. Through these encounters, the other side acquires a face and a name, which leads to a different and more complex understanding and view of the national 'Self' and 'Other'.

Moving from a Conflict Mentality to a Peace Mentality

More than ever today in Cyprus a 'gender-sensitive lens' is required to see both:

- how the conflict was shaped over many decades by gendered assumptions, concepts, institutions and practices; and

- how to initiate appropriate interventions in the active peace processes from the perspectives of both women and men in a new Cyprus, member of the European Union.

Building a peace mentality demands the deconstruction of the conflict mentality, and for this to happen the mobilisation and participation of all segments of the population is needed. This was the context for the efforts by some Cypriot women to establish the Women's Studies Centre in Nicosia in 1985 and the Cyprus Peace Centre in 1991 and by a non-governmental organisation (NGO) to build an international Eco-Peace Village in 1998. In the mid-1990s a number of conflict resolution workshops had addressed women's differing experiences of the conflict through a gender lens and started developing spaces for alternative women's discourses. Up to the late 1990s there had been over 70 bi-communal groups of citizens, professionals, political leaders, trade unionists, students, youth leaders and women active in promoting rapprochement, despite intense political risks at times. In 2002 a diverse group of women formed the NGO Hands Across the Divide (HAD). The partial opening of the Green Line (23 April 2003) and the crossing of citizens to each other's sides was connected to reconciliation efforts at the grassroots level.

The work of Cypriot women discussed below is based on the interconnection between feminist ideology and conflict resolution values. The values of inter-connectedness and relationship building are fundamental in promoting a different view of

Thousands crossed the buffer zone in 2003 when movement restrictions were eased in Cyprus after 30 years
UN Peacekeeping Force in Cyprus

Official diplomacy can no longer ignore citizens' unofficial contribution to peace processes in conflict societies. Women in situations of conflict globally have a wealth of peace-building experience to be utilised and legitimised. For women, peace and security means the elimination of all forms of structural and institutional inequalities and violence.

the conflict and the role of change agents. A recognition of the relationship between the personal and the group, the regional and the international, provides a holistic understanding of the major issues and causes of the conflict. Conflict resolution promotes an analytical view of the conflict, which means considering the 'Other's' perspective and reality to be as legitimate as one's own. It promotes a culture of inclusion and tolerance of the views of the Other.

Through the use of different conflict resolution methodologies and dialogue, men and women from both Cypriot communities have been developing new understandings about the conflict and its interactive nature. The conflict is re-framed as a shared problem to be solved co-operatively. Through this process, men and women from across the divide discover shared fears, concerns, interests and hopes, as well as become aware of the force and impact that their formal and informal socialisation has had on their understanding of 'national history' and the Other, the enemy. The transformation begins when the group engages in joint creative thinking. Their perspective becomes more inclusive, and gradually a new culture is created with a shared identity – that of a peace-builder – that helps smooth out other divisions such as ethnicity, class and age.

Official diplomacy can no longer ignore citizens' unofficial contribution to peace processes in conflict societies. Women in situations of conflict globally have a wealth of peace-building experience to be utilised and legitimised. For women, peace and security means the elimination of all forms of structural and institutional inequalities and violence.

Cypriot Women's Efforts in Peace-building

The background

The women of Cyprus, both Greek and Turkish, have experienced inter-ethnic violence and war, displacement, rape, loss of loved ones, loss of dignity, loss of property and lack of opportunities for economic development. The collective memory of these events differs in time and intensity for each Cypriot community. The two competing nationalisms imported from Greece and Turkey have further separated the two communities. The Turkish Cypriot community felt victimised by the majority in the inter-ethnic violence of December 1963–64 and later in 1967, when thousands of them (one-third of the 120,000) became uprooted and lived in homogeneous enclaves until 1974. Many felt themselves to be second-class citizens experiencing the consequences of unequal economic development.

The Republic of Cyprus (governed by Greek Cypriots only after 1964) proved ineffective in protecting the human rights of all its citizens, thus little loyalty developed toward the state. The politics of fear, mistrust, intolerance and separatism were on the rise. The official inter-communal negotiations that began soon after the internationalisation of the problem did not improve the situation on the ground. In the summer of 1974 the military junta in Greece and its local collaborators staged a coup to topple the Makarios Government, thus giving Turkey the opportunity (translated as constitutional right) to invade the island on 20 July 1974. This resulted in the geographic partition of the island into North and South, which brought about the displacement of one-third of the Greek Cypriots to the South. The issue of return for Greek Cypriots and of violation of international law, human rights and justice are critical in their collective narrative, as is the collective trauma.

The fact is that both communities have experienced violence and war. The missing link to this experience has been to address the bigger question of what inter-ethnic violence and war have done to *all* the citizens of Cyprus, and not just to each ethnic community at different points in time. Conflict resolution thus invites us not only to engage in mutual acknowledgement of the legitimacy of each other's pain and loss, but also to understand the different meanings and interpretations attributed to the 1974 events. For instance, for the Greek Cypriots, 20 July is a day of mourning and renewal of determination to struggle for freedom and return. According to the Turkish Cypriot official narrative, however, it is a day of liberation and independence.

Formation of the Bi-communal Women's Group

The Bi-communal Women's Group (1995–96) made up of 22 women of different ethnic groups, ages, classes and educational backgrounds, held in a workshop which grappled with the

The fact is that both communities have experienced violence and war. The missing link to this experience has been to address the bigger question of what inter-ethnic violence and war have done to all *the citizens of Cyprus …*

The work carried out in cross-ethnic encounters and conflict resolution training workshops points ... to the need for long-term work to bring about changes in attitudes and belief systems and for confidence-building before any claims of reconciliation can be made. The history of the conflict is so deep rooted that, even after a political solution is reached, it will take more than one generation to evolve a culture of multiculturalism and co-operation.

question: 'What contributes to pain and suffering in Cyprus through the eyes of women?' The group used a computer-supported decision-making methodology called 'interactive management'. They worked through three stages of planning and design: (a) analysis of the current situation; (b) goal setting/vision for the future; and (c) development of an agenda for collaborative action. There were four facilitators: a Greek Cypriot man who handled the computer, an American professor, a Turkish Cypriot woman and myself. Some of the basic assumptions of the workshop were that:

- Ethnic communities are heterogeneous and contain many voices;
- Every person speaks as an individual rather than as a representative of his or her community, party or business;
- Debate about political positions is best left to the politicians;
- The opportunity to engage in bi-communal dialogue is a privilege; and
- The purpose is not to solve the Cyprus problem but to create conditions for the solution.

The obstacles as articulated by this group of Cypriot women present a complex picture. The Greek Cypriot politicians' belief – that as soon as the Turkish army withdraws from the northern part of the island the people in both societies will have no problem living together as they did in the past – denies the complexity of the problem and places blame only on the outside. The work carried out in cross-ethnic encounters and conflict resolution training workshops points rather to the need for long-term work to bring about changes in attitudes and belief systems and for confidence-building before any claims of reconciliation can be made. The history of the conflict is so deep rooted that, even after a political solution is reached, it will take more than one generation to evolve a culture of multiculturalism and co-operation.

The Cypriot women produced from their perspective hundreds of obstacles, which can be classified into four broad categories: (a) psychological; (b) structural; (c) historical and political; and (d) philosophical/personal. These, in turn, were sometimes specific to Greek Cypriot women or to Turkish Cypriot women and sometimes shared.

Two of the concerns as learned and internalised by Greek Cypriot women included external interventions in the affairs of the island, with specific reference to the *coup* and the Turkish invasion in 1974, and identification with the glorious Hellenic past. The latter, in their view, provides the basis for a superiority complex in relation to Others, with some considering this factor as undermining the Cypriot part of their identity. Many expressed sadness that the Turkish Cypriot community did not understand their tragedy during the 1974 events: displacement, loss of loved ones and economic catastrophe. Fear of losing their homeland as a result of Turkish expansionist plans was strongly voiced.

The Greek Cypriot women also expressed concern at the lack of understanding by both communities and the continual refusal at the individual and collective levels to forget past events. They felt that "we always emphasise differences" and that there was a lack of attention to a shared past. The show of military power by the state was seen as intimidating people and preventing them from coming out in the open to speak against militarisation.[20] This fear of militarisation relates to their role as mothers as they do not want to bring up their children in such conditions. "We women, because we are mothers, find it more painful to live and raise our children in conditions of insecurity", some said. At the same time they expressed a feeling of failure at not taking advantage of their special role as mothers to contribute to peace-building.

What is evident in such statements and perceptions is that many Greek Cypriot women connect peace with biological difference (childbearing and motherhood). They do not question the role of socialisation in the construction of such expectations and how women in times of conflict are turned into promoters of values articulated by the male-dominant system. From other research (Hadjipavlou, 1995), it can be seen that some Greek Cypriot women are confused about the political ideology and worldview that feminism advocates. They lack a gender consciousness, so there are a number of contradictions. On the one hand, all the women in the group – and this applies to the Turkish Cypriot women as well – described the social organisation of their societies as patriarchal and hierarchical, but on the other hand, they said they were not feminists and believed that women by nature were peace-loving.

The Greek Cypriot women also expressed concern at the lack of understanding by both communities and the continual refusal at the individual and collective levels to forget past events. They felt that "we always emphasise differences" and that there was a lack of attention to a shared past.

123

Both groups viewed the patriarchal structure of social organisation, as well as the absence of women from ... the peace process, as serious obstacles to the functioning of ... representative democracy in Cyprus. Other shared concerns included: social and religious prejudices ... and a lack of institutional support to promote ... understanding of the other's culture.

They did not question their pride in 'offering' their sons to fight for the liberation of their homeland or view this as a gender issue, nor did it occur to them that they could challenge such practices and expectations.

The Turkish Cypriot women expressed strong fear of being dominated by both the Greek Cypriot majority and by Turkey. "We feel like a sandwich between the two", some said. They also felt sadness at the fact that the Greek Cypriot community ignored their plight and did not empathise with their tragedy between 1963 and 1974, which meant being uprooted and enduring economic hardships. They also feared losing the Cypriot part of their identity with the influx of Turks from Anatolia. The lack of international recognition of their situation made them feel isolated from the rest of the world, both in terms of communication and opportunities. Concern was expressed at the composition of the official negotiating team.

Both groups viewed the patriarchal structure of social organisation, as well as the absence of women from decision-making bodies and the peace process, as serious obstacles to the functioning of true, representative democracy in Cyprus. Other shared concerns included: social and religious prejudices, including those around intermarriage, and a lack of institutional support to promote knowledge and understanding of the other's culture. Lack of integrated schools, and the fact that national histories and narratives emphasise crimes committed against the Other, reinforced the conflict mentality.

Another mutual concern voiced was the increase in structural and domestic violence and the lack of sufficient support centres to provide the necessary services and mechanisms for the empowerment of women. They viewed this as closely linked to the militarisation of the island. Many also talked about a reluctance to express their true feelings about the conflict for fear of being labelled as traitors: they resorted to silence or talked only among themselves. Militarism has forced each group to live only in one part of the island and to imagine the other part – creating a psychological split.

Hands Across the Divide (HAD)

In March 2001 a group of Greek Cypriot and Turkish Cypriot women from different NGOs (some of whom had worked together in conflict resolution training workshops before, but most of whom did not know each other) participated in a two-day seminar entitled 'Communication in Divided Societies: What Women Can Do'. The seminar was organised by the British Council in co-operation with Greek Cypriot and Turkish Cypriot women. Thanks to the workshop facilitator, women were encouraged to use the concept of gender as an analytical tool and adopt a 'gender lens' to examine their conflict experiences and peace activities.

The women participants voiced their anger and impatience at the continuing impact of militarism and patriarchy on their daily lives. They decided to launch an international campaign to inform the world about their realities and demand their right to freedom of movement, contact and free communication in Cyprus. The women's voices were clear: "We have had enough. We want to be together and we want it now. We must campaign for our human rights – we cannot depend on the military authorities to give us permission to meet each other."

The group came together again in London (it could not meet in Cyprus because of the ban on bi-communal contact) for a workshop in February 2002. This resulted in the establishment of the first international Cypriot women's NGO, Hands Across the Divide (HAD), with a branch in London comprising diaspora Cypriot women. The overall objective was to promote gender equality and the participation of women in the peace negotiations. This was followed by a historic meeting in the Kreisky Forum in Vienna between HAD and another NGO, the Women's Initiative for Peace, comprising women from Greece and Turkey. For the first time, women from Cyprus, Greece and Turkey came together to share common concerns in promoting peaceful relations in the interest of all three countries.

Differences in ideological positions as well as visions emerged. However, the Greek Cypriot and Turkish Cypriot women formed close alliances and developed a joint agenda in support of reunification: "No matter what political leaders are saying or doing, we are continuing the journey to peace although some may not be ready to go through all that peace entails." As trust and openness to the others' viewpoints increased, the women from all three countries addressed what they have in common as women regarding Greek-Turkish

... the Greek Cypriot and Turkish Cypriot women formed close alliances and developed a joint agenda in support of reunification: "No matter what political leaders are saying or doing, we are continuing the journey to peace ..."

The underlying shared worldview of HAD members is a belief in the values of democracy, which includes an open market of ideas and freedom of speech, gender equality and equal access to resources and opportunities – and the aspiration to live in a united country. Any form of violence is condemned, be it domestic, institutional or state, and there is a strong belief in problem-solving.

Cypriot relations. They agreed to reinforce each other's efforts for peace-building and for women's increased representation in public life.

The underlying shared worldview of HAD members is a belief in the values of democracy, which includes an open market of ideas and freedom of speech, gender equality and equal access to resources and opportunities – and the aspiration to live in a united country. Any form of violence is condemned, be it domestic, institutional or state, and there is a strong belief in problem-solving. HAD is a women's organisation seeking to promote alternative voices and perspectives in a bipolar environment where confrontation and official propaganda prevail. This effort has gone beyond ethnicities, national identities and geographical location.

A further HAD workshop took place in November 2003 at a Turkish Cypriot restaurant close to the Venetian walls in Nicosia (work and thinking are usually combined with food and drink in Cyprus). The facilitator encouraged women to work in pairs to brainstorm. Then each had to choose one main reason for wanting a solution. The answers were recorded on flip charts and became working material for the second phase of the workshop the following week. Box 15 provides some examples that indicate the multi-layered aspect of the conflict, as well as women´s experience within it and desire for change.

These Cypriot women's desires shed light on how the national issue has eclipsed the multiple realities of women's lives in a conflict culture. It is an example of the gendered nature of peace and conflict – a dimension that is not included in the political or formal peace agendas. The solution was negotiated in contravention of UN Security Council Resolution 1325, signed by Cyprus, that calls on States to include women at the peace table so that their perspectives, experiences and concerns are legitimated and included in a future solution.

Box 15 Why Women in Cyprus Want their Country United

Women at the HAD workshop gave the following as their main reasons for wanting a solution to the division of their country:

Identity: I want a solution urgently because I want my identity ... my Cypriot identity. I want to be rid of this suppression I feel now. Women could change society if there were opportunities for women to develop. I want to be sure of having equal rights as a woman and as a person.

Security, opportunities, equality and democracy: I want to feel free to travel in my own country. I want us to be able to present ourselves to the world as one country. I want us to have respect, security and equality .... I want real democracy and freedom of speech. I want to be able to write about unspoken things. I want to write about the rapes, the missing persons, the underground movements. I want us to join the European Union because EU laws may solve some of the inequality problems we face, and we would also have freedom of choice to work anywhere as equals.

Demilitarisation: I want not merely the removal of soldiers, but mental demilitarisation to change our mindset. I don't want it to be just a paper agreement. I want us to really start thinking positive, new thoughts about the Other. I want a land without borders, a single country.

A perspective for a future: communication: I want a future .... I want my right to choose what I do. No passport, no identity cards, no handbag searches. And I want what is mine, my property, to be restored to me. I want people to be able to talk to each other, to communicate ... to share ideas about who we are. I want a peaceful environment, a culture of peace. No more nationalist propaganda. I want to hear what we have in common. I want my right to choose what I want.

[Cypriot women members of HAD] ... *wanted to encourage men to recognise that women can handle power, but that they may exercise that power differently; to encourage men to learn to accept women in high positions where decisions are being made; and to encourage men to share power with women.*

Women and Men in Partnership in a Post-conflict Cyprus

With regard to the changes they wished to see in the relationship between women and men in a post-conflict Cyprus, Cypriot women members of HAD made a number of recommendations. They wanted to encourage men to recognise that women can handle power, but that they may exercise that power differently; to encourage men to learn to accept women in high positions where decisions are being made; and to encourage men to share power with women.

Women also wanted men to redefine partnership with women, sharing responsibilities and housework; being more faithful; changing their perception of women as brainless and sexual objects; and being more emotional and empathetic. They thus expressed a desire that the dichotomy of the private and the public should be eliminated in a future Cyprus and that changes should be made in the socialisation of both women and men in the family and at school. Individual choices should not be defined by one's gender.

In any patriarchal system and within a masculine culture, the way language is used is an important indicator of the kind of relationship that exists between men and women and of the tensions between them. The hierarchical structures that exist within the family and at work need to be rethought in order to establish more healthy relationships between genders, aiming toward more desirable levels of co-operation and companionship.

The findings from a research project on women in all Cypriot communities (Hadjipavlou, 2003) revealed that the most important changes the majority of women would like to see in Cypriot society are for women to be respected as individuals, to share domestic responsibilities and to trust in their own judgement.

As part of the post-conflict and reconciliation process in Cyprus, women also need to acknowledge that men suffer social pressure to prove themselves and to stay detached from their feelings and vulnerabilities. Regarding men as the problem, rather than seeing them as part of the solution, only increases the distance between women and men. Women should learn to be more comfortable with power and the public sphere and understand the role they may have had in reproducing patriarchal values through the upbringing of their children. New socialising practices need to be instituted where both parents participate in their children's upbringing in the household, so that social roles and expectations do not continue to be sharply marked. Women should also learn to trust other women in high positions.

Military parade on independence day in Nicosia
Markus Matzel/Still Pictures

Some Lessons Learned

From the Cypriot women's experience as outlined above, it can be seen that the feminist values of tolerance, understanding, co-operation, empathy and acknowledging the other's truth and reality, as well as the creation of networks to highlight the absence of Cypriot women from high-level decision-making, are very much part of the women's bi-communal peace-building efforts. These values are also an integral part of their efforts to achieve gender equality and fulfilment of their basic human rights and needs. Findings from research surveys (2001, 2003) reveal that Greek Cypriot women are going through a transition phase in which elements of modernity combine with trad-

Gender mainstreaming promotes the advancement of women in all realms of life .... Making this possible is a task to be undertaken by both women and men. If Cyprus is to become a truly democratic, inclusive society and create multicultural spaces where ... women and men can work in partnership and as individuals, then the present power structures ... must be challenged ...

itional and established beliefs. Gender stereotypes are being questioned as a result of women's high level of participation in the workforce, including as professionals, at the same time as they lack representation in the realm of politics and decision-making. Women think that ignoring their experiences and concerns while negotiating the future of their homeland will serve to further sharpen the existing gender inequalities.

Conflict resolution, gender and peace studies should be included at all levels of education, for they provide alternative worldviews and behaviours that promote a peace culture. Both women and men need to work together on gender awareness, to enable the peace agenda to become a gender-sensitive one. 'Masculinity' and 'femininity' as they have been inherited from the past need to be transformed so as to develop a post-militaristic world based on the values of partnership and the power to create separately or together.

Through sharing of personal stories and experiences, a new narrative is being developed among Cypriot bi-communal groups, with a common moral centre: that of mutual concern for building a peace culture and a love for Cyprus through non-violent forms of conflict resolution in all aspects of life. The challenge still remains to communicate these messages to both the decision-makers and the communities at large. Institutional support to building linkages between different societal levels will contribute to this task.

Gender mainstreaming promotes the advancement of women in all realms of life – in the fields of politics, economics, culture and research. Making this possible is a task to be undertaken by both women and men. If Cyprus is to become a truly democratic, inclusive society and create multicultural spaces where gender equality and diversity can flourish and where women and men can work in partnership and as individuals, then the present power structures that still govern relationships must be challenged, as the women in HAD have so aptly voiced it.

My personal journey to peace-building and the choices I have made convince me that the only way to question simplistic, monolithic, patriarchal understandings of 'national interest' and 'national security', is to experience the 'Other', the perceived 'enemy' and realise that the 'enemy' has been socialised in the same way. Individual intervention and a different education can help us overcome and transcend the socially constructed enemy images. We can even use this reflective inner dialogue to enhance our own insights into the victim-perpetrator mentality – and acknowledge that the perpetrator is as much a victim as is the victim a perpetrator. Cypriot women's daily psychological suffocation within the 'different walls' is a testament to the continuing power of militarism and the urgent need for this to change.

Recommendations

- Conflict resolution programmes that share a feminist, holistic approach call for change to come from below as well as from above; conflict resolution must tackle issues of identity, security, political participation, inclusion in decision-making and distributive justice.

- A shared commitment to democratic values, including that of gender equality, can bring women together across divides.

- Women and men must be involved in conflict resolution at decision-making levels.

- Basic human needs must be integrated into peace-building initiatives.

- New gender relationships are needed, i.e. attitudes of men and women towards each other must change. Men must be seen by women as part of the solution, not as the problem; men and women must work in partnership.

- School curricula should include gender sensitisation and parents should play a role in challenging gender stereotyping in children's socialisation.

- Conflict resolution, gender and peace studies should be included at all levels of education as conflict prevention tools.

- Members of bi-communal peace-building groups (comprising women or men, or both) need support, financial and otherwise, and greater acknowledgement from international institutions.

We can ... use this reflective inner dialogue to enhance our own insights into the victim-perpetrator mentality – and acknowledge that the perpetrator is as much a victim as is the victim a perpetrator. Cypriot women's daily psychological suffocation within the 'different walls' is a testament to the continuing power of militarism and the urgent need for this to change.

9 India: Legacies of Dispute

Urvashi Butalia

The Complexities of Women's Experiences of Conflict in India

Attempting to map conflict in India is a daunting task. The country is widely perceived to be reasonably stable with a thriving – albeit often imperfect – democracy and strong civil society and human rights movements. In many ways, the sheer size of India and the diversity of its population mask the gravity of the many conflicts within it, because most of them remain localised. Inevitably, those that touch on cross-border issues and international relations, such as the stand-off on Kashmir, receive much more media and public attention than other conflicts, which are seen to be less 'political' – even though in real terms they may be as, if not more, political.

Almost from the moment of its rather violent birth, the Indian nation-state has been riven by different kinds of conflicts – over livelihoods, resources, land, identity, religion, culture, politics and, more recently, globalisation. If these are the internal fault lines and pressures that India has had to cope with, there have been other tensions around its international borders: with Bangladesh (particularly in recent years); with Sri Lanka (over the Indian Peace Keeping Forces and, more recently, the influx of Tamil refugees); with Nepal, with whom India has an open border (related to trafficking in women and the Maoist insurgency); and with Pakistan (a legacy of the 1947 Partition of India that has led to three wars, where the continuing tension between the two countries also helps draw attention away from very pressing internal problems).

Analysis of these conflicts tends to concentrate on what authors see as the 'real' issues, which are often taken to mean the political issues that underlie the tensions. Despite the fact that it is clear that violent conflict and war all over the world claim more civilian casualties than they do military, there have been few attempts to map the precise extent of this. Conflicts over resources in India, for example, the acquisition of rural land – for industrialisation or mining – mainly impact on the poor. Of these almost 80 per cent are *Dalits* (or untouchables), among whom at least 50 per cent are women. Histories of how social exclusion and marginalisation are heightened by situations of conflict, and how it is the poor and weak who suffer the most, are still to be written.

This chapter does not attempt such a history but rather seeks to throw light on the complexity of women's experiences of, and involvement in, violent conflicts in India. Recent conflicts in India have shown how women and their bodies lie at the core of much of the violence perpetrated. In inter-caste wars, the upper castes routinely rape the women of the lower castes in an attempt to insult the male community and to pollute the caste's 'purity' through defiling women's bodies. In movements for self-determination or nationalist expressions, or in attacks on minorities, the rape and violation of women's bodies is routine. It is only now becoming clear in India that where rape is used as a weapon of conflict, the law is almost wholly inadequate to deal with this. Increasingly, women are also drawn into violent conflicts in other ways, either due to coercion or necessity (as when women in need of money are sometimes forced to act as couriers or become sex-workers) or through conviction (as with the rise of the Hindu right wing in India).

There is also a growing body of evidence – for example, in the north-east of India – of women engaging in the fight for peace. The Naga Mothers' Association, a well-known organisation in Nagaland, has been one of the key forces behind the peace initiatives in that region. And yet, and this is well known the world over, when it comes to sitting around the table and talking peace, women are seldom present. This is why the quality of peace, its meaning in everyday life, is always only partial.

This chapter looks briefly at three regions in India that have experienced different kinds of conflict in recent years. The western state of Gujarat was in 2002 the scene of the organised massacre of thousands of Muslims and the systematic rape and killing of large numbers of Muslim women, acts perpetrated by fundamentalist Hindus. The conflict in the north-western state of Kashmir, which shares a border with Pakistan, has been ongoing almost since Independence and more

Recent conflicts in India have shown how women and their bodies lie at the core of much of the violence perpetrated. In inter-caste wars, the upper castes routinely rape the women of the lower castes in an attempt to ... pollute the caste's 'purity' through defiling women's bodies .... It is only now becoming clear in India that where rape is used as a weapon of conflict, the law is almost wholly inadequate to deal with this.

Roshmi Goswami, an activist from the north-east region of India, pointed out in a conversation that "Women's work patterns make them particularly vulnerable to attacks and atrocities by rival factions [in a conflict], for it is the women who have to go out to collect firewood and water for the family".... It is also clear that more and more women are being drawn into violent conflict, either out of choice or forcibly.

intensely in the last 13 years. In the northern state of Punjab, the early 1980s saw the rise of a militant movement for autonomy and independence, which led to thousands of deaths. Each of these histories provides us with valuable insights into the impact of violent conflict on women.

Feminist analysts and activists have drawn attention to the very complex consequences of violent conflicts for women and children. Not only are they among the primary victims of conflict, but their sex, their social location, their gender roles and their marginalised status in society ensure that they experience the consequences of conflict in very specific ways. For example, as Roshmi Goswami, an activist from the north-east region of India, pointed out in a conversation that "Women's work patterns make them particularly vulnerable to attacks and atrocities by rival factions [in a conflict], for it is the women who have to go out to collect firewood and water for the family".

It is also clear that more and more women are being drawn into violent conflict, either out of choice or forcibly. For some, as in Kashmir, the choice is an economic one. With the loss of male earners, women are forced to find ways of keeping families together: providing information, acting as couriers or providing sexual services may become possible, and sometimes attractive, options. Violence may be appealing for other reasons as, for example, in the 2002 massacre of Muslims in Gujarat in which women actively participated in large numbers. Though women may not have taken up weapons and been directly involved in the violence, some nevertheless supported the ideology behind the attacks and found the violence that it called for acceptable, and something they were willing and even eager to act on.

Gujarat

On 27 February 2002, a train passing through the western Indian town of Godhra became the target of an attack that led to the worst inter-community violence India had seen since the Partition of the country. No one quite knows the exact origin of the incident, but it soon came to acquire a mythology that has grown over time and has more or less obliterated the long history that preceded it and provided its context. A large number of travellers on this particular train were Hindu pilgrims

– men and women – returning from the north Indian city of Ayodhya, believed to be the birthplace of the god Ram, where they had been performing *kar seva* (the Hindu tradition of offering voluntary service at religious places). The history of Ayodhya itself is the subject of controversy that will not be explored here. Suffice it to say that, in a travesty of this tradition, thousands of people calling themselves *kar sevaks* had destroyed the ancient Babri Masjid (mosque) in Ayodhya in 1992, which led to massive violence between Hindus and Muslims in the country.

In Godhra in February 2002, Hindu pilgrims had been returning by the trainload for several days preceding the incident. Apparently, each day as the trains passed by the town of Godhra, a Muslim majority town, several travellers hurled abuse and hate at the inhabitants, accusing them of being anti-national and exhorting them to leave the country.[21] Clearly, something happened on this particular day – and there are many stories about exactly what the provocation was, but none that can be substantiated because people are no longer willing to speak out – which led to people from Godhra (believed to be Muslims) attacking and setting fire to the train. Fifty-nine people, several of whom were women and children, died in this attack.

Within a day, large numbers of Hindus, armed with different kinds of weapons, began attacking Muslims throughout Gujarat, starting with the important cities of Ahmedabad and Baroda. The attack on the train was made worse by an irresponsible and partisan media. In reporting this incident, at least one well-known and widely circulated newspaper published a story (completely baseless) that Hindu women travellers on the train had been raped, their breasts had been cut off and then they had been killed and thrown onto the track. By the time the newspaper retracted this story – publishing, under pressure, a tiny denial in one corner of the paper – the damage had already been done. Male ire had been aroused at this insult to 'their' manhood through the violation of the bodies of 'their' women.

While this initial fiction was quick to acquire currency, the terrible truth of what happened in Gujarat emerged only gradually. In urban areas, Muslim commercial establishments and small businesses were singled out and attacked, entire housing

By all accounts, the police either stood by and watched or encouraged the attacks. The mass rape of women formed a major part of this violence: young and old women were raped ... and many were killed .... Several months later, when ... women attempted to report the rapes, the police refused to accept their complaints, and refused particularly to include the names of individual attackers when the women were able to identify them.

estates with people inside them were set on fire and hundreds of people were killed in gruesome, macabre ways.

By all accounts, the police either stood by and watched or encouraged the attacks. The mass rape of women formed a major part of this violence: young and old women were raped, often in front of their families, and many were killed. There were stories of pregnant women having their wombs ripped apart and foetuses pulled out and destroyed. Several months later, when the violence finally died down and women attempted to report the rapes, the police refused to accept their complaints, and refused particularly to include the names of individual attackers when the women were able to identify them.

Tensions between Hindus and Muslims in India go back hundreds of years. The Hindus see themselves as the 'original' inhabitants of India, and they regard the Muslims as either descendants of 'invaders' or people who converted to Islam, with conversion never being seen as an acceptable choice. This perception persists, despite the fact that for centuries Hindus and Muslims also lived together in relative harmony and have created cultures that are both rich and composite. However, since Partition, hostility between the two communities has worsened. The British Government's decision to partition the country was meant to provide a solution to what the colonial power saw as the problem of Hindu-Muslim animosity, yet the 58 years since Partition provide innumerable examples of worsening tensions between these two communities that periodically erupt into violence.

Both the tension and violence became much worse in recent years in which India was governed by a right-wing majoritarian Hindu Government. The then ruling party, the Bharatiya Janata Party (BJP) and its sister organisations (known as the Sangh 'parivar' or family) made it part of their agenda to ensure that minorities in India learned to 'adjust' and to live by the rules of the majority community. Their first targets were Muslims, but Christians and *Dalits* also came in for attack. Over the years, emboldened by their electoral success at the centre and the weakness of their partners in the shaky coalition that held the Government together, the BJP began to experiment with the 'Hinduising' of particular parts of the country. The western Indian state of Gujarat, home to Gandhi and known for its economic success, was one of the states selected for such an experiment. Over the years, cadres of the BJP's sister organisations, the Rashtriya Swayamsevak Sangh, the Vishwa Hindu Parishad and the Bajrang Dal systematically spread hate, using intimidation tactics against minorities and frightening people into living in clearly demarcated areas. For example, in the capital city of Ahmedabad, certain areas were demarcated as Hindu or Muslim and it became rare for Hindus and Muslims to live in the same locality. The systematic campaign of spreading hatred and fear was in full swing when the incident of the attack on the train took place.

One of the remarkable and disturbing things about the Gujarat massacre was the participation of women. In virtually every instance of violence, women were to be found among the attacking mobs or lending support through the preparation of weapons and petrol bombs. Later, when fact-finding teams went in to survey the situation and to prepare reports, they found that while Hindu women at first seemed sympathetic to the plight of Muslim women victims of sexual violations, it did not take them long to express the hate-filled propaganda of the Hindu Right. This asserts, among other things, that Muslims do not believe in family planning and because they have many children, they will soon overtake the Hindu population. A mere look at the population percentages – 80 per cent Hindus as opposed to 12 to 15 per cent Muslims – shows the invalidity of such a claim, but when mythologies are being constructed, they have little to do with truth. Further, those women who chose to espouse violence insisted that their 'grievances' should be taken into account by institutions like the National Human Rights Commission.

The Gujarat massacre left hundreds of Muslim families homeless and destitute. For women, this has meant an increased burden of work, and for those who lost husbands it has meant taking on the responsibility of earning to keep the family together. Struggling to do this in a public sphere that is anti-women is no easy task. And for women's organisations working in the area, the business of putting together the fabric of daily life to enable women of different ethnic communities to work together to tackle the real issues of their lives – such as poverty, food security and health – is a formidable challenge.

Two particular questions are raised by the Gujarat massacre related to the problems faced by women's organisations that

One of the remarkable and disturbing things about the Gujarat massacre was the participation of women. In virtually every instance of violence, women were to be found among the attacking mobs or lending support through the preparation of weapons and petrol bombs.

have attempted to intervene. First, when all evidence of rape or sexual assault is destroyed, how can the law be mobilised and used to bring the perpetrator to account? What does justice mean in this regard? Second, how should women's organisations respond to victims who told them that their priority was not justice (a concept in which they had little faith) but they simply wanted to get on with their lives? At least, they said, they were alive. Some asked the activists not to record their stories, because this made them more vulnerable, not only to the attackers who were still at large but also within their own community where they would forever be labelled as 'raped women'. These are questions to which activists have not yet found satisfactory answers.

Punjab

The legacies of division left behind by Partition touched the eastern state of Bengal and the north-western state of Punjab particularly, both of which suffered not only an exchange of population but also a division of their properties. Thus the new, truncated eastern Punjab (which fell in India following Partition) was a much reduced landmass from the erstwhile undivided Punjab. With the division and the exchange of population, Punjab also suffered a demographic and cultural impoverishment, becoming mainly a Sikh and Hindu state.[22]

While conflict between Hindus and Muslims is increasingly recognised as a 'fact of life' and is therefore almost 'acceptable' in India, conflict between Hindus and Sikhs – the third largest religious minority in India and one that maintains close ties with and shares a culture and sometimes also a language with majority Hindu India – was something most people would not have imagined. But they did not bargain for the political appropriation and takeover of most movements by vested political interests.

In the early 1980s a movement for the assertion of Sikh identity began to use violence as a means of achieving an independent state: Khalistan, the land of the Khalsa, or the pure. To the then ruling party at the centre (the Congress, led by Indira Gandhi), this provided an opportunity to edge out the party that was in power in the state (the Akali Dal). It provided support to the Sikh activists, a measure that eventually rebounded on the centre, with the movement for Khalistan turning increasingly militant and taking to arms. As this grew and gathered support, the state brought in harsh measures to quell it, banning many organisations, arresting suspected militants, using draconian laws against them and denying them rights. During this period, a number of national security laws were introduced to meet the so-called terrorist threat, with thousands of arrests and disappearances taking place. Very soon, Punjab became an unsafe place to live in, visit or even travel through.

By 1984 the violence had so escalated that the army had to be called in, and its personnel were given orders to shoot to kill if they saw anything suspicious. It was the army that, under orders from Mrs Gandhi, stormed the Golden Temple, the holiest of Sikh shrines, where militants had taken shelter. This attack killed the militant leader, Jarnail Singh Bhindranwale, and led in turn to Mrs Gandhi's own assassination in reprisal by her personal bodyguards, both Sikhs. Massive anti-Sikh riots followed her assassination, particularly in the capital city of Delhi, and thousands were killed. Militancy continued for some years after Mrs Gandhi's death, but by the early 1990s it seemed as if some semblance of normality had returned to Punjab. Random killings of innocent people, search and seizure operations, enforced disappearances and arrests were a thing of the past (although Amnesty International documents show that torture is still common in Punjab).

But had peace really returned? Was normalcy really that or was it hiding something else? During the period of militancy, young boys who joined the movement became heroes in their families and communities. Disappearances of young men, violations of human rights, the role of the army, the political negotiations that inevitably are a part of such conflict have been widely discussed and written about. What remains hidden, however, is the experience of women. Rape by the army and security forces stationed in Punjab received some attention. A much more difficult subject to address, however, was the fact that as more and more young men joined the movement, and as they began living a life on the run, women became fair game. Militants hiding out in houses would often demand that the women of those homes, and especially the young girls, be made available to them. Fear of reprisals prevented families from

During the period of militancy, young boys who joined the movement became heroes .... Disappearances of young men, violations of human rights, the role of the army have been ... widely discussed .... What remains hidden ... is the experience of women. Rape by the army ... received some attention. A much more difficult subject ... was the fact that as more and more young men ... began living a life on the run, women became fair game.

Many women who were taken away by the militants became 'unmarriageable' once 'peace' returned .... Faced with the responsibility of having to look after them, some families became a new source of their oppression .... [F]or those women who were either married to or associated with militants it became impossible to return to 'normal' society. Even today, there are villages in Punjab where the wives and partners of militants are pariahs.

speaking about this, and the mythology of heroism that attached to the young men also acted as a silencing device.

Punjab is mainly an agricultural state, and over the years the fear of fragmentation of landholdings has led to the enactment of laws whereby women have very little share of property. They are encouraged to give up whatever claims they may wish to make, being told that they need to make a contribution to holding the family, and the family property, together. Many women who were taken away by the militants became 'unmarriageable' once 'peace' returned and they were able to come back to their families. Faced with the responsibility of having to look after them, some families became a new source of their oppression. If this was the condition of 'normal' women, for those women who were either married to or associated with militants it became impossible to return to 'normal' society. Even today, there are villages in Punjab where the wives and partners of militants are pariahs. Socially isolated, they continue to face harassment from the police and are often seen as being 'sexually available'. This makes life difficult not only for them, but also for their children. Social isolation is also the fate of those women who willingly took part in the militancy, for their betrayal was seen to be worse by virtue of being voluntary.

These and other experiences are only now beginning to come to light more than a decade since some semblance of 'normalcy' has returned to Punjab. Even women's groups have been reluctant to address these questions, perhaps because there is a perception that sympathy with militancy and an espousal of violence on the part of women cannot be countenanced.

Kashmir

For over fifteen years, Kashmir has been caught in the grip of a conflict that, from its beginnings as a militant movement fighting for self-determination, has rapidly turned into a battle involving at least 100 different militant factions and groups, with the Indian security forces pitted against them. The situation is no longer one of a simple demand for self-determination. Instead, there are groups who believe Kashmir must ally with Pakistan (and who are supported, both financially and in terms of training, by Pakistan, which has led to a worsening of the already strained relations between the two countries) and others who are committed to an independent state. All 'sides' in this battle use violence, and it is the people of Kashmir whose lives are deeply affected by this.

A father crouches with his two children in the shadow of a soldier from the Indian security forces in Kashmir
Martin Adler/Panos Pictures

There are many interpretations of how this conflict began and from which moment it can be dated. However, what is widely recognised is that the current phase of Kashmiri separatist nationalism began at the end of the 1980s with young men and women coming out into the streets in large numbers. Over the years, however, the nature of the movement, as well as the actors within it, have changed radically. Paid mercenaries and militants have entered the picture, the sheen and romance of militancy for many young men in Kashmir has worn off and militant attacks on ordinary people have become commonplace. Repression and counter-insurgency have been swift to follow, and it is estimated that between 60,000 to 70,000 people have died and some 4,000 are missing.

Large numbers of Kashmiri women have the dubious distinction of being labelled as 'half widows'. These are women whose husbands are missing and who have been unable to trace them. Officially, because they cannot produce a dead body, they are not considered widows. But because they are leading single lives, they are seen as half widows. Not only is this not a very pleasant appellation, it also means that these women cannot claim the compensation that the state makes available to women who are widowed as a result of violence,

Large numbers of Kashmiri women have the dubious distinction of being labelled as 'half widows'. These are women whose husbands are missing and who have been unable to trace them. Officially, because they cannot produce a dead body, they are not considered widows.

The young men who make up [the armed forces] have left behind wives and families ... and this is often used as an excuse to explain their participation in sexual violence .... In the early 1990s ... the Rajputana Rifles were said to have raided a small village called Kunan Poshpora where 30 women were allegedly raped. Later, a state-sponsored fact-finding team asserted that the women were lying and there had been no rape.

militancy, etc. Because the conflict in Kashmir is long standing, it is easier to see the effect of continuing violence on the health of women: stress and trauma are commonplace and, because of the general atmosphere of fear and uncertainty, trust has almost completely disappeared. Hospital services are unavailable or minimal and women, who may be tardy in seeking medical care in normal times, are reluctant to visit institutions functioning on a skeleton staff to ask for help with such nebulous illnesses as depression, trauma and stress.

Continuing militancy and violence have ensured the presence of the armed forces and of special units of both the police and the army. The young men who make up these forces have left behind wives and families whom they seldom see, and this is often used as an excuse to explain their participation in sexual violence against Kashmiri women. In the early 1990s a unit of the army, the Rajputana Rifles were said to have raided a small village called Kunan Poshpora where 30 women were allegedly raped. Later, a state-sponsored fact-finding team asserted that the women were lying and there had been no rape. Facts are hard to come by in times of conflict and Kashmir is no exception. Whatever the truth of the incident – and the state-sponsored team has been proved wrong many times – the reality is that, even today, there are no men who will come forward to marry the 'raped' women of Kunan Poshpora. While the army has, in recent times, attempted to establish some control over its cadres, members of other forces have no such controls. In addition, it has become increasingly clear that levels of domestic violence have risen considerably in the state.

Hard Questions for the Women's Movement

These three brief accounts in no way do justice to the complex experiences of women caught in situations of armed conflict. As activists have often pointed out, women play multiple roles in such situations. They are among the primary victims of such conflict, but they are also often its agents. Any study of conflict needs to look beyond the women who are victims to those who are caught in a difficult situation, either out of choice or otherwise. These include the wives/partners of militants or of men in the security forces; and they also include those who are willing and active participants, such as the militant cadres in the north-east made up of strong, articulate, committed women. Society in general, and women activists in particular, need to be aware of the difficult situations into which violent conflict throws women and be prepared to address this.

These issues are particularly important for the women's movement and women activists. For example, the rise of the Hindu right wing, and its successful mobilisation of women, has thrown into question for activists a much cherished belief in a commonality of women's experience that cuts across caste and class and had been seen as one of the strengths of the Indian women's movement. In the wake of the communal carnage in Mumbai, activists in that city have asked what they would do if, after seeing militant women in the streets being violent towards other communities, they were required to provide medical aid and legal counsel to the same women in matters of domestic disputes, problems over dowry and so on. Would they react to them as women or as actors spreading hatred and violence?

The increasing involvement of women in situations of violent conflict has forced women activists to ask other questions. A journalist, Manimala, visiting Kashmir some years ago, was accused by Kashmiri women of having been indifferent to their fate. Why, they asked her, had people from India (specifically women) not bothered to visit Kashmir and talk to women there, to try and understand their pain? The accusation had some truth in it: the early 1990s, when violence in Kashmir was at its height, was also the period when the women's movement in India was at its peak. Yet activists concerned with questions of identity and violence within the home, and active on those questions in other regions, did not pay much attention to Kashmir and what was happening there. One reason for this could be that Indian feminists have not really confronted their own nationalism. The 'anti-national' movement in Kashmir in some ways made the women within it, especially those who may have taken on the ideology of the group who sought independence or allegiance with Pakistan, suspect and therefore less 'worthy' of attention on the part of feminists.

These and other key questions are now being raised and addressed by women activists all over India, in an attempt to understand not only what happens to women who are caught in the midst of conflict – conflict usually created by men but which draws in women in many ways – but also what has guided their own reactions. It is only when they understand this and begin to address the question that the first steps can be taken towards resolving conflict and restoring peace.

Recommendations

- New laws must be introduced to prosecute those who use rape as a weapon of war.

- The media need to be more responsible in reporting acts of violence: they must avoid incitement to race hatred and violence by refusing to publish or broad-cast exaggerated, uncorroborated or false stories of atrocities committed against women and children.

- 'Half-widows' (those whose husbands are missing, presumed dead in armed combat) must be able to claim widows' compensation.

- Efforts need to be made to counter increasing tendencies of eve-teasing, sexual innuendo and other manifestations of misogyny that are preventing women from engaging in economically productive and political activities.

- The activities and achievements of women's peace movements need to be given greater recognition and attention in the media.

- The unwritten and unrecognised histories of marginalised groups, including those of women, need to be recorded and acknowledged.

- Feminists need to begin to confront their own nationalism.

10 Jamaica: The Search for Survival and Respect in the Hostile World of the Inner City

Herbert Gayle

Over the past 50 years there has been increasing awareness that freedom and dignity are among the basic needs of human beings. No one can live a normal life in bondage, segregated or subjugated, dehumanised or disrespected. Jamaica's rate of development since independence has been relatively good. This is clearly shown in the published quantitative data on the country. The problem, however, is that progress has bypassed a whole group – the very poor – the most desperate being those in the inner city. While data show that two-thirds of those below the poverty line reside in rural communities, this is only so because the system of measuring poverty does not take into account the value of 'ole yam bush', backyard gardens and other forms of subsistence, the obvious practice of sharing or community, and the various uses of family land, all unique to rural areas. In sum, the urgent concern in Jamaica is that of urban poverty.

A Glimpse of the Problem of Violence

An urban poverty crisis

According to the 1998 Crime Report from the Statistical Department of the Crime Office, Jamaica, approximately 82 per cent of all homicides committed in the country in 1997 and 76 per cent in 1998 occurred in Greater Kingston – which is the home of just over one-third of the population. What is also interesting to note is that the overwhelming majority of the remaining 18 and 24 per cent of homicides for those years were committed in the 'new' urban centres such as Montego Bay, the second city. Violence in the capital city is very

According to [Jamaica's] Crime Office, approximately 82 per cent of all homicides committed in the country in 1997 ... occurred in Greater Kingston – which is the home of just over one-third of the population .... [T]he overwhelming majority of the remaining ... homicides ... were committed in the 'new' urban centres ...

The 1980 General Elections in Jamaica saw over 900 persons killed due largely to the violent activities of youths of Kingston, who were used as mercenaries by the two main political parties. As Gunst (1999) documented, many of these youths were forced to leave the country at the end of the political tumult. They fled mainly to the UK and the USA – and have been blamed for worsening the problems of drugs and violence there.

concentrated. Four divisions in 'Downtown Kingston', covering a rather small area of just over 16 square miles, accounted for 54 per cent of homicides in 1997. This segregated area is the heart of the violence and corresponds perfectly to the heart of the urban poverty map of the city. It comprises just over 200,000 people, or just under 8 per cent of the 2001 population. It is clearly the most densely populated area in the country.

The following factors generally characterise the inner city, though some communities outside the centre also face the grave problems of crime and violence and, despite their location, bear the same characteristics in varying degrees (Chevannes and Gayle, 1998):

- dense population – with over 60 per cent under the age of 30;

- high unemployment rate – averaging over 30 per cent (twice the country's average);

- low education – 50 per cent not completing secondary school;

- poor housing – with over 40 per cent living in tenements, over 30 per cent in one-bedroom dwellings, and many in shacks or 'improvised dwellings';

- poor sanitation – over 5 per cent without flush toilet or water closet, more than one-third without piped water, skips overflowing and garbage on the street and in gullies; and

- poor infrastructure – poor or no telephone services, poorly surfaced or unpaved roads and pathways and few or no active institutions, except political ones.

A young male phenomenon

The 1980 General Elections in Jamaica saw over 900 persons killed due largely to the violent activities of youths of Kingston, who were used as mercenaries by the two main political parties. As Gunst (1999) documented, many of these youths were forced to leave the country at the end of the political tumult. They fled mainly to the UK and the USA – and have been blamed for worsening the problems of drugs and violence there. This has put a strain on social and political relations between Jamaica and both countries. The violent behaviour of a few Jamaican youths has encouraged a worsening of cultural prejudices, which is manifested in long interrogations and searches at airports and other checkpoints, among other stressful situations. Between 1995 and 2000 almost 11,000 persons were deported back to Jamaica, largely for crimes committed abroad. This has resulted in a crisis for Jamaican society as it lacks the resources to deal with the problem.

Roadblock laid by JLP supporters, Kingston, Jamaica
Herbert Gayle/Partners for Peace

Data from the Statistical Department of the Crime Office, Jamaica, reveal that during 1996 and 1997 over three-quarters (79.5 and 78.5 per cent respectively) of the arrests for murder were of persons under the age of 30. The same can be said for other violent crimes such as shootings and robberies. Police reports list drug and gang feuds as the main factors accounting for over one third of all murders since the mid-1990s, but show that levels of domestic or interpersonal disputes are also high.

Though extreme, the life situation of inner-city males in Jamaica is not unique. Some Caribbean and African inner-city males in London have a similar story. Fifty-six per cent of the 148 persons killed by the gun in London between 1993 and 1999 were black, although black people account for 7.5 per cent of London's population. The table below does not break down the information by gender; nonetheless, information from police sources tells us that the accused and victims are overwhelmingly males. Further, it reveals that the vast majority (62 per cent) of the black victims in London are below the age of 30.

... the life situation of inner-city males in Jamaica is not unique .... Fifty-six per cent of the 148 persons killed by the gun in London between 1993 and 1999 were black, although black people account for 7.5 per cent of London's population.

147

... violence in Jamaica is a predominantly male-against-male phenomenon ... [and] in a middle-income island paradise with one of the highest life expectancies, 5 per cent of the population, overwhelmingly males, cannot expect to live to age 40.

Homicides by Age of Black Victims in London, 1993–1999

Age	Homicides	Percentage	Cumulative
0–15	31	10.3	10.3
16–30	155	51.7	62.0
31–60	107	35.7	97.7
61 >	7	2.3	100.0
Total	300	100.0	100.0

Source: Metropolitan Police Service, London

Despite the fact that some communities are plagued by domestic violence, mainly against women, violence in Jamaica is predominantly a male-against-male phenomenon. For example, in 1996 there were 920 violent deaths: 16 children, 88 women and 816 men. If 342 male fatalities by traffic accidents – compared to 69 female – are added to that, it is obvious why there has been a growing concern for the Jamaican male. In addition, it is alleged that the police consistently killed over 100 persons per year in the 1990s – almost all males from the inner city. It thus becomes clear how it is possible that in a middle-income island paradise with one of the highest life expectancies, 5 per cent of the population, overwhelmingly males, cannot expect to live to age 40. For young men in the inner cities, therefore, life is an oxymoron: sorrow and death in the land of sunshine and long life. The primary factor associated with the problem faced by both inner city males of Kingston and black youth in London is isolation or segregation.

Construction of the Problem

Figure 1 (page 147) provides a graphic representation of the various elements of the problem.

Historical infrastructure

A European first sighted Jamaica in 1494. By 1655, when the English drove out the few poorly-organised Spaniards who had settled on the island, none of the indigenous Tainos remained alive. They had either died from infectious diseases carried by the Spanish conquerors or they had been murdered. They were replaced by African slaves.

Figure 1: Construction of the Problem in Jamaica

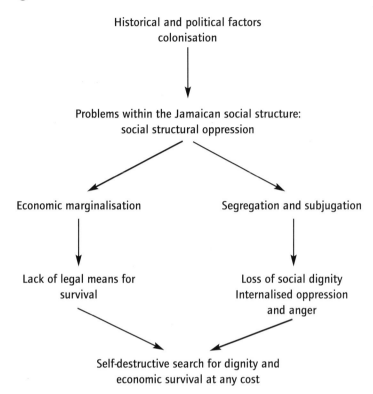

Over the next two centuries, violence was the main mode of control on the slave plantations and, not surprisingly, the Afro-Jamaicans responded by revolting against planter authority; hence our national heroes were 'resistance fighters'. In fact the resistance in Jamaica was so strong that sugar became unprofitable. After Emancipation in 1838 the British planter class relied heavily on a well-constructed political network to maintain control. The Governor, the Assembly, the Governor's Council and the Local Militia all served the dual purpose at the various levels of protecting the planter class and controlling the freed Afro-Jamaican population.

For more than a century, from 1838 to Universal Adult Suffrage in 1944, this group of freed people had no political representation and were abused in a variety of ways, including the use of physical violence by the planter class. This was a period of unrest and two major uprisings occurred. Paul Bogle led the first in 1865. The freed men took up arms to compel the planter class to listen to their plight. The success of this

... violence is central to the construction of Jamaican society. In 1980 violence became a national crisis, but the seeds had long been sown. Today violence remains a means of expressing frustration, of dealing with disagreements and of seeking economic and social gain. The 1980s marked ... a heightened sense of the economics of violence, as it became profitable for the urban poor to kill each other.

revolt gave the planter class reason to construct a para-military police force. Paradoxically, this militant band of 'street executioners', comprised of Afro-Jamaicans, was used to crush its own people. Any form of open protest could be met with instant death, especially if it threatened the life of the planter class. This legacy still haunts the Jamaica Constabulary Force, which continues to be seen largely as the oppressive agent of the ruling class and bears the name of 'Babylon'. In 1938, when the second uprising occurred, the level of violence used by the state against the disadvantaged sugar workers was phenomenal.

In accounting for the violence in some developing countries, Fanon stated:

> *The policeman and the soldier, by their immediate presence and their frequent and direct action, maintain contact with the native and advise him by means of rifle-butts and napalm not to budge ... the agents of government speak the language of pure force. The intermediary does not lighten the oppression, nor seek to hide the domination; he shows them up and puts them into practice with the clear conscience of an upholder of the peace; yet he is the bringer of violence into the home and into the mind of the native.* (1963: 29)

The actions of government agents of force have clearly served the purpose of reinforcing the pain of the colonial history of Jamaica. It is fair to say that they have led the natives to think that society was meant to be violent; that it was an effective way to get things done. This becomes clear when you examine any of the many informal systems of justice found in the inner city. I have been told repeatedly by inner-city youths that the violence carried out in these 'community systems' is learned from the society. The claim these youth make is that, unlike the legal system, the community system is impartial. In fact, violence is central to the construction of Jamaican society. In 1980 violence became a national crisis, but the seeds had long been sown. Today violence remains a means of expressing frustration, of dealing with disagreements and of seeking economic and social gain. The 1980s marked the advent of more sophisticated weapons to kill and a heightened sense of the economics of violence, as it became profitable for the urban poor to kill each other.

The socio-economic construct

There is no doubt that the social structure of Jamaica fosters violence: sharp class differences, a partial and almost ineffective system of law, intense concentrated poverty, a major gap between material goals and the legal means to achieve them, and socialisation of males to be 'tough'. The means of expression and achievement open to the urban poor, and especially the youth, are extremely limited when compared to their middle-class, 'uptown' counterparts.

According to Fanon (1963), the community of the urban poor is one of ill fame, peopled by men of evil repute: a world without space where men live on top of each other and build their huts on each other. They are always in each other's face. Their life is miserable, and if they forget their misery the media does a tremendous job of reminding them of their position, failings and sins. The urban poor are envious of the uptown folk and the uptown folk know it. Often when their glances meet, the rich ascertain bitterly, always on the defensive, "They want to take my place". This is very true, for "there is no [inner city youth] who does not dream at least once a day of setting himself up in the [uptown man's] place" (ibid: 30). The rich man therefore feels more comfortable having the urban poor controlled and segregated. The dreaming youth is vulnerable to recruitment into drugs and gangs of all sorts – into anything, including political warfare, that promises him something. He sings, "When mi win de Lotto mi a go buy a big house ova deh soh". His concern is to get out, and he is in fierce competition with those around him who wish to do the same. He gets very irritated by their being constantly 'in his face' for, as told to me repeatedly, "Dem caan help me up is only help down". This economic hunter, failed and ridiculed by his middle-class political leaders, vents his frustration on his neighbour – not only because his neighbour is competing for the same scarce benefits, but also because his neighbour is just like him. This is why he places a low value on his neighbour's life.

It also explains why a macho, homophobic youth in Central Kingston covered me with his body in order to protect me during a drive-by shooting incident in 1994. Only when the shooting had subsided and all danger had gone would he get off me. His explanation for this strange behaviour was, "It better

The dreaming youth is vulnerable to recruitment into drugs and gangs of all sorts – into anything, including political warfare, that promises him something. He sings, "When mi win de Lotto mi a go buy a big house ova deh soh". His concern is to get out, and he is in fierce competition with those around him who wish to do the same.

Boy dancing at a mourning ritual for a youth killed in South St Andrew, Jamaica
Herbert Gayle/Partners for Peace

you live than me. Me already dead in a way. Your life more important than mine". Since then it has been repeated to me several times as an explanation of why inner-city youths are so quick to kill each other, yet reluctant to treat the life of the uptown folk with the same value. They are often merciless towards their inner-city competitors whose lives are equally 'not worth a shit'. Any tool – the more powerful the better – that can help the inner-city youth stand above their neighbours is welcomed. The gun is therefore not just a weapon; it is a tool of economics and power (Gayle, 1996). Inner-city youth go to great lengths to 'Maggle pon dem matey', or compete with each other. This is a part of how they 'cry for respect', and it often involves violence.

Merton (1968) presented Western societies as materialistic with particular success goals, but without the legal means for all to achieve them. This leaves the excluded individuals or groups to respond in one of five ways (four of which are deviant) to this situation (see Box 16). The non-deviant response is to conform and seek to achieve these goals by normative means, though with no guarantee of success. Criminologists have paid most attention to the deviant responses of innovation and rebellion, as these imply acts of violence against others. The reality is that the dispossessed will express their frustration in a variety of ways that threaten the stability of society.

Jamaicans are highly innovative. Probably the most important example here is that of the illegal drug trade, which is

Box 16 The Deviant Responses of the Excluded

Merton (1968) discussed the four ways in which the individual or group may deviate, as follows:

1. *Innovation.* This is an attempt to achieve the material goals by any means possible. It is most likely to be selected by persons of the lowest stratum who are least likely to succeed otherwise because of their position and also due to problems in their socialisation.

2. *Ritualism.* This is especially the response of lower-middle-class persons who are socialised in such a way that they find it easier to reduce their goals than attempt to innovate or use illegal means to achieve them.

3. *Retreatism.* This response applies to persons who retreat from society out of the frustration that comes with recognising that they do not have the means to achieve the material goals of society. This group includes outcasts, drug addicts and alcoholics, and those who do the ultimate: commit suicide.

4. *Rebellion.* Here the individual or group rejects both goals and means and set their own. They no longer live by the rules of society or aspire to the goals set by the dominant group.

A number of scholars have made a strong connection between the illegal drug trade in the Caribbean region and the ... use of guns and other weapons by young men to harm or kill each other .... [T]here is a connection between drug-related violence and political violence in Jamaica .... [M]any of the young men who were recruited by political parties in the 1980s have now entered the drug trade ... under the guise of politics or within the old political network.

an enormous economic enterprise. A number of scholars have made a strong connection between the illegal drug trade in the Caribbean region and the importation and use of guns and other weapons by young men to harm or kill each other. They have also found that there is a connection between drug-related violence and political violence in Jamaica. While the latter has been declining, the former seems to be escalating. The connection appears to be that many of the young men who were recruited by political parties in the 1980s have now entered the drug trade, and have done so either under the guise of politics or within the old political network. Hence it has been found that some acts of violence have been for both political and drug-related reasons.

Headley (1994) argued that people are often killed because

Urban violence ... seems to have a strong economic motive .... Young males are often expected to earn an income at any cost. According to this argument, therefore, the vast majority of males involved in economic or hustling-related violence could be expected to have a poor educational background and lack the other skills needed for employment in the formal sector.

they stand in the way of a person attempting to achieve an economic goal. Urban violence, therefore, seems to have a strong economic motive. The immense pressure placed on young males to provide for the family has important implications for economic-related crimes. Young males are often expected to earn an income at any cost. According to this argument, therefore, the vast majority of males involved in economic or hustling-related violence could be expected to have a poor educational background and lack the other skills needed for employment in the formal sector.

Much of human action seems to be driven by economic and political motives. It would seem that man would manipulate whatever tools are made available within the material and knowledge reservoir of a society in order to survive and seek respect. The problem of violence in Jamaica can be resolved, but there has to be a commitment on the part of a number of players involved.

Recommendations

- Jamaica's wealth needs to be distributed more equitably.

- The Government should address the plight of the poor by direct policies aimed at providing them with opportunities for realising a better quality of life.

- The Government must address the problems facing inhabitants of particular inner-city areas – including unemployment, overcrowding, poor housing and sanitation, all of which contribute to stress, frustration and anger that may express itself in violence.

- Resources must be directed to young men to encourage them to regard their lives as valuable and to assist them in developing skills so that they do not have to resort to crime to support themselves and their families.

- Greater efforts must be directed at assisting the police in fostering more amicable and supportive partnerships with communities. Concurrently, the police must take steps to make crime ineffective.

11 The Pacific: Gender Issues in Conflict and Peacemaking

Pamela Thomas

Over the last 15 years political and ethnic conflicts in Bougainville, Fiji Islands, Solomon Islands, Timor-Leste and West Papua, together with escalating crime and violence, have shattered the long-held illusion of a peaceful Pacific. Currently efforts are in progress to maintain peace, re-establish law and order, rebuild infrastructures and help individuals recover from the mental and physical trauma of conflict. In the Solomon Islands, Australia, New Zealand and other Pacific Island countries are helping to restore the rule of law, re-establish the court system, convict former militants responsible for violent crimes and rebuild the health system. In Papua New Guinea, police training is being provided in an attempt to improve law and order. In Bougainville, Fiji Islands and Vanuatu support is being provided to NGOs to work at community level to build peace, restore confidence and work towards a situation of normalcy.

What is seldom given adequate consideration is the role that Pacific Island women have played, and continue to play, in establishing communication channels between warring parties, in restoring and maintaining peace, in rebuilding communities and in working to overcome the physical and psychological trauma of conflict. The stories of Pacific Island women's experiences that have been told in villages, at meetings and international conferences, and in their poems and papers all provide important lessons for the future. These stories show that there is still limited recognition of the ways in which gender relates to the processes and impacts of conflict, peacemaking and peacekeeping or of the very different roles women and men have played in these processes.

For Pacific Island women and children, the end of war has not meant an end to conflict or an end to hardship. Conflict

> *What is seldom given adequate consideration is the role that Pacific Island women have played, and continue to play, in establishing communication channels between warring parties, in restoring and maintaining peace, in rebuilding communities and in working to overcome the physical and psychological trauma of conflict.*

Informal women's groups, small NGOs and church women's groups initiated a number of ... innovative activities aimed at ending conflicts .... They arranged all-night vigils in the Solomon Islands and multi-ethnic peace marches during curfews in Fiji Islands; they advocated for peace and women's solidarity across the Pacific; and they lobbied political leaders and commanders of the different warring factions.

has meant long-term displacement, food shortages, more female-headed households, chronic physical and psychological trauma, unwanted pregnancies and poor health. For children, it has meant a generation without education or health care, long-term food deprivation, lack of cultural identity and lack of beneficial male role models.

The Causes of Conflict

Pacific Island women have identified the following major causes of conflict, some of which resulted from the colonial establishment of nation states that incorporated different tribal and ethnic groups. These are:

- increasingly unequal access to land, paid employment and economic resources, particularly when inequality is based on ethnicity;

- centralisation of resources and services;

- lack of involvement in decision-making and authority;

- a weakening of traditional methods of dispute resolution; and

- the growth of a 'Rambo' culture of violence and guns among young unemployed men.

Pacific Women and Peacemaking

Informal women's groups, small NGOs and church women's groups initiated a number of brave and innovative activities aimed at ending conflicts and alleviating their terrible impacts on the community. They arranged all-night vigils in the Solomon Islands and multi-ethnic peace marches during curfews in Fiji Islands; they advocated for peace and women's solidarity across the Pacific; and they lobbied political leaders and commanders of the different warring factions. Women went behind the 'army' lines to speak with soldiers to remind them of the damage they were causing their families; ran the gauntlet of the rebel no-go zones in the Solomon Islands; smuggled food into Honiara during the blockade; provided information to Fijian women about the Constitution; and worked towards addressing the social and economic devastation of 10 years of war in Bougainville. Community-based women's NGOs are now involved in helping displaced families and women heads of households start small income-generating activities. However, in no Pacific Island country were women either consulted or included in any of the formal peace or restoration talks.

While assistance in restoring law and order and rebuilding infrastructure is meeting with considerable success, Pacific women believe that some peacemaking efforts by outsiders are hampered by lack of knowledge of appropriate communication strategies or of the language that is acceptable to previously warring parties. Outsiders involved in peace processes have not always been aware of all the factors underlying a conflict, or understood the situation and perceptions of all parties concerned. The role of the parties around a peace table is frequently not clearly understood by anybody. Agreement as to the nature and function of these roles needs careful negotiation by donors, the parties to the conflict and all other stakeholders.

... in no Pacific Island country were women either consulted or included in any of the formal peace or restoration talks.

Restorative Justice Meeting, Lalapipi Village, Gulf Province
P Howley Collection

The use of specific words and the 'naming' of events and groupings can inflame tensions in ways that are largely unrecognised. For example, the widespread use in the media of the description 'racial' to describe the conflict in Fiji Islands and the use of 'Indian/Fijian ethnic events' served to reinforce the racial nature of the problems, hiding the reality of tensions within ethnic groups.

There are growing concerns among Pacific Island women about the popularity of violent videos, the increasing acceptability of sexual violence and the glorification of the gun-toting macho 'Rambo' image as a role model for young men.

Violence and the Media

For the last 30 years, the impact of media violence on young people has been widely discussed, with recent acknowledgement among medical professionals in the United States that it can encourage violent behaviour among young people. There are growing concerns among Pacific Island women about the popularity of violent videos, the increasing acceptability of sexual violence and the glorification of the gun-toting macho 'Rambo' image as a role model for young men. Little is being done to address this situation, and indeed it is a difficult situation to address. There is growing recognition that true peace will only come about when men decide not only to physically hand in their guns but to clear guns and the Rambo image from their minds. Viable economic and social alternatives will need to be put in place before this occurs.

Domestic Violence and Male Control

The relationship between domestic violence and a growing culture of violence and national conflict is an issue of discussion among Pacific women. Socialisation of children, particularly boys, is an area of concern. Women's status, women's roles, national and international legislation and the way it is interpreted and implemented are all underlying factors that relate to an increase in conflict.

Control of political, religious, economic and social processes in the Pacific region, including in Australia, are still overwhelmingly male. The growing culture of violence, which can start in the home and includes abuse of children, combined with the lack of legislation or the ability to police domestic violence, augurs ill for the future. A recent AusAID appraisal of violence against children in the Pacific outlines the likelihood of child abuse escalating to more widespread conflict. This is borne out by research in Australia and Melanesia showing that abused children often become abusive teenagers and then violent adults (Dinnen, 2001).[23]

Recommendations

- Gender must be recognised as a key factor in the processes and impact of conflict.

- Women's peace-building activities need greater acknowledgement and consideration.

- Women must be included in peace talks.

- Care must be taken not to reinforce racial tensions by attributing armed violence to ethnic divisions in a way that obscures more complex sources of conflict.

- Attention must be given to the socialisation of boys into stereotyped images of ideal masculinity, including their overexposure to violent videos imported from abroad.

- Legislation is required to tackle domestic violence.

12 Papua New Guinea: Women in Armed Conflict[24]

Helen Hakena

The political crisis in Papua New Guinea (PNG) has its origin in the early 1960s when a special prospecting authority was granted for exploration in the Panguna area, despite the objections of the land's traditional owners: women.

Brief Historical Background

The political crisis in Papua New Guinea (PNG) has its origin in the early 1960s when a special prospecting authority was granted for exploration in the Panguna area, despite the objections of the land's traditional owners: women.[25] In 1964 the Australian mining company CRA began drilling for minerals, and in 1972 a massive copper mine was opened on Bougainville's Crown Prince Range. The Panguna Copper Mine was operated by Bougainville Copper Ltd, owned by CRA. A crater 6 km long and 4 km wide was gouged out of the mountain and millions of tons of rubble were tipped into the Java River Valley. The chemical effluent from the copper concentrator was poured directly into the Kawerong river, which ran green and changed its course. The once fertile valley became completely barren and Panguna became known as the 'Valley of Tears'.

It was against this background of destruction that the discontent and distress of the Bougainville people grew. Added to this were the stresses of rapid modernisation, which was changing Bougainville's economy from one of subsistence to one that was cash-based; an education system that was creating expectations that were not being met; high unemployment; and a large imported workforce to work on the mine, which was creating 'squatter' townships around Arawa, Kieta and Toniva. The Rorovana people, the Panguna landowners and others were being denied the right to protect their land, houses and other property because the Australian Colonial Administration was assisting Bougainville Copper Ltd to establish and develop the Panguna Mine. The treatment of the landowners and others by the Administration and mine officials alienated them from the PNG political leadership.

The first and most serious political decision was reached on

1 September 1975, when Bougainvilleans declared their independence from PNG. The event demonstrated the people of Bougainville's cultural unity and identity and a widespread reluctance among them to be railroaded into a united PNG. A compromise peaceful solution was made when the Government offered partial self-determination to Bougainville through the formation of the North Solomons Provincial Government.

The Bougainville crisis became critical in late November 1988 when militant landowners took to the jungle and caused damage to property. The militants demanded the closure of the mine, 10 billion Kina in compensation and the secession of the North Solomons Province from PNG. The Panguna Mine ceased operation in May 1989 and a State of Emergency was declared in June. The Bougainville Revolutionary Army (BRA) was also formed about that time. In 1990 the national Government withdrew all its services from Bougainville. This included the withdrawal of the security forces. A total sea and air blockade was imposed on the entire province. This was the beginning of the war.

The Effect of the Crisis on Women in Bougainville

Before the crisis, Bougainvillean women were very assertive of their rights and organised themselves into groups, mainly village groups that in general ran along religious lines (as they still do today – in fact they are as strong as ever). Bougainvilleans were peace-loving people. There was authority in the communities and violence was rarely heard of. The rule of law was adhered to and human rights principles were respected and promoted. The level of respect shown to women was very high.

This was partly because of the high esteem in which our culture and customs, such as our matrilineal tradition, were held. These were blended with Christian principles and teachings such as "love one another as you love yourself". These precepts have guided our way of living for a long time.

The emergence of the crisis changed all this. We learned that civilians, especially women and children, become the primary targets of groups who use terror as a tactic of war. Women suffer from gender-based violence. We learned that the magnitude of violence against women during and after the crisis was overwhelming. Our women from day one of the conflict felt these

We learned that civilians, especially women and children, become the primary targets of groups who use terror as a tactic of war.

As the crisis intensified, women's rights were severely abused. Chiefs no longer had power and authority in their communities. Power was now in the hands of young men because they had guns. So women ... were raped and tortured in front of their husbands and children. Young girls were the most threatened and vulnerable, as they could be raped, humiliated and forced to do all sorts of things against their will under the barrel of a gun.

changes, especially in terms of the types of violence that were inflicted on them by combatants, both by the rebels – the BRA – and by members of the PNG Government security forces.

As the crisis intensified, women's rights were severely abused. Chiefs no longer had power and authority in their communities. Power was now in the hands of young men because they had guns. So women's security was threatened both outside and inside their homes. They were raped and tortured in front of their husbands and children. Young girls were the most threatened and vulnerable, as they could be raped, humiliated and forced to do all sorts of things against their will under the barrel of a gun.

Such sexual abuse had never been heard of in Bougainville before. But militarisation and the presence of weapons during the crisis brought about this new kind of brutality. During the crisis women were attacked and raped because they were related to political adversaries or simply because they were at home at the wrong time when government soldiers or rebels arrived. For example, five young girls from my village were abducted and taken for questioning to the jungle nearby by members of the BRA because they were suspected of having affairs with some members of the PNG defence forces. Four managed to escape, as they knew the surrounding environment, but the fifth was not so lucky. She was raped.

Women's voices silenced

Women were not free to work in their gardens because of fear of being sexually harassed. Freedom of movement, freedom of association and freedom of speech were restricted and controlled.

Permission had to be sought from the 'authority' of the day before meetings or peace protests could be convened. In 1990, when the women from my community of Hagogohe arranged for a peaceful march where over a thousand women were to air their views about lack of services caused by the total blockade on the island, they were told by the 'authority' of the day, the BRA, that peace was not possible. The women leaders who were arranging the peace march were each taken to secret locations where they were verbally abused and threatened for trying to organise the march, which never took place.

On 15 May 2003, I was confronted and threatened by some

senior members of the BRA, who warned me not to continue with the Provincial Women's Meeting that I was co-ordinating to gauge women's views on peace-related issues such as weapons' disposal, withdrawal of the Peace Monitoring Group and the wording of the Constitution.

Increased domestic violence and health problems

We learned from the crisis that violence against women did not arise solely out of the conditions of the conflict, but rather it was directly related to the violence that existed in women's lives during peacetime as well. Sexual violence is common during peacetime, but in times of conflict and post-conflict it is more prevalent and more brutal.

In addition, some women have suffered injury and unwanted pregnancies resulting from sexual violence; resulting in psychological damage such as anxiety and post-traumatic stress disorder and even suicide. Apart from the atrocities committed, there were also health consequences from the breakdown of services and lack of human and material resources and medicine. The physical health and psychological well-being of women and girls were affected in terms of pregnancy, childbirth and menstruation. For example, the total blockade imposed by the PNG Government interrupted the supply of sanitary protection to the women of Bougainville, making it difficult for them to leave their homes during menstruation.

Women and the Peace Process

Despite having important roles and responsibilities in Bougainvillean culture, women have been excluded from peace committees. They have struggled to participate in disarmament meetings as well as in the formal political peace process, both of which have been dominated by men. However, although they have been excluded from negotiations, women have continued to advocate and lobby for peace on Bougainville.

The LNWDA

The Leitana Nehan Women's Development Agency (LNWDA) was formed in 1992 (formally launched in 1995) with the goal

Despite having important roles and responsibilities in Bougainvillean culture, women have been excluded from peace committees. They have struggled to participate in disarmament meetings as well as in the formal political peace process, both of which have been dominated by men. However, although they have been excluded from negotiations, women have continued to advocate and lobby for peace on Bougainville.

Laying wreaths on the Stone of Reconciliation, Arawa, Bougainville
National Newspaper

of creating a world safe for women and children. Our motto was 'Women weaving Bougainville together'. In 1994 we received support from the International Women's Development Agency (IWDA), and in 1998 the two organisations jointly developed a project called 'Strengthening Communities for Peace', which has been funded by AusAID since 2000. In 2001 we were awarded the Millennium Peace Prize for women in recognition of our contribution to preventing war and building peace (see Box 17).

Box 17 LNWDA and the Millennium Peace Prize

On International Women's Day 2001, International Alert and the United Nations Development Fund for Women (UNIFEM) presented the first Millennium Peace Prize for Women. The award – made to six individuals and organisations – was the first of its kind to specifically honour the vital role that women play in peace-building and the indispensable contributions that women have made to resolving and preventing violent conflict.

The citation to LNWDA read: "Leitana Nehan have been key to the process of peace negotiations and reconstruction in Bougainville, Papua New Guinea since the mid-1990s. In 1992, under the slogan 'Women weaving Bougainville together', they began rebuilding the trust that had eroded between neighbours and within communities.

By building relationships between young people, their workshops have helped heal the deep rifts caused by the war. They have challenged the police to shift their attitudes and focus their concerns on the issue of violence against women, for the Government to allocate funds for public awareness and studies concerning the root causes of violence and for churches to openly condemn violence and oppression against women."

Source: www.international-alert.org/women/old_website_two/millennium_peace_prize.html

LNWDA recognises the strong connection between violence against women and the militarisation of Bougainville society. Because of this, we are working not only with women but also with men, youths and entire communities towards reconciliation and freedom from violence. Building relationships among young people from different communities has been one of our approaches to healing the rifts created by the war. LNWDA works with ex-combatants, and we encourage men to be involved in our work to assist their recovery, to 'balance the teams' sharing of experiences', to involve men in building peace and to offer role models to other young men in the community. We now have 1,500 volunteers.

Seventy of the volunteers travel on foot in teams of seven from village to village across 150 selected communities and schools in the 10 districts of Bougainville. The aim is to strengthen communities for peace, and the topics we cover include domestic violence, sexual assault, rape, sexual abuse, sexual harassment, incest, homebrew alcohol, violence and integral human development.

Part of this work involves 'youth mobilisation', where we bring people together to share ideas. Over the years, we have been able to bring together 'hard core' rebels out of guerrilla fighting and into the women-led peace movement. For example, teams in Buka, Paruparu, North West, Selau/Suir, Buin and Siwai are made up of ex-combatants. The young ex-combatants are proving very loyal to the women's movement and LNWDA, and their involvement in the programmes is seen as part of their recovery and rehabilitation. The anti-violence workshops help boys and young men to understand that the guns and violence of their childhood are not a necessary part of their futures. LNWDA also uses male volunteers to run awareness workshops on violence against women and to share their experiences.

Our workshops for young women bring together participants from all over Bougainville to socialise, share ideas and concerns, and learn. The workshops encourage young women who have lived with violence for 15 years to speak out and to learn about their bodies and discuss issues of concern to them. They provide a safe environment for young women to discuss their feelings and to realise they are not alone. LNWDA's awareness work in communities and schools on the problems

... [W]e have been able to bring together 'hard core' rebels out of guerrilla fighting and into the women-led peace movement .... The young ex-combatants are proving very loyal to the women's movement and LNWDA, and their involvement in the programmes is seen as part of their recovery and rehabilitation. The anti-violence workshops help boys and young men to understand that the guns and violence of their childhood are not a necessary part of their futures.

Although many Bougainville women went through suffering, trauma and violence during the crisis, they were able to bring families and communities together by providing healing and recovery services and organising solidarity networks across families, clans, communities and districts .... The power of command and respect for women was felt in the real times of need, when society was not functioning normally.

encountered by women and girls has led to a decrease in the number of victims in the areas served by our volunteers.

A vital part of our awareness work is on 'homebrew', an extremely potent locally-made liquor, 90 per cent alcohol, that did not exist in Bougainville before the war. It is a problem all over the island, and is closely linked to high rates of violence against women. Young men drown themselves in homebrew alcohol to try to forget their negative experiences.

Since 2000, LNWDA has been providing counselling services, including trauma counselling for women and girls who have experienced violence, rape and sexual abuse, as well as individual and couples' counselling. Much of the counselling is provided by counsellors who visit communities and schools in their districts.

Our popular weekly 20-minute radio programme, broadcast on our local radio station, Radio Bougainville, addresses these issues as well as selected current affairs topics that we believe can assist in building peace. The programme has an estimated audience of around 10,000 people out of the total population of 200,000. We have received written confirmation that the radio programme is also being heard by people from the neighbouring Solomon Islands.

One programme included in our Strengthening Communities for Peace project, and one that is increasingly popular, focuses on integral human development. It deals with the spiritual, mental, emotional and physical development of the whole person. Besides this project, we also conduct training on capacity-building, HIV/AIDS awareness and proposal writing.

Building peace and promoting reconciliation

Although many Bougainville women went through suffering, trauma and violence during the crisis, they were able to bring families and communities together by providing healing and recovery services and organising solidarity networks across families, clans, communities and districts.

The power of command and respect for women was felt in the real times of need, when society was not functioning normally. Women's groups – community-based organisations, youth and church groups – played a major role in building peace and reconciliation at both the local and national level. Women became the first peace negotiators and promoted dialogue. They did not set conditions when they negotiated peace. Women leaders attended international seminars and conferences, where they talked openly about the atrocities inflicted on women. They also used international fora to call for peace. Individual women and women chiefs used their influence to negotiate peace in their communities.

Everything the women did – whether it was attending a meeting, praying, struggling to keep their families alive or comforting other women – had to some degree a positive influence on the peace process in Bougainville. In the heart of all wars, it is women who have the strength to survive. The women of Bougainville proved this by going into the jungle to persuade their sons, husbands and their other relatives to avert war. They were not frightened. This happened all over Bougainville.

In October 1990 the women of Selah in north Bougainville organised a peace march where they petitioned the PNG Defence Force and BRA to put down their arms and begin peaceful negotiations. They then organised an all-night peace vigil to protest in silence about the violence. It is estimated that about 5,000 people, including some members of the BRA, attended the vigil. Another peace initiative took place in Buka in 1993, where the Buka women told the leaders of all parties to carry out peaceful negotiations. In Siwai, south Bougainville, BRA leaders and members were also petitioned to stop the war and to allow people out of their bush camps.

In August 1994 the Catholic Women's Association of Bougainville organised a reunion for the Catholic mothers of Bougainville, where women were encouraged to pray, talk and negotiate with parties involved in the conflict in order to stop the fighting. More than 2,000 women from all over Bougainville attended the reunion, a sign of unity, confidence, courage and determination to move the peace process forward.

After attending the Beijing Conference in 1995, we organised a Silent March in Buka. Defying the State of Emergency, more than a thousand women participated in protest against the war and against the use of rape as a weapon. We were stopped by the PNG Defence Force twice. They wanted to arrest the leader of the march and asked, "Who is your leader?" We said, "All of us are leaders. We all own the march." The soldiers could not arrest anyone.

After attending the Beijing Conference in 1995, we organised a Silent March in Buka …. [M]ore than a thousand women participated in protest against the war and against the use of rape as a weapon. We were stopped by the PNG Defence Force twice. They wanted to arrest the leader of the march and asked, "Who is your leader?" We said, "All of us are leaders. We all own the march." The soldiers could not arrest anyone.

When the issue of the disposal of arms was raised, the women of Bougainville were told bluntly by the ex-combatants that weapons disposal was not a women's issue. The guns were owned by them .... Therefore they had the authority to deal with them, even to the point of not disposing of or surrendering them .... [T]hese ex-combatants forgot that ... women were victims [of the conflict].

The women of Bougainville's success in contributing to the achievement of peace was due primarily to how we combined traditional and modern ways of reconciliation.

Weapons disposal

When the issue of the disposal of arms was raised, the women of Bougainville were told bluntly by the ex-combatants that weapons disposal was not a women's issue. The guns were owned by them. They bought some of them, they made some of them and they died because of them. Therefore they had the authority to deal with them, even to the point of not disposing of or surrendering them.

But these ex-combatants forgot that the women themselves were also affected by the conflict and that women were victims. The women of Bougainville had exprienced trauma, violence, rape, suffering and death. So the women voiced their views

Weapons being handed in, Siwai, Bougainville
Peace Monitoring Group

and concerns and organised meetings to discuss the issue of weapons disposal. On 15 May 2003 the LNWDA held a meeting attended by more than 200 women from all over Bougainville. Issues discussed included weapons disposal. At the meeting the women unanimously agreed that all weapons should be destroyed, not containerised.

Challenges that Women Face

The main challenge that women have faced while doing peace-building work is protecting those working at grassroots level who are victimised by both sides in the conflict and therefore face great difficulties. Their security and safety are not guaranteed. Another challenge is the instability of the current political situation, the frequent changes in government and the division of civil society along political lines, with different groups seeking control of peace initiatives. This not only impedes information sharing, but also means that activities may be duplicated or have contradictory impacts. A third challenge is that women are not included in decision-making committees in peace time but are used more so during conflict.

We also feel great pain to know that our attackers, the people who killed our husbands and male relatives, and raped, tortured and mutilated our people, have not been punished. Many of these people are running around freely amongst us. It is as if they are being rewarded for the crimes that they committed.

We believe that gender mainstreaming needs to be improved in times of peace-building. It needs to start from the very beginning of a peace-building mission to ensure that structures and programmes are designed to address the different needs of women and men for protection, assistance, justice and reconstruction. In conclusion, I would like to make a few recommendations that we believe can bring about some changes in how peace can be achieved and, more particularly, how atrocities can be minimised.

On 15 May 2003 the LNWDA held a meeting attended by more than 200 women from all over Bougainville. Issues discussed included weapons disposal. At the meeting the women unanimously agreed that all weapons should be destroyed, not containerised.

Recommendations

- Psychological social support and reproductive health services for women affected by conflict need to be an integral part of emergency assistance and post-conflict reconstruction. Special attention should be provided to those who have experienced physical trauma, torture and sexual violence. This was lacking on Bougainville.

- Gender equity should be recognised in all peace processes, agreements and transitional governance structures. International and regional organisations and all parties involved in peace processes should advocate for gender parity, maintaining a minimum of 35 per cent representation of women in peace negotiations, and should ensure that women's needs are addressed in all peace agreements.

- An international truth and reconciliation commission on violence against women in armed conflict should be set up as a step towards ending violence. Convened by civil society and supported by the international community, the commission would address crimes that have been left unrecorded.

- Domestic violence should be recognised as systematic and widespread in conflict and post-conflict situations, and a multi-sectoral approach should be adopted in addressing its impacts.

13 The Mano River Union Sub-region: The Role of Women in Building Peace

Christiana Solomon

Women's Invisibility as Peace-builders

1 *Baby strapped to her back, holding another child by the hand, she flees into the bush.*

2 *Smartly dressed, document folder open in front of her, she discusses with rebel leaders.*

If asked which of these two images corresponds to the international community's view of African women, most people's answer would undeniably be the first. But the reality is that African women are deeply involved in peace efforts in some of the most violent areas in the world – in this case, in the Mano River Basin comprising Guinea, Liberia and Sierra Leone – sometimes at great personal risk.

Although it is known anecdotally that women are very active in peace-building activities at grassroots level and staff non-governmental organisations (NGOs) that include peace programmes, analytical studies about their positive contributions in this field are still scarce. Because of this lack of scholarship, there is insufficient documentation on women peace-builders as role models, female practitioners do not get the recognition they deserve and women are grossly under-represented as negotiators in conflicts.

One reason for this invisibility of women's peace-building activities is that grassroots organisations seldom document their work, and when they do the publication and circulation of their work is often outside mainstream circles. This chapter is therefore intended to be a contribution to documenting key information about women peace-builders in the Mano River Union (MRU).[26] It also grew out of a concern that there was a lack of accountability to practitioners among researchers.

> *... the reality is that African women are deeply involved in peace efforts in some of the most violent areas in the world ... sometimes at great personal risk.*

The Mano River Basin occupies a total land area of 429,000 sq. km, with a population of approximately 14 million people. The countries share similar histories, heritages, cultures and ethnic groups, with certain differences. The artificial borders of African states means that some of these ethnic groups were divided between the countries. This arbitrary division gave ethnicity critical salience in the politics of the 'new' states and complicated the conflict in the Basin.

Working as a civil society activist in Sierra Leone, I met many academics who were investigating the war and its impact, particularly on women and children. They requested access to subjects, and my organisation[27] granted this in the belief that widespread dissemination would raise international awareness of the conflict situation and the determinant role of women in seeking peaceful means to end the war. However, there has been a high degree of failure of researchers to provide feedback to the subjects.

The Mano River Union Sub-region: An Overview

The MRU was established on 3 October 1973 under the Mano River Declaration, initially between Liberia and Sierra Leone. At this stage it formed primarily a customs' union, designed to allow the free movement of people and products and to foster a union for economic sub-regional co-operation and social integration. Guinea joined the Union in 1980. The MRU derives its name from the Mano River, which divides Liberia and Sierra Leone and also runs through Guinea. Economic integration was seen as the best means of maximising the potential benefits of development projects and overcoming the disadvantage of small size. The focus was less on security issues as the three countries were relatively peaceful and stable, and in 1986 they signed a Non-Aggression Treaty.

The Mano River Basin occupies a total land area of 429,000 sq. km, with a population of approximately 14 million people. The countries share similar histories, heritages, cultures and ethnic groups, with certain differences. The artificial borders of African states means that some of these ethnic groups were divided between the countries. This arbitrary division gave ethnicity critical salience in the politics of the 'new' states and complicated the conflict in the Basin.

The sub-region is richly endowed with resources such as bauxite, gold, diamonds, iron ore, rubber and arable land, as well as marine, fishery, forestry and water resources. Despite this immense wealth, its human development and social indicators are among the worst in the world. The UNDP Human Development Report 2003 ranks the countries among the world's least developed and they are also classified as Heavily Indebted Poor Countries (UNDP, 2003).

The nature of domestic politics in the sub-region has been based on a patron-client system of governance driven by informal networks through which state resources are appropriated to support and consolidate regimes in power and their followers. The history and politics of the three countries have been characterised by the complex interconnectedness of resources, ethnicity, factionalism and conflict. Their political histories have alternated between a one-party state (Sierra Leone), military regimes (Liberia) and periodic attempts at democratic governments.

The invasion of Liberia by dissident forces from neighbouring Côte d'Ivoire in 1989 sparked off a series of chain reactions that later had a 'spill over' effect in Sierra Leone on 23 March 1991 and cross-border skirmishes into Guinea from both Liberia and Sierra Leone in 2000. Explanations for the outbreak of the wars in Liberia and Sierra Leone are mostly ethnic or resource-based respectively. Looking beyond the immediate triggers, however, the conflicts were rooted in the nature and type of state formation, the nature of domestic politics and increasing economic, social and political polarisation. The rhetoric of social justice and greater equity developed by the warring factions was sufficiently appealing to recruits to mobilise them to stage an armed social protest.

The conflicts are complex because of the web of shifting military and political alliances that have been established over the years among the three Governments and the various armed opposition groups. As a result, they are intertwined and have shown a ready potential to spill over and destabilise neighbouring countries. Moreover, the conflicts have been characterised by unparalleled human rights violations, blatant disregard for international norms and laws pertaining to the conduct of war, and heinous war crimes.

Today, the MRU is severely fractured and the once lofty goals of economic integration and peaceful social coexistence are in tatters. Years of bloody war in Liberia and Sierra Leone have produced catastrophic consequences in the sub-region: forced migration of hundreds of thousands of people, deaths, large-scale suffering and gender-based violence, added to which internal political upheaval in Guinea makes peace and stability in the sub-region seem a far-fetched dream.

... the conflicts have been characterised by unparalleled human rights violations, blatant disregard for international norms and laws pertaining to the conduct of war, and heinous war crimes .... Years of bloody war in Liberia and Sierra Leone have produced catastrophic consequences in the sub-region: forced migration of hundreds of thousands of people, deaths, large-scale suffering and gender-based violence ...

*Refugee women from Sierra
Leone in Liberia*
Refugees International

Women Building Peace in Sierra Leone

The women's movement in Sierra Leone became vibrant from 1994, when women began defining their agenda for the 1995 Beijing Conference. It was during this process that they identified the need to organise in support of the peace process and take an active role in Sierra Leone's transition to democracy from military rule. Women's groups, such as Women Organised for a Morally Enlightened Nation and the Women's Movement for Peace, began mobilising and galvanising civil society support for peace and democracy. They rejected the National Provisional Ruling Council (NPRC) junta regime and promoted democratisation as a key to resolving the conflict in the country and also to combating structural or covert violence. Massive street demonstrations were organised around the country and press conferences were held where women expressed their condemnation of the ongoing conflict and called for its speedy and peaceful resolution. They were instrumental in the positive outcome of the National Consultative Conference of August 1995 (known as Bintumani 1), which set elections for 26 August the following year.

The palace coup in January 1996, however, saw the new Head of State attempting to cancel the planned elections, arguing that peace should be won before elections could take place. Women again took the lead in protesting this new turn. They countered that elections are an event, whereas peace is an ongoing process. Thus, elections could occur in parallel to peace negotiations. A second Consultative Conference, popularly referred to as Bintumani 2, was proposed. Women leaders launched a sensitisation campaign, holding rallies and meetings to convince the population to vote in favour of holding elections. They wrote position papers and issued press releases unequivocally reaffirming their commitment to elections. Despite attempts by the military to sabotage the conference, it went ahead as planned and its outcome was pro-elections. This victory came at some cost to the women: all were verbally abused, some received death threats and others were publicly flogged or physically assaulted.

Bintumani 1 and 2 significantly contributed to the heavy turnout for the 1996 elections. Again, attempts by the military and rebel forces to derail the elections were foiled by the women. Acting as observers and presiding officers, they encouraged the electorate not to be intimidated but to cast their votes amidst atrocities and severe human rights violations. Ironically, while working for peace and democratic elections, these groups failed to ensure their own inclusion on electoral lists. Most women, despite their activism in the peace process, were not yet ready to run as individual candidates for political positions. This resulted in the election of only two women parliamentarians and two appointees to ministerial positions.

Women's groups have played a critical role in mediating to help end the war in Sierra Leone. They actively pursued dialogue with rebel leaders and worked to bring them to the negotiating table. They employed diverse methods, including:

- private lobbying and public advocacy;

- listening to the grievances of the rebels, while at the same time expressing condemnation of the human rights abuses they had committed;

- sending messages of peace and reconciliation through the media to both sides of the conflict to demonstrate their impartiality;

- admonishing the Government to listen to the rebels;

- rallying support among members of civil society organisations; and

- mobilising to influence the rebels to negotiate and agree to elections.

Women in the provinces went into outlying villages singing songs and calling on rebels to stop fighting. They met secretly with the rebels in the bush to convince them to come out and lay down their arms. One such meeting was discovered by the military, and the women who had gone to meet the rebels were massacred in the cross-fire (OECD, 1998).

During the Armed Forces Revolutionary Council (AFRC) interregnum, Sierra Leonean women in exile in Guinea organised and won the propaganda war against the AFRC junta. They disguised their voices or used pseudonyms, out of concern for the safety of their relatives and friends still living in Sierra Leone, to send anti-junta messages on Radio Democracy,

Women in the provinces went into outlying villages singing songs and calling on rebels to stop fighting. They met secretly with the rebels in the bush to convince them to come out and lay down their arms. One such meeting was discovered by the military, and the women who had gone to meet the rebels were massacred in the cross-fire ...

> *[Women] infiltrated the junta, exposing crucial information about its activities, including its involvement in arms deals and smuggling of diamonds and the names of its international partners. Some were caught. They were either tortured before being killed, together with their families, or were gang-raped. The lucky ones fled to neighbouring Guinea before they could be arrested.*

98.1 FM. They organised demonstrations and mobilised the international community to intervene. Women who had stayed behind in Sierra Leone sustained the civil disobedience organised against the military junta. They could not organise as a group, but some of them acted as undercover agents. They infiltrated the junta, exposing crucial information about its activities, including its involvement in arms deals and smuggling of diamonds and the names of its international partners. Some were caught. They were either tortured before being killed, together with their families, or were gang-raped. The lucky ones fled to neighbouring Guinea before they could be arrested.

In the aftermath of the 6 January invasion of Freetown in 1999, women's groups participated in the delivery of humanitarian assistance. The Campaign for Good Governance (CGG) paid for rape victims to receive medical attention, the Sierra Leone Chapter of the Forum for African Women Educationalists (FAWE) set up a number of counselling units to assist rape victims, the Sierra Leone Association of University Women (SLAUW) supplied non-food items to young displaced mothers and the Young Women's Christian Association (YWCA) organised feeding programmes for displaced women in the camps.

During the crisis in May 2000, when 500 UN peacekeepers were kept hostage by the Revolutionary United Front (RUF), the Women's Forum organised a Peace March to the residence of the RUF leader, Foday Sankoh. A task force member delivered a statement condemning the RUF for taking the peacekeepers hostage. The women suffered verbal harassment and death threats from Sankoh's bodyguards, who indicated that the key actors were marked for death. Two days later, during a mammoth civil society march against Sankoh, his bodyguards opened fire on demonstrators, killing several and wounding dozens more. During this period, the women of Liberia wrote to their Head of State requesting his intervention to secure the release of all hostages taken by the rebels, including the UN peacekeepers.

Despite the determinant role they had played to end the war in Sierra Leone, women were under-represented, even as observers, during the Lomé peace negotiations. In fact, the only woman's signature on the Accord was that of the

Organisation of African Unity representative. Unfortunately, she was representing a regional body and was not Sierra Leonean.

Women Building Peace in Liberia

Liberian women have not only been victims of the country's civil war but have also played an active role to end it. In 1994 the Liberian Women's Initiative (LWI) was established as a pressure group to speak out against the war (Anderlini, 2000). They adopted the strategy of taking a unified stance on issues relating to the war, focusing on the need for disarmament before holding elections. They conducted meetings, organised demonstrations and presented a range of position statements to the Economic Community of West African States (ECOWAS) and the rebel leaders. They led successful sit home strikes in protest at agreements they felt appeased the leaders of warring factions. They were present at the talks that led to the Accra Clarification of the Akosombo Agreement in 1996. They also protested against and rejected the roles of former US President Jimmy Carter and UN Special Envoy Gordon-Somers who, they felt, were undermining the conference's relevance by encouraging the warring factions to meet separately. They formulated a plan for enhancing the incentives for disarmament, but complained that neither the UN nor ECOWAS had studied their plan or considered incorporating it into their own programme of actions.

As the viewpoints and actions of the LWI became more critical, members experienced increased antagonism from the warring factions. The women suffered harassment, looting and death threats, which forced all the prominent leaders to flee Monrovia before the violence erupted.

The Mano River Women's Peace Network

Another important way that women have been organising for peace in the MRU is in the construction of cross-community alliances, finding common cause despite tensions, cultural divides and different nationalities. The Mano River Women's Peace Network (MARWOPNET) is one such example. It is a combination of all the strategic partnerships and networks of

Despite the determinant role they had played to end the war in Sierra Leone, women were under-represented, even as observers, during the Lomé peace negotiations.

Another important way that women have been organising for peace in the MRU is in the construction of cross-community alliances .... They are credited with bringing together the three Heads of State for the first time in July 2001 to discuss peacekeeping ... as fighting ... in one country spilled into the next .... This marked their breakthrough in political decision-making processes. Consequently, they have since been allowed to participate in the ECOWAS and MRU summits.

women in Guinea, Liberia and Sierra Leone to ensure successful implementation of their platform for peace.

However, these cross-community alliances are not limited to women-to-women exchanges. The women have created strategic alliances with other members of society, in particular the political elites. They have appeared at peace conferences and addressed senior officials of the three Governments directly to argue for attention to their concerns and emphasise the overall importance of women to the peace process. They are credited with bringing together the three Heads of State for the first time in July 2001 to discuss peacekeeping along their borders as fighting and refugee traffic in one country spilled into the next. They were instrumental in getting the presidents of the three countries to meet as a confidence-building measure. This marked their breakthrough in political decision-making processes. Consequently, they have since been allowed to participate in the ECOWAS and MRU summits.

MARWOPNET also continues to research conditions in the sprawling refugee camps and conduct leadership training for women working in local peace groups and at the community level. As important as their high-level approaches to political leaders is their work in travelling the country, going into villages and huts and speaking directly to women about what they need to rebuild their lives, whether more rice or more counselling.

The Network was awarded the United Nations Prize for Human Rights for 2003 by the UN General Assembly in recognition of its outstanding achievement in human rights.

Obstacles to Women's Participation in Governance

In post-conflict situations, there have been numerous calls for women's increased involvement in decision-making processes. However, implementation of these laws and good intentions often runs into major obstacles. At the social level, the new discourse of gender equality may run counter to existing social norms regarding gender roles. In Sierra Leone, for example, local authorities and male members of society, particularly in the Northern Province, may discourage or forbid women from participating in political activities. Moreover, the fact that the division of labour has not changed in favour of women also poses practical limitations on the possibilities for their active involvement in formal peace politics. In addition, as Nobel Peace Prize winner Rigoberta Menchú so aptly put it, "It's very important to be an elector. But what really matters is to be eligible". How then can women make themselves eligible? Note that the emphasis here is on women being more proactive.

Moreover, at the government level, the problems include a lack of financial resources and a lack of gender awareness or even political will among senior officials, mostly men. Governments must move beyond rhetoric and translate into practice what they preach.

Liberian refugees in Sierra Leone
Refugees International

Recommendations

• Women should network actively and strategically nationally, regionally and internationally in order to achieve our vision. MARWOPNET has served as a flagship in this area. Similar alliances on policy-relevant issues should be established in the region.

• Women should learn to support each other. They should learn to talk to one another and use 'focus meetings' and other similar fora to discuss and map out collective strategies for political enhancement and, more importantly, implement those strategies.

• Women should support female candidates for public office to ensure that women have a voice at the political level.

• Women in the provinces should be encouraged and supported to participate actively in democratic governance, conflict resolution and peace-building processes. Whether they are literate or not is immaterial. There is a role for them to play by engaging them in the debates, as they are more competent to mobilise women in the rural areas and articulate their needs and interests.

Recommendations (continued)

- Traditional socio-cultural institutions should be enhanced and utilised to impact positively on the post-war transition. The Elder tradition, for example, acts as a guardian of societal norms and provides structures of authority, dispute settlement, reconciliation and governance. Secret societies also have nationwide networks. They can be utilised to build women's capacity in conflict resolution and peace-building.

- Competent women must be included as senior officials in national institutions, such as National Commissions for Human Rights, and in disarmament, demobilisation and reintegration (DDR) programmes so that specifically female requirements, such as provisions for menstruation and childbirth, are taken seriously.

- Institutional support and increased capacity-building should be provided to women's organisations working actively on governance, human rights, peace and gender issues.

14 Sierra Leone: Women in Conflict Resolution and Post-conflict Reconstruction

Kadi Sesay

Without equity, we will not have global stability. Without a better sense of social justice, our cities will not be stable. Without inclusion, too many of us will be condemned to live separate, armed, frightened lives. Whether you broach it from the social or economic or moral perspective, this is a challenge that we cannot afford to ignore. There are not two worlds, there is one world. We share the same world, and we share the same challenges. The fight against poverty is a fight for peace, security and growth for all of us. (World Bank, 2000)

The message is clear: conflicts, instability and social disintegration are a direct result of poverty, inequity, marginalisation and exclusion, poor governance, and violations of human rights and the rule of law. Many conflicts in Africa lend credence to this. The outbreak of a rebel conflict in Sierra Leone in March 1991 can be largely attributed to these factors. The devastating effects of many of these wars should make all of us learn the bitter lesson that investing in improving the living conditions of a country's population – men, women and youth – is far less expensive than managing a conflict resulting from not doing so.

Sierra Leone's fortunes have been shaped by many years of mismanagement, inefficiency, declining competitiveness, an unacceptably low quality of life and gender inequality, culminating in a brutal war resulting in human carnage unprecedented in its history. The war has caused extensive destruction of the country's meagre socio-economic and physical infrastructure, leading to a further deterioration in the living conditions of the people and widespread poverty.

Consequently, although endowed with immense natural and human resources, Sierra Leone is now classified as one of the poorest nations in the world. It ranks 177th and last in the

... conflicts, instability and social disintegration are a direct result of poverty ..., poor governance, and violations of human rights .... The devastating effects of ... these wars should make all of us learn the bitter lesson that ... improving the living conditions of a country's population – men, women and youth – is far less expensive than managing a conflict resulting from not doing so.

Child soldier of the SLA in Makeni, Sierra Leone
Sebastian Bolesch/Still Pictures

UNDP's human development index (UNDP, 2004). Successive administrations did try to implement policies and programmes aimed at redressing these imbalances. Unfortunately, they had minimal impact on the lives of the majority of Sierra Leoneans because of the prolonged conflict, poor governance and a weak political, economic and social situation.

The diplomatic and military efforts of the international community at critical moments of the conflict in Sierra Leone made it possible for the country to survive. However, the view of many is that the international community should have intervened much earlier to put out the fires of this war before it engulfed the whole country and caused loss of life and destruction on a scale that many found inexplicable. A response to Sierra Leone's plight half as swift as that of the West to the conflicts in Kosovo or Macedonia could have saved thousands of lives and a great deal of property.

In addition to international responses, partnerships for conflict prevention and resolution must emanate from within if the efforts for peace are to be sustainable. And Sierra Leoneans' responses to military rule and the war are examples of domestic partnerships critical for conflict resolution.

The official diplomatic efforts that eventually drew the Government of Sierra Leone and the Revolutionary United Front (RUF) into formal peace negotiations and led to the Abidjan Peace Accord in 1996 and the Lomé Agreement in July 1999 were preceded and complemented by a range of domestic initiatives aimed at a peaceful settlement of the conflict. Any analysis of the political situation in Sierra Leone must take into consideration the imaginative minds, heroic efforts and unwavering determination of many Sierra Leonean women, as well as others, together with their democratically elected Government, to defy all odds and keep the nation state afloat.

Women Taking the Lead

The period 1994–1998 marked a turning point in the history of Sierra Leone with regard to the role of Sierra Leonean women, and civil society in general, in the democratisation process. In 1994 the Sierra Leone Association of University Women (SLAUW) proposed that women's groups meet regularly for networking, information-sharing and collective action on issues of common concern. In 1995 SLAUW participated in a series of teleconference discussions, enabling women to learn about initiatives taken by other Third World women in similar conflict situations. The women resolved to take action for peace.

The strategy was for direct intervention in the then political situation on the ground. The women's groups agreed that the national crisis facing Sierra Leone, with a rebel war in progress, was too serious to be left to the military Government in power. Their argument was that women were natural peacemakers who could bring unique skills into resolving the conflict.

The Sierra Leone Women's Movement for Peace (SLWMP) led a campaign of appeals to the National Provisional Ruling Council (NPRC) military Government and the rebels: they organised marches, prayers, rallies and meetings with the Government and with members of the international community to apply pressure for a negotiated settlement to the war.

The women's peace campaign put the issues regarding the handling of the war into the public domain in a non-partisan and non-confrontational manner that made public debate of contentious issues possible without fear of automatically offending the Government. As a result of the women's intervention, a negotiated peace settlement became a respectable option that offered both the Government and the rebels the opportunity to climb down from entrenched positions without loss of face.

The women of Sierra Leone took the lead in the democratic process, encouraged by other civil society groups who believed that the military were more tolerant of being challenged by women than by men. At the two National Consultative Conferences (Bintumani 1 in 1995 and Bintumani 2 in 1996), civil society groups, especially women's groups, explicitly and passionately demonstrated their rejection of the continuation of military rule in Sierra Leone by unanimously voting for democratic elections to precede peace negotiations – all done in the face of harassment and danger.

The Women's Position Paper prepared for the Bintumani 1 Conference led the way for the removal of the military in 1996 through democratic elections. The most significant of the women's views was the statement that only a recall of the

The period 1994–1998 marked a turning point in the history of Sierra Leone with regard to the role of Sierra Leonean women, and civil society in general, in the democratisation process. In .... 1995 SLAUW participated in a series of teleconference discussions, enabling women to learn about initiatives taken by other Third World women in similar conflict situations. The women resolved to take action for peace.

Another significant move that gave women a public voice was the Government's creation of the National Commission for Democracy (NCD) in 1994, the first National Commission to be chaired by a woman. The NCD and the Interim National Electoral Commission were the twin Commissions that managed the country's transition to democracy between 1994 and 1996.

national Consultative Conference could authorise a postponement of the elections. Women succeeded in creating an independent voice that articulated a non-partisan, female perspective on a wide range of fundamental issues.

The unanimous will of the people forced the NPRC Government to hold multi-party elections on 2 March 1996, ushering in the Government of President Ahmad Tejan Kabbah. When President Kabbah's Government was toppled by a military-rebel coalition, the Armed Forces Revolutionary Council (AFRC), on 25 May 1997, the regime was again denounced and rejected by the citizens, including women, with the support of the international community. In February 1998 the AFRC-led rebel junta was driven out of power by the Nigerian-led forces of the Economic Community of West African States Ceasefire Monitoring Group (ECOMOG).

Civil society groups played a key role in the democratisation process and the resolution of the conflict in Sierra Leone by creating domestic partnerships. In addition to the women, the Inter-Religious Council became one of the most visible and effective local groups trying to build a bridge between the opposing parties. Churches and mosques around the country preached against the barbaric nature of the violence. Muslim and Christian men and women co-operated in an effective partnership and used their religious influence and mandate to prevail on both the rebels and the Government to find a peaceful resolution to the conflict.

Another significant move that gave women a public voice was the Government's creation of the National Commission for Democracy (NCD) in 1994, the first National Commission to be chaired by a woman.[28] The NCD and the Interim National Electoral Commission were the twin Commissions that managed the country's transition to democracy between 1994 and 1996.

Consultations with Civil Society

The NCD, which later became the National Commission for Democracy and Human Rights (NCDHR), having made a strong statement condemning the 6 January 1999 invasion and destruction of Freetown, was mandated by the President to solicit and record the public's views on the way the peace negotiations should go. Following persistent calls for dialogue as a means of achieving peace, a three-day National Consultative Conference on the Peace Process, with representatives from all sectors of civil society, was organised by the NCDHR in Freetown on 7–9 April 1999.

The specific objectives of the conference, attended by 250 participants from 16 civil society groups, were:

- to elicit the views of civil society from all the regions in Sierra Leone on the peace process; and

- to obtain a national consensus on how to end the conflict and achieve lasting peace.

It was during these consultations that the decision in favour of a blanket amnesty, with certain conditions, was reached by consensus as a way of achieving lasting peace and reconciliation. The report of these consultations became one of the documents consulted by all parties before and during the talks. The views of civil society were therefore critical.

Following the report of the national conference, the NCDHR held further consultations to enable civil society to participate in the talks. The following measures were taken:

- A female civil society representative was made a member of the Government negotiating team to represent and defend the views of civil society during the talks. The NCDHR conducted the selection process for the representative.

- The chairperson of the NCDHR (a woman) was also appointed by the President to represent human rights organisations in the Government's peace negotiating team. There were thus two female peace negotiators in the Government team – an unprecedented inclusion.

- The NCDHR facilitated the process of ensuring that more than 10 members of civil society groups attended the talks as observers and successfully influenced the parties to the talks through persuasion at the most critical moments.

- The chairperson of the NCDHR chaired the Socio-Economic and Human Rights Committee during the Lomé peace negotiations.

Recognition of the role played by members of civil society saw

Government poster to promote peace and reconciliation, Freetown, Sierra Leone
T Voeten/International Labour Organization

The resolution of the conflict owed a great deal of its success to the vibrancy of civil society, especially women's and religious organisations.

them slated for significant roles within the Lomé Agreement as members of the Commission for the Consolidation of Peace, the Commission for Diamonds and other structures.

The resolution of the conflict owed a great deal of its success to the vibrancy of civil society, especially women's and religious organisations. The recognition of the role played by NCDHR saw its female chairperson elevated to the position of Minister of Development and Economic Planning in 1999.

Adopting a Regional Approach

As the role of Liberia in the conflict in Sierra Leone became increasingly questionable, and it was recognised that the causes and consequences of conflict and instability transcend national borders, the women of the Mano River Union (MRU) of Guinea, Liberia and Sierra Leone decided to combine their efforts and work together to ensure that they had a say in the decisions that would affect them and play a greater role in building peace in the sub-region. They launched a joint peace initiative: the Mano River Women's Peace Network (MARWOPNET) in May 2000 (see Chapter 12).

In each of the MRU countries, women have been active in promoting peace at various levels. For this reason, Femmes Africa Solidarité (FAS) believes that women can lead the process of reconciliation in the MRU and build confidence among the peoples of those countries. To this end, FAS has adopted a regional approach to facilitate dialogue among women and to give them the opportunity to build greater unity and partnerships and strengthen their respective organisations and movements. A meeting in Abuja brought them together to share experiences and build consciousness, and a sub-regional peace-building programme was launched.

In the course of the meeting, participants reviewed the various peace initiatives and peace processes instituted by the Economic Community of West African States (ECOWAS) and the Organisation of African Unity and were introduced to the new ECOWAS mechanism for conflict prevention, management and resolution, peacekeeping and security. They also learnt about existing mechanisms for conflict management and resolution at the sub-regional and regional levels and examined ways in which they could build partnerships.

Momentum was maintained by immediate follow-up actions to the Abuja meeting, including attendance by a delegation of MARWOPNET at the Mano River Summit in Conakry, Guinea. They made a presentation to the Heads of State emphasising the importance of involving women in the attainment of durable peace in the region. Even more strategically, the Network held bilateral meetings in July 2001 with the three Heads of State to lower the tension and the seeming rise in hostilities, following which the President of Guinea agreed to meet with the President of Liberia (something he had not been prepared to do before). This remarkable breakthrough led to the MRU Foreign Ministers Meeting in August 2001 as a prelude to a Summit of the three Heads of State.

The untiring efforts of the women and other groups within civil society are complementary to sub-regional, regional and UN peace initiatives together with the support of multilateral and bilateral agencies. But first and foremost, the leaders of the three countries and their peoples, including all the parties to the conflicts, must be prepared to give sustainable peace a chance so this sub-region can move forward to meet the international goals for the reduction of poverty by 2015. This is possible if, among other things:

- resources are used for the development of the individual countries and not to raise blood money to devastate individual countries or the sub-region;

- the people are allowed to freely elect their governments through fair and free-from-fear elections;

- civil society behaves as it should, as a watchdog for the people, and does not turn itself into either an opposition party or a government-in-waiting; and

- leaders are elected who work for the good of the nations.

Women and Democracy

Clearly, no one can write about the bitter struggle for democracy in Sierra Leone without mentioning the brave efforts of the many women who stood up even at the risk of personal danger. I believe the real gains derived from this struggle for

... the Network held bilateral meetings in July 2001 with the three Heads of State to lower the tension and the seeming rise in hostilities, following which the President of Guinea agreed to meet with the President of Liberia .... This remarkable breakthrough led to the MRU Foreign Ministers Meeting in August 2001 as a prelude to a Summit of the three Heads of State.

... the real gains derived from this struggle for democracy actually rest on the public affirmation and respect for the crucial public role of Sierra Leonean women in this endeavour. Women have become a more visible political force to be taken seriously, though this affirmation and recognition still need to be translated into more public positions for women.

democracy actually rest on the public affirmation and respect for the crucial public role of Sierra Leonean women in this endeavour. Women have become a more visible political force to be taken seriously, though this affirmation and recognition still need to be translated into more public positions for women.

If democracy is government by all of the people – decision-making in which people play an equal role – then women are entitled to true democracy in which the advantage of their numbers makes them the single most formidable force in Sierra Leone. Women should take on more challenges, be part of the forces formulating polices that control their lives and should be reminded that, as the majority, they can use their votes to transform events and their society.

There is now a chance for women to optimise the current enabling factors and set aside stereotyped images created by society due to their gender. Women should refuse to be intimidated by unconstructive remarks, and instead they should forge ahead in unity towards more active participation in decision-making processes and positions.

Women should play an active role in the consolidation of our democracy, which they have helped to build. This involves safeguarding the independence of the judiciary, fostering a free and responsible press, supporting NGOs – including political parties – and building a strong civil society. Consolidation means affirmative action to include all segments of the population, particularly women, in all the institutions of governance and democracy.

All this can only be achieved, first, if women are given a chance to serve; and, second, and sometimes even more importantly, if women are willing and prepared to come forward. To really change the nation, women must run for elective office across the board from local government to national government. They must support other women running for office and share strategies and tactics that work. Women must forge alliances with other women, particularly elected officials, entrepreneurs and women in NGOs.

"Africa is overflowing with women leaders", notes the leader of a Dakar-based NGO. "They lack only the training and the means to bloom." This highlights the next big step needed for advancing the position of women in Sierra Leone: strengthening their capacity and skills and expanding their opportunities to more fully develop their leadership roles.

In South Africa, the first woman Zulu chief in the Province of KwaZulu/Natal won Supreme Court backing to defeat a challenge to her appointment. She said, "In African traditional practices, women keep their eyes lowered demurely". This is what she was doing, although she was the Chief and men were (among) her subjects. One day, however, she looked them in the eye, and never lowered her gaze again. To sustain democracy, this is what Sierra Leonean women ought to do too.

A woman in Sierra Leone receives her ballot to vote
Carter Center photo

Involving Women in Consolidating the Peace

There are daunting problems confronting Sierra Leone: consolidation of the peace; rehabilitation of the infrastructure; reintegration of ex-combatants; resettlement of the displaced (external and internal); post-conflict reconciliation; and consolidation of advances in democratic governance. These are key challenges that, if thoroughly addressed, could transform the country.

Women's involvement in consolidating the peace is especially important because they are the widows and carers left behind to rebuild their families and the nation after the war. Moreover, studies have shown that women have different ways of approaching conflict and can more easily build bridges to restore confidence. Women realise that they are the major victims of this conflict and are therefore taking steps to involve themselves in the processes of peacemaking and peace-building.

Women should be peacemakers in Sierra Leone, not by standing with a gun but by teaching peace and reconciliation. They should be everywhere encouraging peace and talking about reconciliation, not revenge. The role of and respect for mothers as the carriers of cultural values need to be re-established. Women must play the role of preachers for the message of forgiveness and reconciliation – so as to consolidate the peace – and be watchdogs for the sustainability of democracy.

Recommendations

- Women should demand resources and legal recognition to rebuild their lives, as well as participation in peace-building, conflict resolution and early-warning mechanisms, citing both their traditional peacemaking roles and their right to equal involvement.

- Women should monitor arms purchases, as African military expenditure needs to be reduced for the sake of development, and the destruction of the arms collected from the ex-combatants after the DDR programme.

- Mechanisms should be created for the systematic participation of women in all peace processes at the national, regional and sub-regional levels.

- To consolidate the peace women should follow the stated agenda of:

  - active involvement in conflict resolution;

  - active involvement in reconciliation initiatives, including advocacy against landmines and human rights violations against women and children;

  - a strong embrace of the political process;

  - building of strategic alliances that can unite women across ethnic, social and economic barriers; and

  - heightened demand for greater national investment in education for both boys and girls.[28]

15 Sri Lanka: Mother Politics and Women's Politics

Neloufer de Mel

Background: The Reign of Terror

From 1987 to 1990 the south of Sri Lanka lived through a time that has come to be known as the 'reign of terror'. The society was in crisis. The Janatha Vimukthi Peramuna (JVP), in its bid to capture state power, began a violent campaign of threats, intimidation and assassination to assert its supremacy. It targeted the state – the military, police and bureaucracy – as well as politicians and activists classified as 'traitors to the nation' because of their support for the Indo-Lanka peace accord that brought Indian peacekeepers into the country.

The United National Party (UNP) Government launched an equally brutal counter-offensive. Because the police force had been particularly targeted by the JVP, the police and other security personnel had a vested interest in revenge and were motivated to extinguish the JVP. Those targeted, however, were not only members of the JVP (many youth were killed on mere suspicion of being JVP sympathies), but also men who worked for the opposition Sri Lanka Freedom Party (SLFP) in its various organisational committees. Words denoting 'terror', the 'disappeared' and 'torture chamber' entered the popular vocabulary (Perera, 1999:19). Security personnel and paramilitary groups like the Black Cats and Kola Koti (Green Tigers), specially formed to eliminate the JVP, conducted what is analogous to a scorched-earth policy.

The Presidential Commission into Involuntary Removal in the south of the country found evidence of 7,239 cases of 'disappearances' since January 1988 from an alleged 8,739 cases reported to it. Of these, 4,858 cases were at the hands of state forces and 779 were JVP instigated (Commission of Enquiry, 1997). Journalists and scholars who have written on the 'reign of terror', however, have placed the numbers of deaths much higher, at around 40,000 (Gunaratne, 2001:312). The north

The women of the south faced the trauma of seeing their sons, husbands and brothers either taken away or brutally killed in front of their own eyes .... It was the women who went and confronted the authorities because they were afraid that if the remaining men went, they too would be detained.

and east were also theatres of civil war, resulting in over 60,000 casualties, half of them civilian, with 55,000 maimed; over 750,000 people, mainly of Tamil origin, dispersed into the diaspora; and nearly 1 million Sri Lankans, mostly Tamil and Muslim but Sinhalese also, were internally displaced, many of them in camps (Jeyaraj, 1999: 25).

Box 18 One Woman's Experience During the Reign of Terror in Sri Lanka

This is the story of one woman we interviewed who lives in the Matara district:

"I was living at my brother's house when he was attacked and killed. I was in an utter state of shock, but I went to the police station to lodge an entry. Before going I asked my 10-year-old daughter to wait in the house with her younger brother and sister until I returned, but she wanted to go with me as she was frightened. At the police station they refused to take down my entry. Then I heard a big sound and people shouting. I ran back to find that they had set fire to our house. My other two young children, nine and seven years old, died in that fire. I had to be hospitalised that day. My eldest daughter lives with the guilt of being a survivor of the attack in which her two younger siblings died. When I returned from hospital, the children had already been buried. The authorities refused to give me death certificates, saying that it was not possible as inquiries had not been held into the circumstances of their deaths."

The women of the south faced the trauma of seeing their sons, husbands and brothers either taken away or brutally killed in front of their own eyes (see Box 18). Others either witnessed their men being shot and/or burnt alive, or lived in fear of the sound of the revving engines and knocks on their doors that foretold their husbands and male relatives being arrested and dragged away. Very soon, women began to search for their men in the camps where detainees were housed. It was the women who went and confronted the authorities because they were afraid that if the remaining men went, they too would be detained. For many of them the search was in vain. Their men were not produced, and the authorities were indifferent to their appeals.

A Shift in Focus for Women's Groups

As with women's movements elsewhere, the contemporary Sri Lankan women's movement: comprises women of diverse origins and occupations; diverges as much as it converges on some issues; spans a cross-section of state and non-governmental personnel, as well as professionals, academics and political party members; and has used varied methods of struggle.

Amrita Basu has noted that: "Even women's movements that ultimately define themselves as autonomous from male-dominated parties and institutions are often closely intertwined with broader movements for social change" (1996, Introduction). These movements have had varied goals and encompass a range of activities, including trade unionism, consumer protection and demand for civil liberties, employment and equal opportunities. In Sri Lanka in the 1980s, campaigns for equal pay for women in the tea plantations, elimination of night work for women in the Free Trade Zone and the campaign for enhanced maternity benefits were some of the prominent activities.

By the late 1980s and early 1990s, however, under the severe state and non-state repression, women's groups in Sri Lanka had shifted their feminist demands to the language and principles of human rights. Despite the multiplicity of NGOs focusing on a diverse range of women's issues – and the presence of women's organisations that supported the war effort and continue to do so even today – a broad coalition of women's groups had formed around this issue.

The Women's Action Committee (WAC) responded to the conflict by organising several workshops, campaigns and lobbying strategies linking women's rights to human rights, with the ultimate goal of establishing a far-reaching democratic culture within Sri Lanka (Samuel, 1998:9). It championed the right to self-determination of the Tamil people and raised consciousness about the consequences of the war. WAC collaborated with a group of women academics and professionals

By the late 1980s and early 1990s ... women's groups in Sri Lanka had shifted their feminist demands to the ... principles of human rights .... The WAC responded to the conflict [with] ... strategies linking women's rights to human rights, with the ultimate goal of establishing a far-reaching democratic culture within Sri Lanka ...

Tamils, who fled their village due to fighting in 1994, at an IDP camp
Refugees International

The goal of MDL was a broader platform of unity within Sri Lanka that all mothers and daughters – in the south as well as north and east of the country – could join. It lobbied for a negotiated settlement to the ethnic conflict and the war.

(comprising journalists, lawyers, doctors, administrators, writers and artists) to call for a negotiated settlement to the ethnic conflict and a cessation of hostilities. This effort resulted in a petition signed by over 100 women, published in 1984 in the name of a new collective called Women for Peace. As the war escalated during the 1980s, measures at counter-terrorism such as Emergency Rule, the Prevention of Terrorism Act (under which arbitrary arrest and detention took place) and the Public Security Ordinance (which permitted the disposal of bodies by the security forces) came into force, Women for Peace and WAC protested against these measures, held vigils and worked for humanitarian aid to those displaced by conflict.

The Indo-Lanka Accord of July 1987 proved a turning point in Sri Lanka's recent history. The presence of the Indian Peacekeeping Forces (IPKF), although welcomed at first by women of WAC, drew immense hostility from a nationalistic JVP comprising a Sinhala constituency in the south. Immediately after the IPKF arrival, the JVP began a sustained campaign of political assassination, arson and enforced work stoppages. It protested at the 'Indian occupation' of the country and the 'sell-out' to India by the UNP Government. Women who belonged to WAC and were also involved in other community organisations that challenged Sinhala nationalist positions were threatened and harassed by the JVP. Many of them had to leave their homes in the provinces, where they were known, for the anonymity of the city.

Under such an onslaught WAC could not survive, and from 1987–1990 there was a period of hiatus, hiding and inaction until members regrouped with others to form Mothers and Daughters of Lanka (MDL), indicating that women were willing to take up the challenges posed by militant nationalism and state authoritarianism. The goal of MDL was a broader platform of unity within Sri Lanka that all mothers and daughters – in the south as well as north and east of the country – could join. It lobbied for a negotiated settlement to the ethnic conflict and the war. Its name was not without controversy; there were women who protested against the use of 'motherhood' as a coalescing factor. However, the name stuck and MDL launched an appeal addressed to the state, the JVP and the Liberation Tigers of Tamil Eelam (LTTE) to "stop all killing" (Samuel, 1998: 10).

'Mother politics' was to become an even greater force in the wake of the formation of the Mothers' Front and its challenge to the state during the years 1990–1992.

The Mothers' Front

The Mothers' Front has been, arguably, the most visible and potent women's protest movement in the history of post-colonial Sri Lanka. It brought together women from different regions in the south of the country who united across caste and class barriers. Several women from urban-based NGOs gave the movement support and leadership. It was inaugurated on 15 July 1990 in the southern town of Matara, taking its inspiration from Latin American Mothers' Fronts. Following that example, and recognising the potential of politicising motherhood in a situation of anarchy, they held their first meetings with the mothers and families of the disappeared. Their immediate goals were to try to find the disappeared and obtain the release of those detained without charges. They demanded death certificates and compensation for those who had been missing for over a year. They pledged to try to alleviate the misery of the women who had suffered personal trauma and were now in tremendous economic difficulties with the loss of their breadwinners.

The meetings were an enormous success. Within six months of its inauguration, branches of the Mothers' Front had been formed in ten other districts. By 1992 it had 25,000 members. The UNP Government was disturbed enough by these series of events for the President himself to openly declare sympathy for the mothers whose children had been led astray by undesirable elements. He told the mothers that many of their children were being rehabilitated in the camps in which they were held, implying that the state had taken over the responsibility of undoing the deficiencies of their bad mothering. The Defence Minister openly blamed the mothers for having failed their duty to their children and the nation, chastised them for taking part in demonstrations and stepped up police surveillance on the group (De Alwis, 1998: 187–92).

From then on the Mothers' Front and the UNP Government were locked in antagonistic combat, with each responding to the other's tactics, claims and counter-claims. In July

The Mothers' Front has been, arguably, the most visible and potent women's protest movement in the history of post-colonial Sri Lanka. It brought together women from different regions in the south of the country who united across caste and class barriers.

1992, the Government responded to the challenge by inaugurating its own Mothers' Front. Thus the agitations of the earlier Mothers' Front marked a singular achievement in bringing the agenda of human rights before the public. The UNP Mothers' Front may have focused on its own dead, but it was nevertheless forced to follow the terms of reference set by the original southern group.

What this also indicates is that both Mothers' Fronts had begun to acquire a distinct political tone by the end of 1992. That there were women who felt that the UNP Mothers' Front provided them refuge at a time of need shows that the original group did not do enough to cut across political party lines and recruit mothers of all those who were killed and had disappeared, irrespective of their political affiliations. In all the resolutions unanimously passed at its first convention on 19 February 1991, it was the President and the UNP Government who were named as adversaries. Neither the JVP nor the LTTE were called on, as non-state militant groups engaged in terrorist activity, to halt violence. Rather, the demand was once again to the Government to disarm all armed groups. In this, there was a failure to keep to its goal of being an independent watchdog.

In addition, its actions fell short of forging interlocking political and cultural links that would have brought together all mothers – not just in the south, but also the north and east where Tamil youth were disappearing by the day at the hands of the state armed forces. While there had been a Jaffna Mothers' Front active in the mid-1980s, engaged in earlier moves to get their sons out of detention camps and the clutches of the security forces, and some women from the north and east took part in the Mothers' Front rallies in Colombo, there was no effective networking between these groups thereafter, under a broad umbrella of a united Mothers' Front.

When pressed to comment on this lacuna and the absence of Tamil women in the Front, all the women we spoke to said that they had not met any Tamil women at their Mothers' Front activities. Many of them, however, said that it would have been good if Tamil women, too, had joined because these mothers shared a common concern and common grief.

If the Mothers' Front had been able to achieve a broader

coalition that united Sinhala and Tamil women from all regions, including the north and east, it might have survived to become a powerful protest movement working for peace and a negotiated settlement to the ethnic conflict. By taking the 'impure' and the 'non-citizen' into its ranks, it could have challenged both dominant Sinhala and Tamil nationalisms, at the same time drawing on nationalism's sense of solidarity to forge a strong feminist, coalition politics. However, its focus on the single issue of disappearances in the south became so intimately connected with ousting the President and the UNP from power, that when the President was killed by an LTTE suicide bomber on 1 May 1993 and Chandrika Kumaratunga became President as head of a People's Alliance in November 1994, the Mothers' Front all but fizzled out. It still maintains a presence today but it no longer holds centre stage. On the other hand, it can be argued that the Mothers' Front achieved what it had to in its day and, as with all shifting coalitions, the movement fragmented into different organisations with diverse foci. Instead of calling themselves Mothers' Fronts, many of these groups now work around the issues of widows and women as heads of household.

As already noted, the numbers of women who joined the Mothers' Front were impressive. They included not just mothers but also the widows and sisters of the disappeared. Numbers and rallies aside, however, it was the unorthodox nature of the Mothers' Front protests that radically challenged the UNP Government. Many of the bereft women had supplicated the gods and goddesses at temples (*devales*) in their local districts, seeking answers to and solace for the disappearance of their loved ones. What the Mothers' Front was able to do as an organisation was to convert essentially private quests and pilgrimages into highly public and politicised religious rituals. It held two successful marches in March and April 1992 that led to the Devinuwara and Kataragama *devales* where women heaped curses on the President in revenge for the loss of their loved ones.

Mother Culture

In her work on the women's movements in India, Raka Ray observed that protest movements are influenced as much by

If the Mothers' Front had been able to achieve a broader coalition that united Sinhala and Tamil women from all regions, including the north and east, it might have survived to become a powerful protest movement working for peace and a negotiated settlement to the ethnic conflict.

*Women and children in an
IDP camp, Sri Lanka*

Rawwida Baksh/Commonwealth
Secretariat

*In a culture
where
motherhood is
valorised, the
appeal to
mothers to come
together as
protectors of their
sons, searching
for the truth
of their
whereabouts,
proved most
compelling, as
the numbers of
the movement
proved.*

local cultures, histories and institutions of politics as by other social movements (1999:8). The complex cultural field of motherhood in Sri Lanka played a central role in the formation of the Mothers' Front, its success and, at the same time, its vulnerability to attack and appropriation. In a culture where motherhood is valorised, the appeal to mothers to come together as protectors of their sons, searching for the truth of their whereabouts, proved most compelling, as the numbers of the movement proved. The value of motherhood also gave the women moral and emotive power as victimised mothers in a culture supposedly deferential and respectful to them. Their marches on the streets and beseeching of gods and goddesses pointed to the transgressions of the state in this regard. The public looked on in awe and sympathy as aged mothers marched together with younger women, weeping and wailing, proclaiming their loss in a highly public display of private grief.

Motherhood was also valorised within the JVP ideology to which some of these mothers had lost their sons. The JVP men, caught in the ambivalence towards the family within socialist orthodoxy that both criticised and valorised it, nevertheless by and large remained stuck in traditional patriarchal prescriptions for women. The JVP poetry of the 1980s is another case in point. Many of the 'mother-son' poems had the poet-subject appropriating the role/voice of a mother, who pledges to protect her rebel son even if she eventually loses him. She understands her sacrificial loss in terms of a larger gain as he is "Fighting for a world/Where all live and die as equals". In this way motherhood, and the mothers' espousal of the JVP cause, were used to legitimise the JVP. A photograph of old mothers taking part in the JVP May Day rally in 1981, published in the JVP newspaper *Niyamuwa*, reinforced this message (Gunasekera, unpublished).

When these mothers demanded justice for their disappeared sons, they were seen as legitimate supplicants with the full weight of moral authority behind them. Mother-value and the successful politicisation of motherhood by the Mothers' Front have also been repeatedly appropriated by women politicians. In the run-up to the 1994 presidential election, Kumaratunga – herself the daughter of an assassinated father and widow of an assassinated political leader/actor – "cleverly articulated the mothers' suffering as both a personal and national experience" (De Alwis, 1998: 198–99). Following her election, she appointed a Presidential Commission on Disappearances in 1995, and the two MPs who had spearheaded the Mothers' Front were appointed cabinet ministers.

President Kumaratunga's success in using the theme of motherhood, and in particular her claim to have the support of the Mothers' Front, demonstrates the enormous political potential of motherhood for those politicians who want to claim it. Conversely, even when, as already noted, (bad) motherhood was the focus of the UNP's retaliation against the Mothers' Front, motherhood remained the yardstick by which to judge these women.

That motherhood was placed at the very centre of both the protest discourse and counter-discourse, caused concern among some urban sections of the Sri Lankan women's movement. The form of the mothers' protests was another factor that created unease. Whether mothers should appropriate frenzied weeping and revengeful curses as public political strategy became a topic of debate on the grounds that these images reinforced a stereotype of women as hysterical.

A number of questions come to mind as to the legacy of the Mothers' Front, the ways in which it changed individual women's lives and its influence on the Sri Lankan women's movement in the twenty-first century.

Legacy of the Mothers' Front

A number of questions come to mind as to the legacy of the Mothers' Front, the ways in which it changed individual women's lives and its influence on the Sri Lankan women's movement in the twenty-first century.

The sense of community fostered by these organisations by bringing the bereft women together was important, for many of them did not receive the expected support from their village communities and extended families. As a study of women who became heads of household in the context of political violence and terror in the Moneragala and Hambantota districts shows, the very fabric of a community itself ruptures at a time of generalised violence (Perera, 1999: 53). People were reluctant to come forward to help the bereaved. Poverty was another reason for withholding support, but patriarchy was at play too.

Given that men are the link in kinship networks, their disappearance/death meant that their relatives became estranged or even hostile to the surviving wives and children. In the Hambantota district, of 50 women interviewed only 10 main-

In the Hambantota district, of 50 women interviewed only 10 maintained cordial links with their husband's families. Quite often, the dead husband's brothers or parents took over the land his wife and children had lived on. As the legal titles of these lands were not in the wives' names, they had no alternative but to return to their parents.

tained cordial links with their husband's families. Quite often, the dead husband's brothers or parents took over the land his wife and children had lived on. As the legal titles of these lands were not in the wives' names, they had no alternative but to return to their parents. Thus, even their marital material entitlements were lost to them. Moreover, existing cleavages of caste, class and differences in political affiliations within a village became sharpened in this context of violence. Competition among families and traders, and intra-caste conflict, manifested itself in betrayals of the other to the security forces or the police, so that much of the violence at this time originated from within the village and its intimate community (ibid).

The women who came together under the umbrella of the Mothers' Front therefore found a welcome provision of collective support they sorely lacked in their immediate neighbourhoods. While some women said that it was primarily to seek economic support that they first went to a meeting of the Mothers' Front, they nevertheless received comfort from the collective spirit of the women and discussions of their similar problems.

There are several common factors among the testimonies of women interviewed about the Mothers' Front and their experiences of the conflict. Their initial trauma, now conveyed more in terms of economic despair due to unemployment or, at best, a meagre income, is coupled with the responsibility of single parenthood. It is significant, however, that none of the women mentioned the separatist war as a factor influencing their economic status. The absence of their men meant that theirs were not households from which males were recruited into the army. Thus the war has not offered them employment prospects or direct income. They did not speak either of the spiralling cost of living as a direct consequence of the war. This points to a conspicuous silence on the part of politicians, the media as well as certain NGOs and community development organisations, who work in these areas but have failed to encourage a significant peace movement among the Sinhala people in the south with awareness of the exact economic, social and developmental costs of the war.

Pro-war nationalist sentiment is the other reason a peace movement has not taken hold. Interestingly, none of the women with whom we spoke overtly subscribed to a Sinhala ethno-nationalism that insists that the LTTE/Tamils must be militarily defeated. All of them acknowledged that Tamil women had undergone similar suffering, and wished the Mothers' Front had accommodated more of them within its ranks.

While the collective spirit of the Mothers' Front and its ancillary organisations provided the women comfort and solidarity, and brought into the public/political sphere ordinary wives and mothers who had not been politically vocal before, it is clear from their testimonies that this vocalising also made them targets of attack from within their own communities. They were noted with suspicion, and for some the stigma of being single women was keenly felt. Their children were ostracised at school, marking a climate of mistrust and the suspension of normative socio-cultural codes at a time of crisis, which did not spare even the children from a hostile gaze.

The women of the Mothers' Front were also quite often confronted with the accusation of being anti-national. While they may have been silent on the separatist war or unable to forge links with women from all regions in the country, their efforts were nevertheless aimed at reinstating the distinction between the state and the nation by insisting on a form of governance that was internationally accountable on the issue of human rights.

The Future of the Women's Movement in Sri Lanka

The experiences of two other women's groups point to the potential within the contemporary Sri Lankan women's movement for building a platform for intra-regional coalitions. This notion of cosmopolitanism is particularly apt when the rapid globalisation of the economy and the mass media are also taken into account. These make the borders between village and town, province and metropolis increasingly porous and blurred. The two organisations are the Women's Development Foundation (WDF), based in Kurunegala, and the Uwa Welassa Govi Kantha Sanvidanaya (Uva Welassa Women Farmers' Organisation) based in Buttala. They show that there were women's organisations that existed before the 'reign of terror' that were able to cross over from strategic and practical women's issues to human rights and back. Their interest and

The women of the Mothers' Front were ... quite often confronted with the accusation of being anti-national. While they may have been silent on the separatist war or unable to forge links with women from all regions in the country, their efforts were nevertheless aimed at reinstating the distinction between the state and the nation by insisting on a form of governance that was internationally accountable on the issue of human rights.

Soon after the 1983 anti-Tamil riots, the PWF worked towards Sinhala-Tamil ethnic reconciliation. With the outbreak of the ethnic war, the 1987 Indo-Lanka Peace Accord and its aftermath of civil unrest, the PWF committed itself to a pro-Accord position as a first step towards a peaceful resolution of the ethnic conflict.

activities in forging links with Tamil plantation workers, Tamil women of the north and east, as well as southern women from other provinces, seek to pare down the fixed boundaries within nationalist ideology and ethnic divides towards an alternative view of society and how it should be constructed. These are moves that have made them distinct from other political or single-issue-centred groups and have ensured their long-term survival within Sri Lankan civil society.

The WDF traces its origins to the Progressive Women's Front (PWF), which began in 1982. By 1984, the PWF had begun working in agricultural communities. It organised women into Women Farmers' Societies and ran pre-schools for the children of women working on the sugar plantations. The activities of these women and their participation in public demonstrations and strikes attracted the hostility of the community's men at first, but the women stood their ground. Their strategy was not to be confrontational, since the men were important members of the community, but to seek a consensus on their common issues and methods of protest (Sumika Perera, personal communication, 2000).

Soon after the 1983 anti-Tamil riots, the PWF worked towards Sinhala-Tamil ethnic reconciliation. With the outbreak of the ethnic war, the 1987 Indo-Lanka Peace Accord and its aftermath of civil unrest, the PWF committed itself to a pro-Accord position as a first step towards a peaceful resolution of the ethnic conflict.

After the difficult years of 1987–1990, members of the PWF re-organised in 1991 to form the WDF, which set up its own widows' societies. Its activities became more focused on the issue of minority rights and women's rights as human rights. Its monthly journal, *Athwela* (Chain of Hands) repeatedly published articles by women throughout the 1990s arguing for an end to the war and a political negotiation to the ethnic conflict. The articles highlighted the suffering of women living in the border areas and conflict zones, and went hand in hand with the WDF's lobbying among the mainstream political parties, such as the People's Alliance and UNP, for a negotiated settlement to the war. *Athwela* also highlighted the need for strengthening democratic practice and severely criticised election violence.

Dialogue through cultural exchange was a strategy the PWF

had adopted in the 1980s. Street theatre was an attractive means for communicating a message, and its use of mime, sound and visuals surmounted the barriers of language. It was cheap to produce, mobile and was an entertaining and creative medium that could be both insightful and didactic in getting its message across to the audience.

The women of the Uva Welassa Govi Kantha Sanvidanaya participated in a study tour of Batticoloa town, in the conflict zone of the eastern province, in July 1999. They stated that this was been greatly beneficial in understanding and gathering information on the problems confronting Tamils living in conflict zones, particularly Tamil women. They saw for themselves a town under strict military rule, with army checkpoints and constant surveillance. They commented on the sense of solidarity they felt with the Tamil women who staged a demonstration while they were there, demanding the right to live without fear. They thought that the Tamil women at the demonstration were heartened by their support, and also felt that the participation of Tamil women in their local campaigns would strengthen their own struggle. However, the prevailing security situation prevented such coalition-building on a regular basis (interview, Buttala, July 2000).

While the need for strategic alliances and coalition-building around different issues between Sinhala, Tamil and Muslim women was acknowledged by the women of the Uva Welassa Govi Kantha Sanvidanaya, a cultural exchange among the communities, commensurate with these strategic alliances over political issues, has not taken place. The barrier of language was offered as a reason. When asked whether forms of art cannot overcome linguistic barriers, the women expressed reservations. Why does cultural exchange lag behind strategic alliances? One reason is that unless the culture one wishes to acculturate is associated with power, there is little incentive to learn from it. The colonial elite adopted European culture because it was strategic and useful to do so. It provided access to social mobility and political power. The Sinhala women of Buttala see little reason, at this present moment in Sri Lanka's story of nationalism, to understand Tamil cultural paradigms. Despite their expressions of solidarity, the wide gap that they felt existed between them and the Tamil women of Batticoloa also points to the fact that the legacy of nationalism on both

The women of the Uva Welassa Govi Kantha Sanvidanaya participated in a study tour of Batticoloa town, in the conflict zone of the eastern province, in July 1999 .... They commented on the sense of solidarity they felt with the Tamil women who staged a demonstration while they were there, demanding the right to live without fear.

... work with the Mothers' Front ... and with Tamil plantation labour and Tamil women farmers living in the border areas of the south-east, shows that the basis for a radical challenge to the constraints of nationalism is there to be built on.

sides prevents the two communities from exchanging a deep cultural understanding that would preserve and cherish their differences but on an equal basis.

The fact that the women of both the WDF in Kurunegala and the Uva Welassa Women Farmers' Organisation in Buttala have been able to show solidarity and support for each other's struggles, as well as work for women's rights as human rights, indicates an enabling mobility across varied issues. Their work with the Mothers' Front (even as they were the target of the JVP), and with Tamil plantation labour and Tamil women farmers living in the border areas of the south-east, shows that the basis for a radical challenge to the constraints of nationalism is there to be built on. To foster this politics, its intrinsic commitment to a variety of goals that could alter how society is viewed and constructed, as well as its intra-regional, class and inter-ethnic potential, will be the challenge for the Sri Lankan women's movement in the future.

Recommendations

- Political parties need to listen to women and respond to women's initiatives;

- Women's groups can promote dialogue through cultural exchange and street theatre using a variety of languages as well as mime, to bring together people from different economic and ethnic groups;

- As women engaging in cross-community initiatives may find themselves clashing with political allies on their own side and therefore experiencing divided loyalties, they may need support from third parties;

- Women's groups locally can find inspiration and solidarity from women's groups across the globe;

- With good leadership and support, women can gain the confidence to become leaders at local and national levels.

Notes

1 This derived from work on a research project with Hilary Charlesworth, 'Feminist Analysis of International Dispute Resolution', supported by a John D and Catherine T MacArthur Foundation Research and Writing Award. A shorter version of the paper was delivered as the Schwarz Annual Lecture at the Ohio State University Michael E Moritz College of Law, September 2002.

2 Article 4 of the Harare Declaration lays out the fundamental principles to which every Commonwealth country subscribes.

3 A more detailed explanation of gender mainstreaming, as well as other terms related to gender, can be found in Appendix I.

4 The other critical areas are gender, human rights and the law; gender, poverty eradication and economic empowerment; and gender and HIV/AIDS.

5 The 48th session of the CSW in March 2004 focused on two themes – this and the role of men and boys in achieving gender equality (see Chapter 3).

6 Addressing the UN Security Council Open Debate on Women, Peace and Security, 28 October 2004.

7 Cited in Steiner and Alston (2000: 1187).

8 Presentation at DPKO panel discussion, 'Gender and Peacekeeping: Practical Tools for Change', New York, 29 October 2004.

9 See, for example, paragraphs 237–238 of the Nairobi Forwardlooking Strategies (United Nations, 1986).

10 See also the report of the expert group meeting on 'Peace agreements as a means of promoting gender equality and ensuring participation of women – A framework of model provisions' (UNDAW, 2003b).

11 As noted earlier, the other theme was 'Women's equal participation in conflict prevention, management and conflict resolution and in post-conflict peace-building'.

12 The Arria Formula enables a member of the Council to invite other Council members to an informal meeting for the purpose of a briefing given by one or more persons, considered as expert in a matter of concern to the Council.

13 Missions to Haiti and Liberia have a gender expert with the Assessment Mission to assess the gender needs of the situation.

14 Timor-Leste became the official name of East Timor after Independence in May 2002.

15 In contrast, the 1995 UN General Guidelines for Peacekeeping Operations had made no reference to gender.

16 Ambassador Anders Lidén, Permanent Mission of Sweden to the UN, presentation at DPKO panel discussion, 28 October 2004.

17 The terms of agreement with the host state under which the PSO personnel are deployed.

18 This is not included in the new 'Gender Resource Package for Peacekeeping Operations'.

19 See also Box 10.

20 Cyprus is considered one of the most militarised countries in the world (more than 5 per cent of its GDP goes to defence spending).

21 Because of the Muslim demand for a homeland, which was realised in the creation of Pakistan, Muslims who chose to stay behind in India are often characterised as being pro-Pakistan, accused of favouring the 'two-nation theory' and are told to 'go home'. This is despite the fact that this 150 million-strong population made the choice to live in India.

22 Prior to Partition the population of Punjab was almost equally balanced between Hindus, Sikhs and Muslims, with Dalits, Christians and other minorities making up smaller numbers.

23 See also Cox, 1992; Government of Australia, 2000a and 2000b.

24 This chapter is based on a speech on the 'Abuse and Violations of Women's Rights During Armed Conflicts', delivered at Port Moresby in September 2003.

25 Bougainville is a matrilineal culture whereby land ownership, which is owned on a clan basis, passes through the female line.

26 The MRU is a political entity, whereas the Mano River Basin is the geographical location of the three countries.

27 Campaign for Good Governance (CGG), a national organisation working on governance, human rights and gender issues in Sierra Leone.

28 The author.

29 Young boys between the ages of 9 and 15 were press-ganged into the war, seduced with drugs and money. Girls' education at the expense of schooling for boys simply replaces one problem with another.

Bibliography

Africa Renewal, Vol.18 no 4 (January 2005).

African Rights (1995). *Rwanda not so Innocent: When Women Become Killers*. London: African Rights.

Anderlini, S (2000). *Women at the Peace Table: Making a Difference*. New York: UNIFEM.

Ankomah A, E Fisher, J Holland, I Ramos and J Whetton (1999). *Illicit Drugs and the Poor in Transit Countries: Case Studies from the Caribbean and South Africa*. Prepared for the European Commission. Swansea: Centre for Development Studies.

Afshar, Haleh (ed) (1996). *Women and Politics in the Third World*. London and New York: Routledge.

Association of Female Lawyers of Liberia and the editors (1998). 'Hundreds of Victims Silently Grieving'. In M Turshen and C Twagiramariya (eds). *What Women Do in Wartime: Gender and Conflict in Africa*. London: Zed Books, pp 129–137.

Axworthy, L (1996). 'Axworthy announces Peace-building Initiative at York'. *Gazette* 27 (11), 13 November. Retrieved on 2 December 2002 from *www.yorku.ca/ycom/gazette/past/archive/111396.htm#gen0*

Baksh-Soodeen, Rawwida (2003). 'Gender, Boys and Education'. In Commonwealth Education Partnerships. London: Commonwealth Secretariat and HMSO.

_____ (2002). 'Gender and Post-Conflict Reconstruction in Sierra Leone: How relevant is gender in shaping Sierra Leone's post-conflict reconstruction agenda in the aftermath of the civil war of 1991–2001?' (LSE 2001/2)

_____ and Linda Etchart (eds) (2002). *Women and Men in Partnership for Post-Conflict Reconstruction: Report of the Sierra Leone National Consultation*, Freetown, Sierra Leone 21–24 May 2001. London: Commonwealth Secretariat. (See also *www.thecommonwealth.org/gender*)

Banglabazar Patrika (1999). 5 December.

Basu, Amrita (ed) (1995). *The Challenge of Local Feminisms: Women's Movements in Global Perspective*. Boulder, CO: Westview Press.

Beevor, Antony (1991). *Inside the British Army*. 2nd edition. London: Corgi.

Beyani, Chaloka (2001). 'Key Issues'. In *Women's Land and Property Rights in Situations of Conflict and Reconstruction. A Reader based on the February 1998 Inter-Regional Consultation in Kigali, Rwanda*. New York: UNIFEM.

Bhagwan Rolls, S (2000). 'Gender and the role of the media in conflict and peacemaking: The Fiji experience'. *Development Bulletin* 53: 62–65.

Bhasin, Kamla (1999). 'Keynote address'. Published in *Options* 19, 3rd Quarter. Colombo: Women and Media Collective.

Billy, A (2002). 'Fighting for a fair deal for women'. *Development Bulletin* 56: 58–62.

Bratt, Duane (2002). 'Blue Condoms: The Use of International Peace-keepers in the Fight against AIDS'. *International Peacekeeping*, 9 (3), Autumn.

Brown, Janet and Barry Chevannes (1998). *Why Man Stay So: An Examination of Gender Socialization*. Kingston, Jamaica: The University of the West Indies.

Boutros-Gali, B (1992). *An Agenda for Peace: Preventive Diplomacy, Peacemaking and Peacekeeping*. New York: United Nations.

Brandon, Ben and Max du Plessis (eds) (2005). *The Prosecution of International Crimes: A Practical Guide to Prosecuting ICC Crimes in Commonwealth States*. London: Commonwealth Secretariat.

Byrne, B (1996). 'Towards a Gendered Understanding of Conflict'. *IDS Bulletin*, 27 (3): 31–40.

Canadian Peacebuilding Coordinating Committee (nd). 'What Activities Constitute Peacebuilding?'. *www.cpcc.ottawa.on.ca/chart-e.htm*

Charlesworth, Hilary and Christine Chinkin (2000). *The Boundaries of International Law: A Feminist Analysis*. Manchester: Manchester University Press.

Chevannes, Barry (2001). *Learning to be a Man: Gender and Socialisation in Some Caribbean Communities*. Kingston, Jamaica: The University of the West Indies Press.

_____ (1999). 'What We Sow and What We Reap: Problems in the Cultivation of Male Identity in Jamaica'. Grace Kennedy Foundation Lecture Series. Kingston, Jamaica: Grace Kennedy Foundation.

_____ and Herbert Gayle (1998). *Solid Waste Management: Profiles of Inner City Communities in the Kingston Metropolitan Area*. Kingston, Jamaica: Faculty of Social Sciences, The University of the West Indies.

Chevannes, Barry and Horace Levy (1996). *They Cry Respect: Urban Violence and Poverty in Jamaica*. Kingston, Jamaica: The Centre for Population, Community and Social Change, Faculty of Social Sciences, The University of the West Indies.

Chinkin, Christine (2001). *Gender Mainstreaming in Legal and Constitutional Affairs*. London: Commonwealth Secretariat. (See also *www.thecommonwealth.org/gender*)

CHT Commission (1997). *Life is not Ours: Land and Human Rights in the Chittagong Hill Tracts, Bangladesh*. Update 3. Amsterdam: International Work Group for Indigenous Affairs (IWGIA) and the Organising Committee, Chittagong Hill Tracts.

Clapham, C (1982). *Private Patronage and Public Power: Political Clientelism and the Modern State*. London: Frances Pinter.

_____ (1976). *Liberia and Sierra Leone: An Essay in Comparative Politics*. Cambridge: Cambridge University Press.

Cockburn, Cynthia and Dubravka Zarkov (eds) (2002). *The Postwar Moment: Militaries, Masculinities and International Peacekeeping*. London: Lawrence and Wishart.

Collier, P (2000). 'Doing Well out of War: An Economic Perspective', in M Berdal and D Malone (eds). *Greed and Grievance: Economic Agendas in Civil War*. London: Lynne Rienner.

Commission of Enquiry (1997). 'Final Report of the Commission of Inquiry into Involuntary Removal or Disappearance of Persons in the Western, Southern and Sabaragamuwa Provinces'. Colombo, Sri Lanka: Department of Government Printing.

Commonwealth Secretariat (2003a). *Integrated Approaches to Eliminate Gender-based Violence*. London: Commonwealth Secretariat. (See also *www.thecommonwealth.org/gender*)

_____ (2003b). 'Strengthening Pacific Partnerships for Eliminating Violence Against Women: A Pacific Regional Workshop Report, Suva, Fiji Islands, 17–19 February 2003'. London: Commonwealth Secretariat.

_____ (2000). 'Recommendations and Strategies for Action of the Pacific Regional Symposium on Gender, Politics and Conflict/Peace, Wellington, New Zealand, 16–19 June 2000'. London: Commonwealth Secretariat.

_____ (1999). *Gender Management System Handbook*. London: Commonwealth Secretariat.

_____ (1998a). 'Recommendations and Strategies for Action of the Asian/European Regional Symposium on Gender, Politics, Peace, Conflict Prevention and Resolution, Brighton, UK, 2–6 March 1998'. London: Commonwealth Secretariat.

_____ (1998b). 'Recommendations and Strategies for Action of the Caribbean Regional Symposium on Gender, Politics, Peace, Conflict Prevention and Resolution, Bridgetown, Barbados, 23–26 November 1998'. London: Commonwealth Secretariat.

_____ (1997). 'Recommendations of the African Regional Symposium on Gender, Politics, Peace, Conflict Prevention and Resolution, 23–26 June 1997'. London: Commonwealth Secretariat.

Concord Times (1995). 27 September.

Coomaraswamy, Radhika (2001). 'Integration of the Human Rights of Women and the Gender Perspective'. Report submitted by the UN Special Rapporteur on Violence Against Women to the UN Commission on Human Rights, 57th Session (E/CN.4/2001/73/Add 2). Geneva: United Nations.

_____ (1997). 'Reinventing International Law: Women's Rights as Human Rights in the International Community'. Edward A. Smith lecture to Human Rights Program, Harvard Law School.

Cox, Elizabeth (1992). 'Campaigning against domestic violence: An evaluation of the Papua New Guinea Women and Law Committee's campaign against domestic violence'. Port Moresby, Papua New Guinea: UNICEF. Unpublished report.

Crossette, Barbara (1999). 'Global Rules Now Apply to Peacekeepers, UN Chief Declares'. *New York Times*, 12 August.

De Alwis, Malathi (1998). 'Motherhood as a Space of Protest: Women's Political Participation in Contemporary Sri Lanka'. In Patricia Jeffery and Amrita Basu (eds), *Appropriating Gender: Women's Activism and Politicised Religion in South Asia*. New York and London: Routledge.

De Groot, G J (2002). 'Wanted: A Few Good Women: Gender Stereotypes and their Implications for Peacekeeping'. Presentation at Women in NATO Forces, 26th Annual Meeting, NATO HQ, Brussels, 26–31 May.

_____ (2001). 'A Few Good Women: Gender Stereotypes, the Military and Peacekeeping'. In Louise Olsson and Torun Tryggestad (eds), *Women and International Peacekeeping*. Special issue of *International Peacekeeping*, 8 (2), Summer. London: Frank Cass.

de Waal, Alex (2002). 'Fucking Soldiers: How Armies Spread AIDS in Africa'. *Index on Censorship*, 205 (4).

Dinnen, S (2001). 'Introduction to Violence in Melanesia'. In S Dinnen and A Ley (eds). *Reflections on Violence in Melanesia*. Sydney: Hawkins Press.

_____ (ed) (2003). *A Kind of Mending: Restorative Justice in the Pacific Islands*. Canberra: Pandanus Press, Australian National University.

Dinnen, S and A Ley (eds) (2001). *Reflections on Violence in Melanesia*. Sydney: Hawkins Press.

El-Bushra, J (2000). 'Transforming Conflict: Some Thoughts on a Gendered Understanding of Conflict Processes'. In S Jacobs, R Jacobson and J Marchbank (eds). *Gender, Violence and Resistance*. London: Zed Books.

Enloe, Cynthia (2000). *Manoeuvres: The International Politics of*

Militarizing Women's Lives. Berkeley, CA: University of California Press.

_____ (1993). *The Morning After: Sexual Politics at the End of the Cold War*. Berkeley, CA: University of California Press.

Evans, Martin and Kenneth Lunn (eds) (1997). *War and Memory in the Twentieth Century*. New York: New York University Press.

Fanon, Frantz (1963). *The Wretched of the Earth*. London: Penguin Books.

Forna, Aminatta (2002). 'Death of a Nation' [Sierra Leone]. *Index on Censorship*, 205 (4).

Forster, Jebbeh (2002). "HIV/AIDS: A Strategy for Sierra Leone." In Baksh-Soodeen and Etchart (eds), op cit.

Galtung, J (1976). *Peace, War and Defense: Essays on Peace Research*. Vol. 2. Copenhagen: Christian Ejlers.

_____ (1971). 'A Structural Theory of Imperialism'. *Journal of Peace Research* 8 (2): 81–117.

_____, Carl G Jacobsen and Kai Frithjof Brand-Jacobsen (2002). *Searching for Peace: The Road to TRANSEND*. London: Pluto Press, 2nd edition.

Gayle, Herbert (1996). 'Hustling and Juggling: The Art of Survival for the Urban Poor'. Department of Sociology and Social Work, The University of the West Indies. Unpublished.

Gilligan, Carol (1982). *In a Different Voice: Psychological Theory and Women's Development*. Reprinted 1993. Boston: Harvard University Press.

Goonesekere, Savitri (1998).'The Conceptual and Legal Dimensions of a Rights-Based Approach and its Gender Dimensions'. In *A Rights-Based Approach to Women's Empowerment and Advancement and Gender Equality*, Workshop Report, UN Division for the Advancement of Women, October.

Gordon, Derek (1989). 'Identifying the Poor: Developing a poverty line for Jamaica'. Working Paper No. 3. Jamaica Poverty Line Project, Planning Institute of Jamaica.

_____ (1986). *Class, Status and Mobility in Jamaica*. Kingston, Jamaica: Institute of Social and Economic Research, The University of the West Indies.

Government of Australia (2004). 'Solomon Islands: Establishing the peace'. *Focus* 19: 14–20. Canberra: AusAID.

_____ (2000a). *Young people say DV – No way*. Evaluation of the National Domestic Violence Prevention Workshops for Young People. Canberra: Department of Education, Training and Youth Affairs.

_____ (2000b). 'Young people and domestic violence'. Fact sheet from national research on young people's attitudes and experience of domestic violence. Canberra: Department of Education, Training and Youth Affairs and the Attorney General's Department.

Gunaratne, Rohan (2001). *Sri Lanka: A Lost Revolution? The Inside Story of the JVP*. Kandy, Sri Lanka: Institute of Fundamental Studies.

Gunasekera, Manisha. 'Gender in Counter-State Political Practice of the JVP 1978–89'. Unpublished MA thesis, University of Colombo.

Gunst, Laurie (1999). *Born fi Dead. A Journey Through the Jamaican Posse Underworld*. Edinburgh: Payback Press.

Hadjipavlou, Maria (2003). 'Inter-ethnic Stereotypes, Neighbourliness, Separation: Paradoxes and Challenges in Cyprus'. In *Journal of Mediterranean Studies*, 13 (2).

_____ (1995). 'Women of Cyprus: Twenty Years Later (1974–1994): A Pilot Study (in Greek)'. In N Peristianis and G Tsangaras (eds) *Anatomy of a Transformation: Cyprus after 1974*. Nicosia, Cyprus: Intercollege Press.

Hakena, H (2000). 'Strengthening Communities for Peace in Bougainville'. *Development Bulletin* 53: 17–20.

Harriott, Anthony (2000). *Police and Crime Control in Jamaica: Problems of Reforming Ex-Colonial Constabularies*. Kingston, Jamaica: The University of the West Indies Press.

Hannerz, Ulf (1992). *Cultural Complexity: Studies in the Social Organisation of Meaning*. New York: Columbia University Press.

Headley, Bernard (1994). *The Jamaican Crime Scene: A Perspective*. Mandeville, Jamaica: Eureka Press Ltd.

Heinecken, Linda (2002). 'Facing a Merciless Enemy: HIV/AIDS and the South African Armed Forces'. *Armed Forces & Society*, 29 (2), Winter.

Hill, Felicity (2002). 'NGO perspectives: NGOs and the Security Council'. *Disarmament Forum*, No. 1: 27–30.

Howley, P (2002). *Breaking Spears and Mending Hearts: Peacemakers and restorative justice in Bougainville*. Sydney: The Federation Press.

Hunt, S and C Posa (2001). 'Women Waging Peace'. Foreign Policy, May/June. *www.foreignpolicy.com/issue_mayjune_2001/Hunt.html*

International Labour Organization (ILO) (2000). *ABC of Women Worker's Rights and Gender Equality*. Geneva: ILO.

IRIN-WA (2004). 'Liberia: LURD commanders want leader replaced by his wife'. 8 January. *www.irinnews.org/report.asp?ReportID=38823*

_____ (2001). 'Interview with Angela King'. 31 October. *www.irinnews.org*

Jalal, P (2002). 'Gender issues in post coup d'etat Fiji: Snapshots from the Fiji Islands'. *Development Bulletin* 56: 28–31.

Jeyaraj, D B S (1999). 'Lions and Tigers'. *Himal*, April, Kathmandu.

Jones, Lucien (1995). 'The Jamaican Society: Options for renewal.' Grace Kennedy Foundation Lecture, Kingston, Jamaica.

Kabeer, Naila (2003). *Gender Mainstreaming in Poverty Eradication and the Millennium Development Goals: A handbook for policy-makers and other stakeholders*. London: Commonwealth Secretariat.

Khan-Melnyk, Antoinette (1994). 'Politics and U.S.–Jamaican Drug Trade in the 1980s'. In B Bagley and O Walker III (eds), *Drug Trafficking in the Americas*. New Brunswick: Transaction Publishers.

Kidu, C (2000). 'Reflections on change, ethnicity and conflict: Family and ethnic violence in Papua New Guinea'. *Development Bulletin* 53: 29–34.

_____ and S Setae (2002). 'Winning and losing: Key issues in Papua New Guinea'. *Development Bulletin* 56: 51–54.

Lederach, J (1997). *Building Peace: Sustainable Reconciliation in Divided Societies*. Washington, DC: United States Institute of Peace Press.

Levy, Horace, Herbert Gayle and Angela Stultz (2001). *An Assessment of Greater August Town for the Purpose of Reducing and Preventing the Incidence of Violent Crime and Increasing Access to Justice*. Kingston, Jamaica: Government of Jamaica's Citizen Security and Justice Programme, Planning Institute of Jamaica.

Liloqula, R (2000). 'Understanding the conflict in Solomon Islands as a practical means to peacemaking'. *Development Bulletin* 53: 41–44.

Mazurana, Dyan (2002). 'International Peacekeeping Operations: To Neglect Gender is to Risk Peacekeeping Failure'. In Cynthia Cockburn and Dubravka Zarkov (eds), op cit.

_____ and Eugenia Piza Lopez (2002). 'Gender Mainstreaming in Peace Support Operations: Moving Beyond Rhetoric to Practice'. London: International Alert.

Meintjes, Sheila, Ann Pillay and Meredith Turshen (2001). *The Aftermath: Women in Post-conflict Transformation*. London: Zed Books.

Merton, Robert (1968). *Social Theory and Social Structure*. New York: The Free Press.

Mertus, Julie (2000). *War's Offensive on Women. The Humanitarian Challenge in Bosnia, Kosovo and Afghanistan*. Bloomfield, CT: Kumarian Press.

Moser, Caroline and Jeremy Holland (1997). 'Urban Poverty and Violence in Jamaica'. World Bank Latin American and Caribbean Studies: *Viewpoints*. Washington DC: The World Bank.

Muktakantha (1999). 6 December.

Nabalarua, E (2002). 'Gender, race and religion in sustainable community development in Fiji'. *Development Bulletin* 56: 28–31.

NGO Working Group on Women, Peace and Security (2004). 'Recommendations for the 2004 Report of the Special Committee on Peacekeeping Operations', New York, 1 April.

_____ (2002a). 'Fact Sheet on Women and Armed Conflict'. Prepared and circulated at the UN on 23 October in conjunction with a UN Press Conference and UN Security Council Arria Formula meeting.

_____ (2002b). 'Security Council Resolution 1325 – One Year On'. *http://www.peacewomen.org/un/UN1325/since1325.html*

O'Conner, James (1985). 'Capital, Crisis, Class Struggle'. In S Resnick and R Wolff (eds), *Rethinking Marxism*. New York: Autonomedia, Inc.

Oguli-Oumo, M, I M Molokomme, M M Gwaba, V Mogegeh and L Kiwala (2002). *Promoting an Integrated Approach to Combat Gender-Based Violence: A Training Manual*. London: Commonwealth Secretariat.

Olsson, Louise and Torun Tryggestad (eds) (2001). *Women and International Peacekeeping*. Special issue of International Peacekeeping, 8 (2), Summer. London: Frank Cass.

Paina, D T (2000). 'Peacemaking in Solomon Islands: The experience of Guadalcanal Women for Peace movement'. *Development Bulletin* 53: 47–49.

Paris, R (1997). 'Peacebuilding and the Limits of Liberal Internationalism'. *International Security*, 22 (2): 54–89.

Patterson, Orlando (1967). *The Sociology of Slavery: An analysis of the origins, development and structure of Negro slave society in Jamaica*. London: Macgibbon and Kee.

Perera, Sasanka (1999). *Stories of Survivors: Socio-Political Contexts of Female-Headed Households in Post-Terror Southern Sri Lanka*. Vol. 1. Colombo: Women's Education and Research Centre.

Perera, Sumika (2000). Interview with Neloufer de Mel. Colombo, Sri Lanka. August.

Peterson, S and A S Runyan (1993). *Global Gender Issues*. Boulder, CO: Westview Press.

Pollard, A (2000). 'Resolving conflict in Solomon Islands: The Women for Peace approach'. *Development Bulletin* 53: 44–47.

Ray, Raka (1999). *Fields of Protest: Women's Movements in India*. New Delhi: Kali for Women.

Rees, Madeleine (2002). 'International Intervention in Bosnia-Herzegovina: The Cost of Ignoring Gender'. In Cynthia Cockburn and Dubravka Zarkov (eds) op cit.

Refugees International (2005). 'Sierra Leone: Promotion of Human Rights and Protection of Women Still Required'. 18 March 2004. *http://www.refugeesinternational.org/content/article/detail/949/*

Regehr, E (1995). 'Rebuilding Peace in War-Torn and War-Threatened Societies: The Challenge of Peace-building'. *Ploughshares Monitor*. December.

Reno, W (1995). *Corruption and State Politics in Sierra Leone.* Cambridge: Cambridge University Press.

Report on Progress made in the implementation of the Beijing, Platform for Action in Africa (Beijing +10), Sierra Leone, August 2004.

Riches, David (1986). *The Anthropology of Violence.* Oxford: Basil Blackwell Ltd.

Rothschild, D (1997). *Managing Ethnic Conflict in Africa.* Washington, DC: Brookings Institutions Press.

Ruddick, S (1989). *Maternal Thinking: Towards a Politics of Peace.* London: The Women's Press.

Ryan, S (1990). *Ethnic Conflict and International Relations.* Aldershot: Dartmouth Publishing Company.

Samuel, Kumuduni (1998). 'Gender Difference in Conflict Resolution: The Case of Sri Lanka'. *Options* 14, 2nd Quarter. Colombo: Women and Media Collective.

Schnabel, Albrecht (2002). 'Post-Conflict Peace-building and Second-Generation Preventive Action'. *International Peacekeeping*, 9 (2), Summer.

Social Development Commission (1998). 'Profile of Communities along the Industrial Belt between Six Miles on the West and Rockfort on the East'. The Research and Documentation Department, Social Development Commission.

Sørenson, B (1998). 'Women and Post-Conflict Reconstruction: Issues and Sources'. WSP Occasional Paper No. 3, June.

Spees, Pam (2004). 'Gender Justice and Accountability in Peace Support Operations: Closing the Gaps'. London: International Alert.

Statistical Department of the Crime Office, Jamaica (1998). Major Crimes Reported Island-wide. Kingston, Jamaica.

_____ (1997). Major Crimes Reported Island-wide. Kingston, Jamaica.

_____ (1996). Major Crimes Reported Island-wide. Kingston, Jamaica.

Statistical Institute of Jamaica (2001). 'Population Census, Volumes 1 and 2'. Kingston: Statistical Institute of Jamaica.

_____ (1991). 'Population Census, Volumes 1 and 2'. Kingston: Statistical Institute of Jamaica.

Steiner, Henry J and Philip Alston (2000). *International Human Rights in Context: Law, Politics, Morals*. 2nd edition. Oxford: Oxford University Press.

Stone, Carl (1992). 'The Jamaican Party System and Political Culture'. In P Lewis (ed), *Jamaica: Preparing for the Twenty-first Century*. Kingston: Ian Randle Publishers.

_____ (1991). 'Hard Drug Use in a Black Island Society'. *Caribbean Affairs* 14.

Thomas, P (ed) (2004). *Development Bulletin* 64: 'Gender and development: Bridging policy and practice'. Canberra: Development Studies Network, Australian National University.

_____ (2002). *Development Bulletin* 56: 'Political participation in the Pacific: Issues of gender, race and religion'. Canberra: Development Studies Network, Australian National University.

_____ (2000). *Development Bulletin* 53: 'Conflict and peacemaking in the Pacific: Social and gender perspectives'. Canberra: Development Studies Network, Australian National University.

Tripodi, Paolo and Preeta Patel (2002). 'The Global Impact of HIV/AIDS on Peace Support Operations'. *International Peacekeeping*, 9 (3), Autumn.

Turshen, M (1998). 'Women's War Stories'. In M Turshen and C Twagiramariya (eds). *What Women Do in Wartime: Gender and Conflict in Africa*. London: Zed Books.

UNAIDS/WHO (2002). 'AIDS Epidemic Update 2002'. *http://www. unaids.org/worldaidsday/2002/press/Epiupdate.html*

UNESCO Press (1999). 'Zanzibar Conference Stresses Importance of African Women's Role in Building Peace on the Continent'. Zanzibar, 17 May. UNESCO press release. *www.unesco.org/opi/ eng/unescopress/99-111e.htm*

United Nations (2004). 'Human Trafficking and United Nations Peacekeeping'. Department of Peacekeeping Operations (DPKO) Policy Paper, March.

_____ (2000a). 'Further actions and initiatives to implement the Beijing Declaration and Platform for Action'. A/RES/S-23/3, November 16.

_____ (2000b). Report of the Panel on United Nations Peace Operations (Brahimi Report), New York, October.

_____ (2000c). 'Report of the Secretary-General on the Implementation of the Report of the Panel on United Nations Peace Operations'. New York, October.

_____ (1996). Report of the UN Secretary General 1996 on the implementation of the Outcome of the Fourth World Conference on Women, 3 September, UN Doc. A/51/322.

_____ (1995). *Platform for Action and the Beijing Declaration*. Fourth World Conference on Women, 4–15 September, Beijing, China. UN Doc. A/CONF. 177/20.

_____ (1993). UN Declaration on the Elimination of Violence against Women, UN General Assembly. A/RES/48/104. 20 December.

_____ and United Nations Children's Fund (UNICEF) (1996). *Impact of Armed Conflict on Children*, Report of Graça Machel, Expert of the Secretary-General of the United Nations. New York: United Nations.

United Nations Children's Fund (UNICEF) (1994). *The State of the World's Children 1994*. New York: UNICEF.

United Nations Commission on the Status of Women (UNCSW) (2004). 'Report on the forty-eighth session (1–12 March 2004)'. Economic and Social Council Official Records, Supplement No. 7 (E/2004/27-E/CN.6/2004/14).

United Nations Department of Peacekeeping Operations (DPKO) (2004). *Gender Resource Package for Peacekeeping Operations*. New York: United Nations.

_____ (2003). *Handbook on UN Multidimensional Peace Operations*. New York: United Nations.

United Nations Development Fund for Women (UNIFEM) (2005). 'Gender Profile of Sierra Leone: The Independent Expert's Assessment on the Impact on Armed Conflict on Women'. New York: UNIFEM.

_____ and the International Legal Assistance Consortium (ILAC) (2004). 'Report of the Conference on Gender Justice in Post-Conflict Situations, 15–17 September 2004. New York: UNIFEM.

United Nations Development Programme (UNDP) (2004). *Human Development Report 2024: Cultural Liberty in Today's Diverse World*. New York: UNDP.

_____ (2000). *Human Development Report 2000*. New York: Oxford University Press.

_____ (1998). *Human Development Report, 1998*. New York: Oxford University Press.

_____ (1997). *Human Development Report, 1997*. New York: Oxford University Press.

United Nations Division for the Advancement of Women (UNDAW) (2003a). 'The role of men and boys in achieving gender equality'. Report of the Expert Group Meeting, Brasilia, Brazil, 21–24 October.

_____ (2003b). 'Peace agreements as a means for promoting gender equality and ensuring participation of women – A framework of model provisions'. Report of the Expert Group Meeting, Ottawa, Canada, 10–13 November.

United Nations Population Fund (1997). *State of World Population 1997*. New York: UNFPA.

_____ (1994). *State of World Population 1994*. New York: UNFPA.

_____ (nd). 'Country Profile: Sierra Leone'. *http://www.unfpa.org/profile/sierraleone.cfm*

United Nations Security Council (2002). 'Report of the Secretary-General on women, peace and security'. S/2002/1154, 16 October.

UN Women's Newsletter, The (2002). 'Report of Gender Advisers' Workshop, Department of Peacekeeping Operations (DPKO), New York, 24–31 October 2002'. *The UN Women's Newsletter*, 6 (4), October–December.

Vyas Mongia, Radhika (1999). 'Race, Nationality, Mobility: A History of the Passport'. *Public Culture* 29.

War and Children Identity Project (2001). *The War Children of the World*. Report #1. *http://www.warandchildren.org/report1.html*

Whittington, Sherrill (2004). 'United Nations Goals for "Gender Mainstreaming" in Post War Peace and Democracy Building: Theory behind Security Council Resolution 1325: Its Implementation in Afghanistan and Iraq'. Women and Post-War Reconstruction: Strategies for Implementation of Democracy Building Policies, Florida International University, 12–13 March.

_____ (2002). 'Report of Gender Advisers' Workshop', DPKO, New York, 24–31 October.

Wood, Mary, Hilary Charlesworth and Christine Chinkin (2000). 'Women and conflict resolution in international law'. *Development Bulletin*, 53: 7–9.

Women's International League for Peace and Freedom (WILPF). 'Women, Gender and Peacekeeping' website: *www.peacewomen.org/un/pkwatch/pkindex.html*

World Bank (2000). *World Development Report*. Washington, DC: World Bank.

World Health Organization (WHO) (1997). 'Violence against Women Information Pack: A Priority Health Issue'. Geneva: WHO. *www.who.int/frh-whd/VAW/infopack/English/VAW_infopack.htm*

Yashin, M (2000) 'Flying Away to the Other Side'. In *Don't Go Back to Kyrenia*. (Collection of Poems). London: Middlesex University Press.

Appendices

I Glossary

Gender

The word 'gender' is not much used in everyday speech, but traditional perceptions of women and men, and of the relations between them, are everywhere inevitably 'gendered' perceptions. People often continue to ascribe certain kinds of behaviour to men and boys and other kinds of behaviour to women and girls, and think of these behaviours as natural rather than learned.

According to a report from the UN Secretary-General (United Nations, 1996):

> 'Gender' refers to the socially constructed roles of women and men ascribed to them on the basis of their sex, whereas the term 'sex' refers to biological and physical characteristics. Gender roles depend on a particular socio-economic, political and cultural context, and are affected by other factors, including age, race, class and ethnicity. Gender roles are learned and vary widely between cultures … [and] can change. Gender roles help to determine women's access to rights, resources and opportunities.

Gender analysis

Gender analysis involves the collection and analysis of sex-disaggregated data that reveal how development activities affect women and men differently and how gender roles and responsibilities affect development efforts. It also involves qualitative analyses that help to clarify how and why these differential roles, responsibilities and impacts have come about.

According to the International Labour Organization (ILO) (2000):

> Men and women perform different roles. So do girls and boys. This leads to males and females having different experience, knowledge, needs, access to and control over resources. Gender roles can result in one sex having an

unequal role in decision-making or being denied the benefits from development. Gender analysis explores these differences so policies, programmes and projects can identify and meet the different needs of women, men, girls and boys. Gender analysis also facilitates the strategic use of their distinct knowledge and skills. It should include qualitative and quantitative data.

Gender blindness

Gender blindness is where we fail to see the significance of gender in a particular situation and, as a result, may: (a) fail to analyse a situation correctly; (b) make decisions of whether to act or not based on incorrect or incomplete information; and (c) not select the most appropriate kinds of action to take.

Gender blindness may result in a failure to disaggregate statistics according to sex, such that an all-male board of selectors may inadvertently appoint a team of all-male personnel to carry out a particular task. In a UN document, statistics may be given as to the number of international police or peacekeepers allocated to a conflict zone without those statistics being sex-disaggregated, so the numbers of women and men appointed to these posts is not indicated.

Similarly, if a team of researchers is consulting local people on their priorities in post-conflict reconstruction and schedules a meeting for the community at a time or location that is not convenient for women, women's opinions and wishes may not be included.

Gender mainstreaming

Gender mainstreaming is the key approach advanced in the 1995 Commonwealth Plan of Action on Gender and Development, which sets out a series of strategies and measures for governments to work towards gender equality. It involves a number of activities:

- Forging and strengthening the political will to achieve gender equality and equity at the local, national, regional and global levels;

- Incorporating a gender perspective into the policy-making

and planning processes of all ministries and departments of government, particularly those concerned with macro-economic and development planning, the public service, and legal and constitutional affairs;

- Integrating a gender perspective into all phases of sectoral planning cycles, including the analysis, development, appraisal, implementation, monitoring and evaluation of policies, programmes and projects;

- Using sex-disaggregated data in statistical analysis to reveal how policies impact differently on women and men;

- Increasing the numbers of women in decision-making positions in government and the public and private sectors;

- Providing tools and training in gender awareness, gender analysis and gender planning to decision makers, senior managers and other key personnel; and

- Forging linkages between governments, the private sector, civil society and other stakeholders to ensure a co-ordination of efforts and resources.

Because gender mainstreaming is a broad spectrum strategy that cuts across government sectors and other social partners, it requires strong leadership and co-ordination (Commonwealth Secretariat, 1999).

II Extract from the Commonwealth Plan of Action for Gender Equality 2005–2015 on Gender, Democracy, Peace and Conflict

3.1   The Commonwealth focuses on four critical areas in this PoA:

I   Gender, democracy, peace and conflict

II   Gender, human rights and law

III   Gender, poverty eradication and economic empowerment

IV   Gender and HIV/AIDS

I Gender, democracy, peace and conflict

3.2   As a Commonwealth fundamental value, democracy is well articulated in various documents, notably in the 1991 Harare Declaration. The Commonwealth promotes and supports democracy, characterised by representative government, equal participation, transparency, accountability and responsiveness to all its citizens, women, men, young and old persons. The importance of transparency should be emphasised because of the negative impact of corruption on women.

3.3   5WAMM in Trinidad and Tobago (1996) recommended that "member countries should be encouraged to achieve a target of no less than 30 per cent of women in decision-making in the political, public and private sectors by 2005". This target was subsequently endorsed by CHOGM in Edinburgh in 1997. Countries with proportional representation systems (e.g. New Zealand and South Africa) have recorded a marked increase in women's representation in parliament, and have encouraged women to pursue and advance political careers. Similarly, decentralisation, with its devolution of power and resources, appears to be creating better access and opportunities for women's effective participation and representation in government. Currently the 30 per cent target will not be achieved by the 2005 deadline. The Commonwealth acknowledges the need to work harder to achieve the minimum target of 30 per cent representation by 2015.

3.4 Many Commonwealth countries have continued to strengthen democratic systems of government, introduced accountability measures, and increased women's representation through adoption and implementation of quotas and affirmative action measures. For example, Uganda introduced a constitutional reform to provide for one woman Member of Parliament per district and one third of local council positions for women. Similarly, India's 73rd and 74th constitutional amendments reserved one-third of all local government seats for women, which has resulted in over 500,000 women being elected to the Panchayat Raj throughout the country. Following the first post-conflict national elections in Sierra Leone in 2002, the percentage of women in parliament increased from 8 to 15 per cent.

3.5 However, many governments remain fragile and need stronger institutional infrastructure to sustain democracy, such as Ombudspersons, electoral commissions, parliamentary oversight bodies, an impartial judiciary to uphold the rule of law and human rights, and adequately trained civil servants, including women. Even where democratic institutions are firmly established, citizens, particularly women, continue to be marginalised and have little access or capacity to influence national policies, plans and programmes. This institutional infrastructure must be supported by explicit and practical capacity-building to ensure that NWMs and CSOs can function effectively.

3.6 Women's participation and representation in the frontline of democracy and peace processes is crucial. For women to be able to influence decisions that affect their lives and those of their families, their political, social and economic empowerment must form part of the democratic ideal that contributes to sustainable development. In fact, since women constitute more than half the population, sustainable development cannot be achieved without them. Democracy and development thus need to be seen as mutually reinforcing goals essential to the achievement of gender equality.

3.7 The Commonwealth Ministerial Action Group on the Harare Declaration (CMAG) is a body set up to monitor and ensure adherence to fundamental values of democracy and good governance, respond to serious and persistent violations of these in member countries and make appropriate recommendations. The Secretary-General's Good Offices, reaffirmed most recently by CHOGM in Abuja in 2003, supports capacity-building initiatives to prevent and resolve conflicts, and to ensure increased women's participation and representation in peace processes.

3.8 In the Commonwealth and globally, armed conflicts within and between states, sharpened by growing threats to human security and assisted by the proliferation of small arms and light weapons, are on the increase. Unequal power relations, lack of access to resources, intolerance and lack of respect for individual rights and freedoms fuel armed and other forms of conflicts. Statistics show that civilian populations are increasingly the targets of a myriad of human rights violations such as trafficking in persons, rape with impunity used as a weapon of war, abduction of girls, recruitment of child soldiers and other crimes against humanity. These actions and crimes, committed by both state and non-state actors, violate conventions and treaties such as the Universal Declaration of Human Rights, the four Geneva Conventions, the International Covenant on Civil and Political Rights (ICCPR), the International Covenant on Economic, Social and Cultural Rights (ICESCR), the Convention on the Elimination of All Forms of Discrimination against Women (CEDAW) and the Convention on the Rights of the Child (CRC), with their various Optional Protocols. The differential impacts of conflicts on women, men and children, and the challenges they create, have profound democratic and developmental implications for all humanity. Women and girls with disabilities in conflict situations are particularly vulnerable and specifically targeted for support.

3.9 The 1995 BPfA identified the effects of conflict on women as one of its 12 critical areas of concern. It affirmed the need to increase women's participation in conflict resolution and peace-building at decision-making levels. It also recommended strategic actions to be taken by governments, the international community, the private sector and CSOs, urging adequate protection of women and children during times of conflict. These recommendations arose principally from a view of women as 'victims' of armed conflict. However, women's active and positive contributions towards peace and conflict resolution processes have more recently also been recognised and documented by the international community. Consequently, the UN Security Council in its resolution 1325 in 2000 made an urgent call for the "equal participation and full involvement of women in all efforts for the maintenance and promotion of peace and security", and emphasised "the need to increase their role in decision-making with regard to conflict prevention and resolution".

3.10 Against this background, the 6WAMM in Delhi (2000) recommended that "the Commonwealth take action in collaboration with other international organisations and civil society to include women at the highest levels of peace-building, peacekeeping, conflict mediation, resolution, and post-conflict reconciliation and reconstruction activities". They encouraged a 30 per cent target of women's participation in peace initiatives by the year 2005. As part of its assistance to countries experiencing conflict, the Secretariat held a Sierra Leone national consultation on 'Women and Men in Partnership for Post-Conflict Reconstruction' in May 2001, following a decade of armed conflict that led to the virtual collapse of the country's social, economic, legal and political fabric. The consultation provided a platform for Sierra Leoneans to share their experiences and views, and define their own solutions so that women, men, boys and girls could work together to create a more democratic, equitable and prosperous future.

3.11 The challenge now is to push beyond numbers and demonstrate the impact of women's contribution to democracy and peace in member countries; promote implementation and accountability for international legal instruments that governments have ratified; harmonise national legislation with international standards as tools for promoting de-facto equality; encourage political parties to adopt the minimum 30 per cent target for women candidates; and ensure women's participation and representation in conflict prevention and resolution, peace-building and post-conflict reconstruction processes. In line with the Commonwealth's comparative advantage, there is need to develop a human rights based approach to citizenship peace education at all levels of society including curriculum development and the promotion of a culture of peace, geared particularly towards young people, to ensure sustainability.

3.12 Consequently, activities in this critical area will focus on:

i. Supporting the adoption, accession, ratification, implementation and monitoring of legal instruments and frameworks related to democracy, peace and conflict.

ii. Strengthening democratic and political systems through achievement of the Commonwealth target of at least 30 per cent of women in decision-making in the political, public and private sectors. This will require a strengthening of institutional capacity. Countries which have already reached 30 per cent should continue to strive for a higher target.

iii. Supporting the development and mainstreaming of gender equality into early warning mechanisms, conflict prevention and resolution, peace agreements, peace-building, reconciliation, post-conflict reconstruction, and disarmament, demobilisation and reintegration processes.

iv. Promoting capacity-building and strengthening partnerships between governments, NWMs, civil society, media, schools, institutions of higher education, religious organisations and other social institutions, regional and international bodies in the promotion of gender equality and tolerance of diversity.

v. Ensuring the collection and dissemination of sex-disaggregated data and integrating gender analysis into policy-making, planning and programme implementation in conflict and post-conflict situations.

vi. Documenting and disseminating good practice in gender equality initiatives in the area of democracy, peace and conflict.

vii. Promoting the funding of programmes that will facilitate the gender-sensitive leadership of young people.

viii. Promoting attention to democracy, good governance, peace, security and the importance of gender issues in the school curriculum.

3.13 Governments are encouraged to take action to:

i   Increase women's representation to a minimum of 30 per cent in decision-making in parliament and local government by creating an enabling environment for women (including young women) to seek and advance political careers and by other measures such as encouraging political parties to adopt a 30 per cent target for women candidates as part of their manifestos and to provide leadership training for women. Governments who have already achieved 30 per cent should strive for much higher aspirations.

ii   Review the criteria and processes for appointment to decision-making bodies in the public and private sectors to encourage increased women's participation and representation. This will require explicit investment into institutional capacity.

iii   Promote standards in the media whereby discriminatory and/or derogatory images and remarks about women are eliminated.

iv   Reduce and eventually eliminate the proliferation of small arms and light weapons.

v   Promote women's full, equal and effective participation at all levels and stages of peace-building processes including formal and informal negotiations and agreements.

vi   Ratify legal instruments, and ensure that national legal frameworks promote and protect women's human rights, and provide redress for survivors of armed conflict, particularly women and girls.

vii   Mainstream gender equality, human rights, HIV/AIDS into the training of peacekeepers, disciplined forces, and law enforcement personnel and their partners into codes of conduct.

viii   Promote and support the work of the Special Tribunals, and ensure that where crimes are committed in situations of armed conflict, all perpetrators are prosecuted, both state and non-state actors.

ix   Address the specific needs of women, men and young persons in conflict situations, especially those of child soldiers, refugees, internally displaced persons (IDPs) and people with disabilities.

x   Provide adequate medical, financial and psycho-social assistance and care for women and men, including culturally sensitive counselling to survivors of rape, sexual assault and other violations.

xi   Implement effective disarmament, demobilisation, rehabilitation and reintegration programmes for ex-combatants that address the specific needs and experiences of women and girls in post-conflict situations.

xii   Promote assistance in mine clearance, and support efforts to co-ordinate a common response programme of assistance in de-mining without unnecessary discrimination.

xiii   Develop peace and citizenship education programmes (including in conflict situations) that promote respect for individual rights and freedoms, gender equality, diversity including religious and cultural diversity, and pluralism.

xiv   Collect, monitor and disseminate with urgency sex-disaggregated data to inform early warning mechanisms and conflict intervention programmes.

xv   Promote the implementation and monitoring of Security Council Resolution 1325.

3.14 The Secretariat will take action to:

i   Assist governments, NWMs, political parties, civil society and other partners to achieve the target of 30 per cent for women's representation in the political, public and private sectors.

ii   Support legislative reviews, policies and programmes including women-specific measures that guarantee equal opportunities and treatment to women and men in all sectors and at all levels.

iii   Support leadership and other capacity-building programmes to enable women (including young women) to seek political office and advance political careers.

iv   Provide policy advice and technical assistance to countries in mainstreaming gender equality at all stages of the peace process, including conflict prevention and resolution, peace agreements, peace-building, peacekeeping, reconciliation, post-conflict reconstruction, and disarmament, demobilisation and reintegration processes. This will require the extension of work in partnerships for post-conflict reconstruction.

v   Support member countries' ratification and implementation of legal instruments that promote and protect human rights, including women's rights, and redress violations in conflict and post-conflict situations.

vi   Support the development of peace and citizenship education (including in conflict situations) as part of school curricula, to promote and foster a culture of peace.

vii   Collaborate with governments, NWMs and other partners to document and disseminate good practice in the area of gender, democracy, peace and conflict.

viii   Collaborate with governments, NWMs and other partners to undertake gender focused research and analysis on the impact of armed conflict on women and girls.

List of Contributors

Rawwida Baksh is Head of the Gender Section, Commonwealth Secretariat. She is the Series Co-ordinator of the Secretariat's Gender Management System series and the new gender mainstreaming series on development issues. Prior to joining the Secretariat, Dr Baksh co-ordinated the Caribbean Association for Feminist Research and Action (CAFRA) and lectured at the University of the West Indies. Her postgraduate studies have included International Relations; Gender and Development; and Socio-historical Linguistics.

Urvashi Butalia was the director and co-founder of Kali for Women, India's first feminist publishing house. She is currently a consultant for Oxfam India, a Reader at the College of Vocational Studies at the University of Delhi and is active in the Indian women's movement. Her main areas of research are partition and oral histories.

Christine Chinkin is Professor of International Law at the London School of Economics (LSE) and an Overseas Affiliated Faculty Member, University of Michigan School of Law. She is an editor of the *American Journal of International Law*. Professor Chinkin has published widely, and her amicus brief to the International Criminal Tribunal for the Former Yugoslavia on the issue of witness protection was cited by the majority judges in the historic decision of Prosecutor v Dusko Tadic.

Niloufer de Mel is Director of Studies, Faculty of Arts, and a Senior Lecturer at the Department of English, University of Colombo, Sri Lanka. She is also a faculty member on the postgraduate Women's Studies programme of the University. Dr de Mel is on the Regional Advisory Panel of the Social Science Research Council, New York, and is a member of several women's groups and initiatives both nationally and internationally.

Linda Etchart is a PhD candidate in the Department of International Relations at the London School of Economics (LSE) in the field of gender, military ethics and international humanitarian law. She lectures in Globalisation and Diaspora at Anglia Polytechnic University, Cambridge, UK. She has previously co-edited with Rawwida Baksh, *Women and Men in Partnership for Post-Conflict Reconstruction: Report of the Sierra Leone National Consultation* (2002).

Herbert Gayle is a PhD candidate in Social Anthropology, School of Oriental and African Studies (SOAS), University of London. He has an MSc in Sociology of Development, University of the West Indies. He has published a number of books on adolescent males and gender roles and is the chairman of Fathers Incorporated, Jamaica.

Maria Hadjipavlou is a Lecturer in the Department of Social and Political Science at the University of Cyprus. Since 1991 she has been an associate of the Program in International Conflict Analysis and Resolution (PICAR) of the Center for International Affairs, Harvard University. Dr Hadjipavlou has published widely in the fields of peacemaking and conflict resolution.

Helen Hakena formed the Leitana Nehan Women's Development Agency (LNWDA) in Bougainville, Papua New Guinea, after witnessing the horrific violence committed against women there. In 2001 LNWDA was awarded the Millennium Peace Prize for its work in assisting communities to develop the means to resolve conflict peacefully and to address domestic violence in Papua New Guinea.

Amena Mohsin is Professor of International Relations at Dhaka University, Bangladesh. Dr Mohsin is the author of *The Politics of Nationalism: The Case of the Chittagong Hill Tracts, Bangladesh* (2002).

Elsie Onubogu is a sociologist and international lawyer with expertise in the area of gender and human rights. She received a graduate degree from the Fletcher School of Law and Diplomacy, Boston, USA. As a member of the Social Transformation Programmes Division of the Commonwealth Secretariat, she is responsible for Gender, Democracy, Peace and Conflict. Prior to joining the Secretariat, Ms Onubogu worked with the United Nations from 1996 in various capacities on legal, gender and development issues. She has written many articles and contributed to publications including the *UNDP Human Development Report*; *Modernisation, Globalisation and the Political Economy: Nigeria's Perspective*, and most recently on *African Development and Governance Strategies in the Twenty-first Century*, a book on strategies for development in Africa.

Victor Pungong heads the Good Offices Section of the Commonwealth Secretariat. He holds a PhD in International Relations from Jesus College, Cambridge. Between 1993 and 1997 he was a Lecturer in International Relations and Comparative Politics at De Montfort University, Leicester. Dr Pugong joined the Commonwealth Secretariat in 1997 as a Senior Political Officer. In May 2003, he was appointed Deputy Director of Political Affairs with responsibility for the Commonwealth Secretary-General's Good Offices Role in conflict prevention and resolution and post-conflict capacity-building. The Section has been involved in good offices engagements with Cameroon, The Gambia, Swaziland, Zimbabwe, Zanzibar (URT), Lesotho, Uganda, Kenya, Guyana, Tonga and Fiji Islands.

Kadi Sesay is Minister of Trade, Industry and State Enterprises in the Government of Sierra Leone (2004), and was previously Minister of Development and Economic Planning. Hon Dr Sesay was Chairperson of the country's National Commission for Democracy and Human Rights (NCDHR). Before that she had been a lecturer and then Head of Department at Fourah Bay College, University of Sierra Leone, for 20 years.

Christiana Tewor Solomon is a Research Assistant at the Africa Centre for Peace and Conflict Studies, Department of Peace Studies, University of Bradford, UK.

Pamela Thomas is Director of the Development Studies Network at the Research School of Social Studies, Australian National University. Dr Thomas is also managing editor of the journal *Development Bulletin*. Her major research focus is women's and children's health and the special and temporary aspects of health service delivery in developing countries.